God, Suffering, and Pentecostals

God, Suffering, and Pentecostals

Marius Nel

Foreword by Hannes Knoetze

WIPF & STOCK · Eugene, Oregon

GOD, SUFFERING, AND PENTECOSTALS

Copyright © 2022 Marius Nel. All rights reserved. Except for brief quotations in critical publications or reviews, no part of this book may be reproduced in any manner without prior written permission from the publisher. Write: Permissions, Wipf and Stock Publishers, 199 W. 8th Ave., Suite 3, Eugene, OR 97401.

Wipf & Stock
An Imprint of Wipf and Stock Publishers
199 W. 8th Ave., Suite 3
Eugene, OR 97401

www.wipfandstock.com

PAPERBACK ISBN: 978-1-6667-3358-7
HARDCOVER ISBN: 978-1-6667-2834-7
EBOOK ISBN: 978-1-6667-2835-4

01/18/22

Scripture quotations marked (NIV) are taken from the Holy Bible, New International Version®, NIV®. Copyright © 1973, 1978, 1984, 2011 by Biblica, Inc.™ Used by permission of Zondervan. All rights reserved worldwide. www.zondervan.comThe "NIV" and "New International Version" are trademarks registered in the United States Patent and Trademark Office by Biblica, Inc.™

Scripture quotations marked (CEV) are from the Contemporary English Version Copyright © 1991, 1992, 1995 by American Bible Society, Used by Permission.

Scripture quotations marked (NRSV) are from the New Revised Standard Version Bible, copyright © 1989 the Division of Christian Education of the National Council of the Churches of Christ in the United States of America. Used by permission. All rights reserved.

Contents

Foreword by Hannes Knoetze | vii
Research Justification | ix
Word of Recommendation | xi
A Word in Advance | xiii
Abbreviations | xv

1. Pentecostals and Theodicy | 1
2. Philosophical-Theological Answers to the Challenges of Theodicy | 21
3. Biblical Answers to Theodicy | 47
4. Pentecostal Thinking about Theodicy | 95
5. Reflecting on God in Theodicy from a Pentecostal Hermeneutical Perspective | 143
6. Reflecting on Evil in Theodicy from a Pentecostal Hermeneutical Perspective | 195
7. Conclusion | 240

Bibliography | 245

Foreword

THIS BOOK IS INDEED timely, especially given the challenges we are facing at present due to the COVID-19 pandemic, where millions of people around the globe have lost their lives, and the gap between the rich and the poor is ever-widening. Moreover, in this contemporary era, the theodicy question has become particularly relevant, where social media and television broadcast the suffering and realities of the world into people's living rooms and lives almost instantaneously.

This book is a masterpiece of integrating and applying material on "theodicy," focusing on a classical Pentecostal perspective of the Apostolic Faith Mission of South Africa (AFM of SA). The word "theodicy" emanates from two Greek words that refer to God (*theos*) and justice (*dikē*). Where is God when the world is suffering? The author draws widely on Christian and historical sources as well as understandings and experiences within Pentecostalism to reflect on the theodicy issue. What makes this study extraordinary is Nel's use of the Pentecostal movement's emphasis on divine healing to study theodicean questions and issues, since the Pentecostal movement rarely commits its thinking in writing. Pentecostals have not published much about theodicy, since their practice disqualifies them from a philosophico-theological undertaking. Therefore their teaching and practice of divine healing are investigated to evaluate a possible theodicy.

Nel develops a solid, scripturally-based framework, or a theoretical structure, from different literature types and biblical texts from both the Old and New Testaments. But God's revelation is not limited to the Bible; God reveals himself through nature, events, other people, and directly into believers' hearts through the moving of the Spirit. Nel attempts to paint a picture of the current thinking among Pentecostals about theodicy. He continues to describe three characteristic levels of discourse when studying a Pentecostal community, namely, "ordinary," "official," and "academic" levels. However, the focus of this book is on academic research with a pastoral warmth that makes it accessible for students, pastors, and academics.

Although different possible explanations for the theodicy question are given, such as testing, free will, and so on, it is Nel's sober understanding of God as the One who is more than we are able to describe in human language. The fact that God is always more than we can grasp is comforting. The other side of theodicy discussed is how Pentecostals respond to the place, role, and influence of evil and the evil one.

Probably the greatest reward to many readers, whether Pentecostal or not, will be the way the author is challenging us to rethink our own, in many instances, distorted views on God and suffering, views that in many cases prevent us from being living witnesses of the hope that lives within us (1 Pet 3:15) in a world in desperate need of hope. Such challenges are costly, for they require transformations in our lives and ministries.

Professor Hannes Knoetze
Practical Theology and Mission Studies
Faculty of Theology and Religion
University of Pretoria

Research Justification

THIS BOOK IS MEANT for academics in the fields of theology and philosophy, for pastors occupied with caring for fellow believers, and for Christian believers faced with the challenges that suffering poses. The book is written in the strange, almost bizarre world established by the COVID-19 pandemic, confronting the world's citizens with the uncertainties of infection and frustrating many economic and financial endeavors. It reflects on the phenomenon of people's suffering due to the prevalence of illness, aging, and death, natural catastrophes, accidents, and other unforeseen circumstances. Suffering and grief have the potential to test religious faith due to the logical challenge of a mighty Creator God who created everything perfect and who is good amidst a world characterized by suffering. The study is based on various resources, including a comparative literature study to ascertain the extent of a Pentecostal theodicy; exegesis of Scriptures to describe the different responses in biblical traditions to the issue; a doctoral study concerned with the historical development of the teaching and practice of divine healing in the Pentecostal movement; and personal reflections about theodicy. It aims to stimulate discourse among Pentecostal scholars, philosophers, and experts in related disciplines, along with pastors and believers. The book suggests strategies for redressing the current lack of responsible theodicean responses among Pentecostals due to the reigning theological perspectives that deny that believers may suffer, irrespective of the brutal reality of many of their members' lives. The author shares the Pentecostal theological premises that God is present in the world, caring for and involved with the life of God's people and answering their prayers. Believers participate in the coming of God's kingdom, even while and despite experiencing suffering. This book roots theological research and reflection about human suffering in real life of both believers and nonbelievers while awaiting the final arrival of the kingdom. The book will stimulate ongoing transdisciplinary research among theologians and philosophers. It will also encourage pastors and believers as believers in God to engage with the existential realities of suffering. The research outcomes are relevant for Pentecostal theology and philosophy.

Word of Recommendation

I GREW UP WITH the conviction that God is all good and always wants the best for everybody. I also vividly recall the many hours we spent as a family at healing services where many preachers from South Africa and abroad would pray for my father, who was partially blind since his childhood, and for my mother. Her one leg was shorter than the other due to medical negligence.

This dualism of the goodness of God and people's suffering, many times due to human choices, either their own or that of others, was part of the reality of our lives. My parents lived from the premise found in the words of Jesus to his followers: "In this world you will have trouble. But take heart! I have overcome the world" (John 16:33 NIV), and the experience of Paul, "In times of trouble God is with us, and when are knocked down, we get up again" (2 Cor 4:9 CEV).

My father is ninety-two years old and now totally blind, yet he still believes God can restore his sight. How do we respond to that? How do we counsel and pray with a family whose young father, the breadwinner, has passed on due to COVID-19-related complications? How do we make sense of the death of a young pastors' couple in a motorcar accident with their three-month-old baby left behind?

As the realities of much suffering and loss worldwide come into our houses and lives every day via social media and television, it confronts us all with uncomfortable questions: Why is there so much suffering and evil in the world? How and why does God allow this to happen?

With this timely, comprehensive, and well-researched book, Marius Nel stimulates much-needed discourse amongst Pentecostal scholars and experts in related disciplines to (again) find solid ground for what we understand and believe about God's interactions and purpose with us as believers and human beings in times of suffering, to assist us in detecting the heartbeat of God in the biblical text in the context of the realities of today.

Dr. Henri Weideman
President
The Apostolic Faith Mission of South Africa
2021–09–14

A Word in Advance

FOR A CHILD TO lose a parent is always traumatic. I was ten years old when my mother died after suffering for an extended period from throat cancer. Our home was not religious; my parents attended church mainly for marriage ceremonies, baptisms, and funerals. However, my mother became religious at one stage, trusting God for her healing that never happened. My father married shortly after her death. The new stepmother was, in many respects, the very opposite of my mother. She introduced me to her Pentecostal church, where I became an enthusiastic convert. Unfortunately, her relationship with my father was also characterized by violent conflicts that lasted for days.

During my first year at university, a friend invited me to visit their farm during the winter holidays. We arrived late on a Thursday afternoon, and later that night, we accompanied her grandmother to her home. On the way, the vehicle was in an accident on the farm road, and I was seriously injured. I suffered memory loss for two or three weeks and could not remember anything about the accident. I only left the hospital after two months and then had several operations to repair some of the damage.

The experience confronted me with the question: Where was God when the accident happened? If God is in total control of what happens in the lives of God's children, why did God not prevent the accident and the many health problems that followed from it? I believed that God showed God's desire to live in a relationship with me by sending Jesus Christ to mend the relationship. Why would such a God of love and grace permit accidents to change the course of those people who belong to God?

Even as a teenager, I was interested in the history of the Jews. When I learned of the Holocaust (*Shoah*) tragedy, I read anything about it that I could. Many Jews lost their faith due to the unthinkable crimes of the Holocaust that crowned many centuries of antisemitism characterized by the violent and widespread hatred of Jews in Europe, especially in Poland and Romania.[1] Even today, when new publications about the catastrophe see the light, I make sure I read it. I found I had to answer the same questions about my own life I heard among the Jewish victims and their progeny. God, as a good God, would not allow evil. God, as an almighty God, does not need to allow evil in the created order. Nevertheless, there is evil in the world, implying that God is not good or not almighty.

During three decades in pastoral ministry, I was confronted many times by the same question. For example, what do you say to parents who found their child dead one New Year's Eve after waking and eating some pills she found in her grandfather's cupboard? Or to a wife and four young children whose husband, a detective, was killed in cold blood after revealing how senior political leaders benefitted from gang-related crime?

Several Pentecostal pastors and evangelists prayed for me for several years after my mishap, claiming healing in Jesus' name but without recognizable results. As a consequence, I became interested in the subject of divine healing. I completed a PhD with a dissertation looking at the development of the doctrine within the church I belonged to the Apostolic Faith Mission of South Africa (AFM of SA). It is the largest Pentecostal church in South Africa, with more than 1.2 million members.

In many worship services, believers still testify about their healing after prayer. It is supported by the practice of Pentecostals to pray fervently for the ill, at times driving demons of illness out of suffering people. Especially in Africa and other countries constituting the Global South, divine healing remains a vital element of Pentecostal practice, an essential part of Pentecostals' fourfold or fivefold gospel that proclaims that Jesus is Savior, Spirit baptizer, Healer, Sanctifier, and coming King.

I asked myself, "Why does a loving God allow God's children to suffer from illness in the first place?" It was clear that believers, just like unbelievers, are exposed to the disastrous consequences of diseases, accidents, natural catastrophes, and economic collapse without any distinction.

The NRSV is used as the preferred Bible translation; whenever another translation is used, it will be indicated.

Thanks are due to Ms. Hester Lombard, librarian at the Faculty of Theology of North-West University library, and her staff for their primarily unsung contribution to research. She and her team contributed to the study with excellent literature searches.

---

1. Arendt, *Origins of Totalitarianism*, 28–29.

Abbreviations

JPTS	Journal of Pentecostal Studies Supplement
JSOT Suppl	Journal for the Study of the Old Testament Supplement
SBL	Society of Biblical Literature
WUNT	Wissenschaftliche Untersuchungen zum Neuen Testament

1

Pentecostals and Theodicy

Introduction

THE QUESTION OF THEODICY is vast and can be approached from several angles. To limit the discussion and prevent it from becoming vague and generalized, this study focuses on several aspects. The first aspect is Pentecostalism and specifically classical Pentecostalism that started in the early decades of the twentieth century[1] with the experience of Spirit baptism evidenced by speaking in tongues. It exists in distinction from the other two waves, the charismatic movement that started in the 1960s in established mainline churches and consisted of the adoption of the Pentecostalization of worship practices, and Neo-Pentecostal churches consisting of independent churches that utilized Pentecostalization along with their own emphasis, consisting of a variety of aspects such as a healing ministry, deliverance, or the propagation of prosperity theology.[2] "Pentecostalization" is defined here as the acceptance of Spirit baptism, accompanied by the occurrence of spiritual gifts such as glossolalia (speaking in tongues), interpretation of tongues, gifts of healing, utterances of wisdom, utterances of knowledge, gifts of faith, etc. (see 1

---

1. "Classical Pentecostal movement" is defined here as the movement associated, *inter alia*, with the example of Pentecostalism that originated at Azusa Street, Los Angeles, in 1906. It emerged from the Wesleyan-holiness tradition and believes in the Spirit baptism evidenced by speaking in tongues, an experience subsequent to conversion and sanctification. It acknowledges that the Spirit's work in the community manifests in charismatic gifts.

2. Nel, *Prosperity Gospel in Africa*, 44.

Cor 12:4–11; 14; 1 Pet 4:11). It realizes in spontaneous worship practices characterized by charismatic phenomena.[3]

The second aspect used to limit the study is referencing one specific Pentecostal denomination from Africa that serves as a case study and representative of the classical Pentecostal movement. The Apostolic Faith Mission of South Africa (AFM of SA) is a significant role-player within the southern African and African Pentecostal movement. In discussing Pentecostal thinking about theodicy in chapter 3, reference is made to empirical work that was completed within this denomination.

The third aspect emphasizes the Pentecostal movement's emphasis on divine healing as a means to study theodicean issues, since the Pentecostal movement rarely commits its thinking about theodicy to paper. To describe the theodicean ideas that function within the movement, one needs to analyze its preaching and teaching, given the underlying presuppositions of God's providence, because it did not publish any significant works on theodicy. Divine healing provides a usable vantage point to define the movement's theodicy, and publications in the AFM of SA are used to analyze its theodicy. Because "there is what seems sometimes like a limitless amount of literature on this subject in Pentecostal and Charismatic circles,"[4] it is necessary to limit its study sensibly, and here it is done in terms of one denomination.

The study represents experimental theology that views the issue of theodicy from a Pentecostal hermeneutical perspective. "Experimental theology" implies that the author engages speculatively in theoretical endeavors. It asks the question, How can one think innovatively in line with the Pentecostal ethos? It does not try to provide traditional answers but to think innovatively and shift boundaries. The author's previous research investigated hermeneutical possibilities, in the same innovative and innovative speculative ways, in terms of other issues, including pacifism, eschatology, the LGBTQIA+ issue, the prosperity gospel, and the creation narratives of Genesis 1–2.[5] It is vital to note that as experimental theology it speculates as to possible meaning and value that hermeneutical considerations may add to traditional interpretations. When it does not subscribe to conventional thinking, it moves in the sphere of speculative thought.

3. Dankbaar, *Kerkgeschiedenis*, 183–84.
4. Torr, *Dramatic Pentecostal/Charismatic Anti-Theodicy*, 60.
5. The research was published by Routledge, LIT Verlag, Wipf and Stock, and Cambridge Scholars.

Mark Cartledge distinguishes three levels of discourse that can characterize the study of a Pentecostal community: an "ordinary," "official," and "academic" level. This study starts with the ordinary found in Pentecostal preaching and teaching. Then, it compares it to the official level, as far as it is available, before proceeding to the academic level. It is motivated by the need for such a study to be based on Pentecostal realities.[6] Therefore, I begin with my own experience and relate it to the church's experience to extrapolate how the Pentecostal movement argues the issue of theodicy. Hopefully, the academic product can help inform the official and ordinary levels of preaching and practice.

The study draws on other disciplines within the theological enterprise to illuminate and clarify theodicy in order to present an alternative theological perspective and resultant practice in terms of the ordinary level. The ethos of the study is Pentecostal beliefs and practices, and the emphasis is on Pentecostals' view of and use of Scripture (hermeneutics) and the practice derived from their theological perspectives on theodicy.[7]

It is legitimate to ask to what extent an interpretation of the teaching and practice of divine healing can provide a perspective on theodicy. Another question is to what extent the use of one Pentecostal denomination as a case study can be used to derive conclusions applicable to the classical Pentecostal movement as a whole. Stephen Torr writes of the dangers inherent in such a study, that it might create a strawman and present it as reality.[8] I agree that a researcher cannot answer such questions because of subjective involvement. However, it is impossible to survey every classical Pentecostal church in the world to assess whether my conclusions are valid or to evaluate whether using one teaching to decide about another doctrine is proper and valid. The next best option is to locate the study to one doctrine and one denomination and trust peers to evaluate the validness of conclusions about Pentecostal theodicy and the alternatives that the study proposes in response to and in line with the new Pentecostal

---

6. Cartledge, *Testimony in the Spirit*, 18–20. The ordinary level represents the voices of participants in the movement, the theology of the people on the ground. The official level is denominational or confessional theology, a second-order reflection on the first-order theology. The confessional level is also informed by academic theology. The academic level is theology that is not tied to confessional theology but shares similar sources and concerns, with a broader agenda that tends to abstract information from them in order to theorize more generally.

7. Torr, *Dramatic Pentecostal/Charismatic Anti-Theodicy*, 8–9.

8. Torr, *Dramatic Pentecostal/Charismatic Anti-Theodicy*, 9.

hermeneutics that has been developing during the last three decades among Pentecostal scholars.

The method applied here, a comparative literary study, examines the teaching of divine healing in historical terms within one denomination to use its conclusions to design a possible doctrine of theodicy lacking in the Pentecostal movement. The research shows that it is possible to analyze the teaching and the practice that accompanied it within the AFM of SA. Resources that are utilized refer to the ordinary and denominational or confessional levels. The literature surveyed represents ordinary theology but reflects at least some of the church's official teaching, as shown in some cases. The study is done within the parameters of academic theology, but the language that is used reflects ordinary or street-level theology.

The second element in the method is to apply the data in terms of the new Pentecostal hermeneutics to develop a doctrine of theodicy within the context that is conducible to the Pentecostal ethos. If the correct practice is rooted in the right belief, as Miroslav Volf believes, then the necessity of developing a valid theodicy becomes clear.[9] This level represents academic theological endeavors.

Lastly, the study intends to highlight how such a theodicy can inform the movement's pastoral and practical response to suffering and the question of divine justice. That is needed for a theodicy to become a more just and responsive reaction to sufferers, especially those who suffer innocently and who, as believers, do not enjoy the church's support for theological reasons. Now the academic discourse moves back to the ordinary level. It must be stated that proposals for a new practice can at most be basic and introductory, given the complexity of suffering in people's lives; A. van de Beek refers to suffering and the accompanying guilt as extremely difficult and complicated issues.[10] The primary focus of the study is academic theology motivated by pastoral sensitivity.

The method represents intra-theological and inter-disciplinary discourse, drawing on other disciplines within the boundaries of theology, but staying within the bounds of theology. The disciplines engaged include hermeneutics, biblical theology, exegetical studies, and Pentecostal

---

9. "Christian practices are *by definition* normatively shaped by Christian beliefs" (Volf, "Theology for a Way of Life," 250). "Practices" are defined in Torr (*Dramatic Pentecostal/Charismatic Anti-Theodicy*, 9) as "things Christian people do together over time to address the fundamental human needs in response to and in the light of God's active presence for the life of the world."

10. Van de Beek, *Why? On Suffering, Guilt, and God*, vii.

theology, used to define the parameters of a biblical theology within the scope of Pentecostal hermeneutics. It is submitted that what Pentecostals believe about God's revelation in the word and its relation to the Bible is not consistent with the way many of them read the Bible and that the Pentecostal practice of theodicy, as demonstrated in its teaching of divine healing, is not consistent with the way Pentecostal hermeneutics suggests biblical data should be used and applied. "Critical realism," as defined by N. T. Wright, is used as a corrective epistemology for Pentecostal hermeneutics.[11] That theodicy is studied implies that a particular engagement with philosophy and philosophical theology is also necessary, as chapter 2 illustrates. As will be shown, the use of philosophical theology in responding to the complex problem of evil and suffering is complex and problematic. That is why chapter 2, with its philosophico-theological responses to theodicy, is followed as a necessity by chapter 3 with its discussion of answers to theodicy that specific traditions and books of the Bible present.

Having shown the boundaries and limits of the study and the employed method, it becomes necessary to define the theme of theodicy before describing some of these boundaries. Lastly, this chapter presents an outline of the book's argument, reflected in the development of the rest of the chapters.

Theodicy

"Theodicy" comes from two Greek words that refer to God (*theos*) and justice (*dikē*). The German mathematician and philosopher G. W. F. Leibniz (1646–1716) was the first to coin a term to refer to the challenge confronting believers who experience difficult circumstances while believing in a God of love who cares for them. He was clarifying Romans 3:4 and Psalm 51:6 and formulated the question: "How can an omnipotent and, at the same time, just and benevolent God allow so much suffering in the world?"[12] Thus, the theodicy asks questions about God's justice and righteousness in the face of evil.[13] How do you defend the justice and fairness of a good God who is all-powerful when suffering befalls innocent

---

11. Stewart, "N. T. Wright's Hermeneutic: An Exploration." See also Allan, "Contemporary Pentecostal Hermeneutics."

12. Welker, "Theodicy, Creation, and Suffering," 280.

13. Hick, *Evil and the God of Love*, 6.

human beings, specifically believers?[14] Theodicy attempts to explain the existence of evil in contrast to the belief in the goodness of the God who involves the divine self in human affairs, as believers accept in faith.

Epicurus, a Greek philosopher, living in the fourth century BCE, was probably one of the first to verbalize the question that theodicy struggles with: "Is god willing to prevent evil, but not able? Then he is impotent. Is god able but not willing? Then he is malevolent. Is god both able and willing? Whence then is evil?"[15] Lactantius (250–325 CE), an early Christian apologist, used the same argument: Either God wishes to avert or take away evil, and is unable, but then God is feeble, which is not in accordance with the character of God. Or God is indeed able to take away evil, and is unwilling, but then God is malicious, which is equally at variance with a benevolent and loving God. Or God is neither willing nor able to take away evil, but then we cannot possibly acknowledge this feeble and simultaneously malicious existence as God. Or God is both willing and able to take away evil, which alone is suitable to God, but then from what source does all the evil in the world come, and why does God not remove it?[16] David Hume (1711–66) summarized the challenge of theodicy in his "Dialog Concerning Natural Religion" in a well-known trilemma: "Is he [God] willing to prevent evil, but not able? Then he is impotent. Is he able, but not willing? Then he is malevolent. Is he both able and willing? Whence then is evil?"[17]

The question has become relevant in an age and day when social media and television carry photos and videos of suffering around the world into people's sitting rooms and lives. Natural catastrophes, terrorist attacks, conflict in the Middle East, cancer diagnosed in a sports star or television personality, being reminded of the horrors of the twentieth century's two world wars and the Holocaust, and other genocides that scarred modern world history led to a general mood of skepticism about

---

14. See important remarks of Crenshaw, "Shift from Theodicy to Anthropodicy," 1–16.

15. Castelo, *Theological Theodicy*, 8. Scott (*Pathways in Theodicy*, 64) extends these questions to include logically and helpfully the following theological-philosophical questions: The origin of evil: how does evil originate? And who is responsible?; The nature of evil: What is the ontology of evil? How does it exist?; The problem of evil: How does evil pose a problem for theology?; The reason for evil: Why does God permit evil? What is the morally sufficient reason?; The end of evil: How will God end evil and/or ultimately bring good out of evil?

16. Quoted in Welker, "Theodicy, Creation, and Suffering," 280–81.

17. Hume, *Dialog Concerning Natural Religion*, 108–09.

God's existence because of the difficulty of explaining why evil exists. It resulted, among other things, in the vibrancy of the New Atheism movement that argues that belief in God and divine existence has become impossible in the face of the immensity of suffering that characterizes human life. Theodicy attempts to reconcile God's presence and what is right and good, considering the evil present in the world. "The task of theodicy is to interpret the reality of evil: to situate it within a meaningful theological matrix. Theodicy simply tries to explain evil."[18]

An example of the problem that theodicy confronts is demonstrated by Job's arguments about God's justice when Job, as a devout believer, lost his possessions and children while unbelievers around him flourished, at least in his perception. One such argument is found in Job 21:7–16, asking why the wicked live on, reach old age, and grow mighty in power. They are safe from fear in their houses because no rod of God is upon them. They spend their days in prosperity and go down to *Sheol* in peace. They do not interact with God and God's ways but ask boastfully, "What or who is the Almighty, that we should serve God?"

A Babylonian book in the Middle-Babylonian language from somewhere between the eleventh to sixteenth centuries BCE, the "Babylonian Theodicy," relates a conversation between two men.[19] They debate the concept of divine justice in terms of a Babylonian worldview. The first man, named the "sufferer" by scholars, is not sure that his piety, holiness, and dedication to the gods benefitted him at all now that his life is characterized by suffering and difficulties. "You are as stable as the earth, but the plan of the gods is remote . . . the mind of the god, like the center of the heavens, is remote. Knowledge of it is very difficult; people cannot know it . . . Though it is possible to find out what the will of the god is, people do not know how to do it."

In the Sumero-Babylonian world, religion taught that when one demonstrates piety, employing prayers, gifts, libations, and offerings, the gods will reward one with good health and prosperity. The sufferer argues that this is not true, as demonstrated by his experiences. The second man, the "friend," disagrees. He argues that one can gain insight into divine wisdom by one's piety, although he agrees that some decisions of the gods might seem incomprehensible. One is not rewarded for one's righteousness with wealth and health but divine grace. His friend's arguments eventually

---

18. Scott, *Pathways in Theodicy*, 54.
19. Lambert, "The Babylonian Theodicy," 63–91.

convince the "sufferer." It was not only in the context of Israel that believers found the belief in a good God irreconcilable with their difficulties.

Amicus Manlius Severinus Boethius (477–524 CE) was a philosopher, Roman senator, and consul who declared himself king of Italy. He asked the question, If God is righteous, why does evil exist? The question became critically relevant when the Great Lisbon earthquake shook Portugal on November 1, 1755, impacting Portugal, the Iberian Peninsula, and northwest Africa, killing an estimated sixty thousand people in Lisbon alone and demolishing large public buildings and countless dwellings over a large area. Many people were at church when the earthquake occurred; the mix of the human catastrophe with religious observance and devotion touched the collective consciousness of Europe, necessitating the question of whether the quake was to be interpreted as a sign of God's wrath. If not, where was God while thousands of church members were worshiping God as the earthquake struck their world and ended their lives? Can this really be Leibniz's "best of all possible worlds"? It led to a widespread skeptical realism, later verbalized in Voltaire's telling *Poem upon the Lisbon Disaster*. Voltaire struggled with how to reconcile the church's easy but unhelpful statements like, "Whatever is, is right because God ordained it," "Don't ask why," "Don't think about it," or "Just have faith,"[20] with the suffering of innocent and helpless, and sometimes powerless, victims of natural disasters, disease, and the ravages of poverty and war. Voltaire writes that it is impossible to explain the nature of moral and physical evil and improbable that anyone would ever understand it.

Along with other philosophers, Voltaire rebelled against the prevalent optimistic fatalism that ascribes everything to divine providence. It eventually led to a shift in premodern sensibilities that ended in New Atheism. These thinkers accept that vast evil exists as an integrated element of the functioning of the world, but then it calls into question the existence of God or that God is both good and all-powerful.

The twentieth century experienced the *Shoah*, one among several such mass murders of people and groups, raising the question of whether the gracious God is powerful enough to direct the world in ways that benefit believers. That vast evil exists nobody would dispute. Now Westerners began to question the existence of God or the character of God. The nature of the world in which human beings lived led to atheism, but it also challenged traditional notions of theism. Daniel Castelo

---

20. Orr-Ewing, *Where Is God in All the Suffering?*, 7.

distinguishes between "holy atheism," which states that God is without excuse in terms of God's goodness and all-powerfulness, given the degree and extent of evil in the world, and "protest atheism," which rejects belief in God unconditionally based on the epistemic and moral needs of the human sense of justice, goodness, and righteousness.[21]

The challenge of theodicy can be analyzed logically as:

> Proposition 1: God exists
> Proposition 2: God is good
> Proposition 3: God is all-powerful
> Proposition 4: There is widespread evil occurring in the world

The problem is reconciling the second and third propositions that qualify the first with the fourth one, throwing doubt on the truth of the first proposition. A good God will not allow evil in the creation, and an all-powerful God would prevent evil, except if the human definition of "good," "evil," and "powerful" differs from divine definitions (used in the Bible to describe God and divine characteristics).

Gottfried Leibniz, for example, assumed that God existed and that God was good and all-powerful. He argued from the position that, in the grand scheme of things, good was more prominent than evil. That is because an infinitely good God created the best or most optimal world; God could do nothing less, given God's character. In accepting that this world is the best there could be, he asserts, "Thus, if the smallest evil that comes to pass in the world were missing in it, it would no longer be this world; which, with nothing omitted and all allowance made, was found the best by the Creator who chose it."[22] In other words, evil is necessarily part of the world that God had created since God permitted it. Evil functions in one way or another to promote the good. Evil must serve the purposes of God; otherwise, God would not have allowed it, concludes Leibniz.[23] Shane Sharp argues somewhat sarcastically that believers accomplish theodicy by performing (what he calls) "imaginary face-work."[24] He defines imaginary face-work as cognitive acts or actions taken to save the face of others. To do so, believers utilize several arguments that justify

---

21. Castelo, *Theological Theodicy*, 14. Castelo also refers to Willis, *Theism, Atheism, and the Doctrine of the Trinity*, chapter 4.
22. Leibniz, *Theodicy*, 128–29.
23. Castelo, *Theological Theodicy*, 10.
24. Sharp, "Monotheistic Theodicy as Imaginary Face-Work," 874.

or excuse face-threatening conduct, that is, to find excuses for God in the face of unjust and innocent suffering by human beings.

Sharp refers to research based on in-depth interviews of sixty-two women from various monotheistic religious affiliations and views. Without exception, the participants believe in a God who is omnipotent and morally perfect. They learned of the attributes of God during their upbringing, beliefs they held before their experiences of intimate partner violence. The participants also shared experiences of suffering in the form of physical, emotional, and/or sexually intimate partner violence. All of them admitted that they initially had trouble reconciling their experiences of violence with their beliefs about the benevolence and omnipotence of God. They confessed that there were times when they prayed, "Why did you let this happen to me, God? Where are you when this happens?" They explained that they found answers to the question in such a way that they were able to maintain their belief about God despite their experiences of acute suffering. They developed a theodicy that consisted of three different types of explanations for God's involvement in their suffering: fidelity to a higher principle, that is, the idea that God bestowed on humanity the ability to make free choices as a higher principle justification to save God's face as a morally perfect actor; ultimate benefit, that is, that God allows individuals to suffer for a greater good; and shifting blame to relieve God of the responsibility for the individuals' suffering by blaming some actor(s) other than God, mainly themselves and Satan.[25] Their purpose was to "save God's face," where the taken-for-granted assumption is that God is all-powerful and morally perfect.[26] This study in social science demonstrates that believers tailored face-saving accounts to their own specific situations, personalities, and biographies. Some argue that God allowed these experiences in their lives to enable them to help others in the future. Others blame themselves for their suffering. By incorporating their personal situations, personalities, and biographies into their excuses and justifications to save God's face, they successfully created accounts that were "personally resonant and thus more cognitively satisfying than abstract theodicean explanations for the existence of suffering."[27]

---

25. Sharp, "Monotheistic Theodicy as Imaginary Face-Work," 873–76.
26. Sharp, "Monotheistic Theodicy as Imaginary Face-Work," 878.
27. Sharp, "Monotheistic Theodicy as Imaginary Face-Work," 879.

As Daniel Castelo argues, such a way of reasoning excuses God from direct involvement as the cause of evil but affirms God's function as the cosmic orderer so that God's goodness and providence would and could not be compromised.[28] However, it does not answer the critical question of whence evil comes.

Other questions posed by the theodicy are: Why is biological life in general, and the lives of individuals and groups of people, invaded by physical and moral evil? Why does God allow that people suffer at all? Why is death an inherent element in all of life? Why is entropy, a state of disorder, randomness, or uncertainty a built-in principle underlying the whole of the universe? To conclude, if God is all-powerful and righteous, why does God allow evil in the created world? Furthermore, if God is loving, why does God not prevent suffering in people's lives, particularly in the lives of believers?

It is essential to define what one means by "God" when arguing about *theo*dicy. Is it the God of deism or theism, the God portrayed by the biblical authors, or the god of theological or philosophical theism?[29] In this regard, Alasdair Macintyre and Paul Ricoeur argue that the God in whom many people in the nineteenth and early twentieth centuries came to disbelieve was not the Christian God but a concept that had been invented only in the seventeenth century.[30]

It is also necessary to define "evil," as it is a central element in theodicy. Many theologians distinguish between three types of evil: metaphysical evil, which refers to all created beings as finite whose earthly power and knowledge is limited, limitations that remain beyond their influence; physical evil, which refers to all possible forms of bodily and spiritual suffering that, although in part related to metaphysical evil, can be treated by medical intervention and a healthy lifestyle; and moral evil, including all forms of evil and injustice caused by people themselves and for which they are directly responsible.[31]

In the case of moral evil, the theodicy question transitions to anthropodicy, asking why people abuse human freedom to act reprehensibly and destructively in moral terms. However, that does not cancel the

---

28. Castelo, *Theological Theodicy*, 10.
29. The argument is further explained in chapter 5.
30. MacIntyre and Ricoeur, *Religious Significance of Atheism*, 14.
31. Welker, "Theodicy, Creation, and Suffering," 281.

question of why a good God created flawed people who choose to do evil instead of good.

The issue of theodicy has gained new significance in the time when this study was completed. Now the financial and health consequences of the COVID-19 pandemic have forced the world to stop and reconsider religious faith as a way to attempt to explain the experiences of hundreds of millions of people implicated by the infection.

Pentecostal Hermeneutics and Theodicy

Like most conservative Protestants, Pentecostals hold a "high" view of Scripture: the Bible is God's authoritative, reliable, and inspired (meaning "God-breathed," 2 Tim 3:16) word. Because the Bible has a divine origin, it serves as the sign and instrument of God's loving address to intelligent creatures.[32] In some sense, it is the word of God ("*sacra scriptura est verbum Dei*") as God's self-revelation and affectionate address to human beings.

Like these traditions, Pentecostals utilize all the traditional principles used for reading the Bible. This includes that one should interpret a passage in light of its immediate context, read it for its function within and as a part of the rest of the book, and read it in light of the historical, social, and cultural context that its language, assumptions, and allusions take for granted and in which the text originated, as well as the original listeners' or readers' social context.[33] It also considers the text's specific genre or literary type and the different theological and ideological traditions and ideological elements in texts. In the last place, the text is interpreted as a part of the Bible's narrative and scope.

The way Pentecostals read the Bible has changed and developed along different lines during the century of their existence. The early Pentecostals read the Bible from their experience of Spirit baptism and the charismatic experiences that followed after being filled with the Spirit. Their experience formed their pre-understanding when they read the Bible; they read it as Spirit-filled people whose lives changed by the experience of Spirit-baptism that they perceived to be a replication of the day of Pentecost (Acts 2). As a result, they found different emphases and shades of meaning in some texts than Protestants or Roman Catholics.

---

32. Webster, *Holy Scripture*, 42.
33. Keener, *Spirit Hermeneutics*, 117.

They read the text as literally as possible, but at the same time, they expected that the Spirit would speak to them about the application of the text to their lives and situation.

However, from the 1940s, the face of the Pentecostal movement changed. Many Pentecostals yearned for acceptance from society and other churches. Previously they were treated as members of a sect and cult and experienced discrimination in several ways. To overcome that hurdle, they vied for the evangelicals' approval, formed alliances with them, changed their behavior and practices accordingly, and eventually accepted how conservative evangelicals read the Bible, or their hermeneutical perspective. Now they read the text literally without considering the historical and social context in which it originated and the social customs it reflects. Instead, they viewed the Bible in a biblicist way, adhering to every word and sentence as divine truths that reflect God's direct and complete revelation. Like legalism, which applies the letter of the law to all situations and people, ignoring individual circumstances, biblicism is rigid and demanding, applying biblical prescripts given for a specific group of people and related to their world to contemporary people.[34] It teaches, among other things, that cremation is immoral, believers should reject the use of all alcohol and tobacco, and women should subject themselves to men's authority. It views the Bible as a science textbook and interprets Genesis 1–2 as literal, that creation originated in a word from God, that God made everything in six days, and that the earth is six thousand years old.

Since the 1990s, Pentecostal scholarship developed a new hermeneutics that connects with how the early Pentecostals had read the Bible and rejected the fundamentalist-literalist hermeneutics of many of the contemporaries. The contemporary Pentecostal hermeneutics is distinctive in several ways, although not necessarily unique to the Pentecostal movement. It reflects what is distinctive and specific about being a Pentecostal and presents what it believes is the Pentecostal ethos, values, and interests.[35] Being a Pentecostal is defined in terms of the experience of a personal experience of Spirit baptism and living a Spirit-filled life, interpreted from the vantage of the day of Pentecost (Acts 2).[36] One of

---

34. Rachel Evans defines "biblicism" as a theory about the Bible that emphasizes its "exclusive authority, infallibility, perspicuity, self-sufficiency, internal consistency, self-evident meaning, and universal applicability." Evans, "Problem of Biblicalism."

35. McKinley, "What Do I Do with Contexts?," 159–71.

36. Keener, *Spirit Hermeneutics*, 4.

the implications of being a Pentecostal is that Pentecostals interpret the Bible with the help and enlightenment of the Spirit, the same Spirit who had initially inspired authors to write it down.

In other words, Pentecostal hermeneutics is dependent on charismatic experiences. In the first place, these charismatic experiences form Pentecostals' pre-understanding (*Vorverständnis*) in reading the Bible, determining the way they interpret and apply it. Second, their ongoing experiences and encounters with the Spirit provide the context in which they read the narratives of biblical events and shape how they read the text.[37] Third, the direction in which they read the Bible is from their experiences to the Bible and back to the practice of their lives, in the same way as the early Pentecostals did. In other words, they do not read the Bible from the perspective of dogmatic truths that the church predefined but from the view and perspective that the Spirit is leading and using the Bible to change and transform their lives.

The second emphasis is that Pentecostals read the Bible with the intent to hear what God is telling them about their present needs and challenges. In other words, they are open to hearing the "voice of the Spirit" while reading the text; they expect that the Spirit would give them insights into what God is telling them at the present moment. The text does not tell readers directly how to apply it to their situation; they expect the Spirit to do so through insights formed in their minds. "The Spirit is active in the life of the whole church to interpret the biblical message in the languages of today. He actualizes the word of God by helping us to restate the message in contemporary terminology and apply it to new situations. The result is that salvation history continues to take effect in us."[38] God's revelation continues in the life and experience of the church through the Spirit.

Sometimes these insights are not necessarily directly connected to the biblical text, but believers understand it as God's will for their lives. They obey these injunctions because they have learned that obeying and following God's voice transforms their lives; to meet God in the Bible changes one's behavior, regulates one's decisions, and sets parameters for one's life.[39]

---

37. Lewis, "Towards a Pentecostal Epistemology," 113–14.
38. Pinnock, "Work of the Holy Spirit in Hermeneutics," 4.
39. Lewis, "Towards a Pentecostal Epistemology," 116.

What is essential for Pentecostals is to "hear God's heart beating" rather than understand what a text's literal meaning is. They know that God is not a prisoner of the Bible, and they do not worship the Bible. Instead, they expect to meet God while reading the Bible and experience that God meets them in the challenges of their situation. The Bible is a book written by human beings, and, like all other human beings, they had their shortcomings and weaknesses, some of which are stated honestly in the Bible. Pentecostals worship God who reveals the divine self through the Spirit, at times (and in their experience primarily) using the Bible to do so. However, God is not limited to the Bible; God speaks through nature, events, other people, and directly into believers' hearts through the moving of the Spirit. When the last chapters reflect on theodicy from a Pentecostal hermeneutical perspective, this principle will be applied.

At times, they see in biblical events something that directly fits their situation and explains the meaning of events in their lives. While some read the Bible as a rational deliberation, Pentecostals' Bible-reading practices are affections-based because they are based on charismatic experiences in and with the text.

Another emphasis in Pentecostal hermeneutics is that one can only read the Bible when the Spirit reveals its truths to the reader. While anyone can read the text, only Spirit-filled people hear the word of God in the text because it is a condition that the Spirit anoints and enlightens them to understand what God is saying to them. Pentecostals know that the Spirit can act in difficult or even impossible ways. They refer to God meeting them in their "spirit," that is, the God-given human ability to communicate and commune with God, apart from their rational and volitional senses. They argue that the Spirit cooperating when one reads the Bible is a condition for the Bible and God's revelation to "happen" in their lives.

What do they mean when they emphasize that the reader should rely upon the Holy Spirit in interpreting the text? This primarily implies that using humanly devised interpretative methods will always be limited because understanding what God says in the text requires divine guidance. French Arrington suggests several helpful ways for interpreters to express their dependence on the Spirit that reflect Pentecostal practices.[40] First, one needs to submit one's mind to God and set one's critical and analytical abilities under the Holy Spirit's guidance. What is required is

---

40. Arrington, "Use of the Bible by Pentecostals," 105.

an openness to the Spirit's witness and to realize that the Spirit transcends human reason. Because the Bible is not an object that believers interpret but a living word that interprets them, studying the Bible should always occur in a context of prayer and worship. Pentecostals acquire knowledge about God not by studying the Bible but by their personal encounters with God. The Hebrew term for "to know" explains it. *Yāda* refers to knowledge that one acquires through experience in a relationship with somebody or something. It is not theoretical knowledge about facts but consists of the actualization of a relationship with God.[41] Pentecostals are not interested in amassing knowledge by reading the Bible; they read it from their desire to "know" God.[42]

Unfortunately, the way Pentecostals read the Bible sometimes indeed leads to subjectivist interpretation of texts. What Pentecostals should do is to keep the two dimensions, experiential-pneumatic (or spiritual-charismatic) and exegetical elements, in balance.[43] They may not overemphasize the experiential and pneumatic at the cost of the mind's contribution to the reading process. Furthermore, the Bible should serve as the objective standard; they should submit all interpretations to it. Pentecostals believe it is true that God still speaks today, and when God speaks, God has more to say than just what is written in the Bible. However, God's revelation will never contradict the Bible; after all, the same Spirit who had inspired the Bible's authors now reveals God.[44] At the same time, individuals must submit their interpretation of Scripture to the faith community's understanding of the text.

Pentecostals try to restore the way the New Testament church functioned because they believe that the outpouring of the Spirit led to the ongoing revelation of Jesus to his disciples in contemporary times. Thus, they interpret their world in terms of the biblical world and share Jesus' and the disciples' worldview, as far as it is possible, given the distance in time and situation. They deliberately shape their identity by connecting and associating with the biblical characters and their historical encounters with God. Because they accept that they continuously live in the biblical

---

41. Jones and Jones, "Yielding to the Spirit," 112.

42. Grey, *Three's a Crowd*, 159.

43. It is acknowledged that although an objective reading of the biblical text (for instance, always finding the original intention of the author) is impossible, what is needed is an interpretation that relies upon a consensus among believers within the same tradition from ancient times to the contemporary day.

44. Archer, "Pentecostal Hermeneutics," 148.

experience, they believe the same Spirit still leads them and reveals God to them as in biblical times. When they testify about God and their charismatic experiences, they use biblical language. They fuse the ancient and contemporary horizons of understanding uniquely because their world coincides with that of biblical figures. Pentecostals view themselves as the restoration of the early church in recent times. They interpret "being Pentecostal" as being Spirit-centered and Spirit-focused, miracle-affirming, and praise-oriented.[45] They expect to share the experiences with God that biblical characters had and interpret the Bible as the means to find answers to their pressing questions.[46] The implication is clear, that the meaning of the biblical text may move beyond the scope of the authors' intent and that the author did not necessarily always fully understand what they wrote, as underscored by the way authors in the New Testament quote and apply texts from the Old Testament. The Spirit may explicate a text for contemporary readers in a new and refreshing way, generating a new meaning for a new context. However, it remains important to remember that it will always be in line with the biblical metanarrative.[47]

Pentecostals who believe that the Spirit still reveals God organize their worship gatherings by leaving ample space for the Spirit to interrupt them at any moment. They reject a formal liturgical structuring of worship services because they believe it will rob the Spirit of the freedom to intervene at will.[48] They think that the worship services should always be spontaneous and allow anyone to participate because the Spirit may intervene at any time and in any way. Anyone may join and participate in the service by testimony, song, prayer, or a charismatic word (gift of the Spirit, or *charisma*). All believers are part of the priesthood and prophethood bought by Jesus's blood, despite gender, age, or level of (theological and other) education.

How they read the Bible also determines how Pentecostals do theology. They confess, like most Protestants, that the Bible is the standard that defines faith and practice,[49] but at the same time, they express their doctrines in terms of their experiences with God.[50] When they think

---

45. Jacobsen, *Thinking in the Spirit*, 12.
46. Bultmann, "Problem of Hermeneutics," 79.
47. Lewis, "Towards a Pentecostal Epistemology," 113.
48. Davies, *Immoral Bible*, 253.
49. See discussion in Nel, "Pentecostal Movement's View," 2.
50. Ellington, "Pentecostals and the Authority of Scriptures," 34.

about doctrines, they do it in terms of experiences that the Bible describes and that they have applied in their lives. Therefore, a condition for doing theology is that one should be Spirit-filled, spending one's time studying the Bible in worship and listening prayer. It is crucial for them not to have clearly defined doctrines qualified by propositions but ongoing encounters with God and continuous revelation. In their practice, creeds do not function at all, and doctrines are subjected to believers' personal encounters with God.

It is important to remember that the Pentecostal hermeneutics views the Bible as a witness to revelation and not revelation itself. Revelation only happens when the Spirit moves and changes believers' reading into a word that they perceive as directly from the heart of God. And only when reading the Bible results in a revelation applicable to the current situation does the Bible *become* the word of God. Pentecostal hermeneutics is Christocentric, in line with the self-identification of classical Pentecostals with the fourfold or fivefold Full Gospel of Jesus Christ as Savior, Sanctifier, Spirit Baptizer, Healer, and Coming King. It acknowledges that Jesus Christ is God's true and final word, the one through whom God revealed the divine self. In relation to Jesus, the Bible is God's secondary, written word that needs the enlightenment of the Spirit of Jesus to interpret and understand it correctly.

Although their view of the Bible and its inspiration differ in several ways from Karl Barth's, they share some elements. Barth emphasized that the human character of the Bible, with the author's experiences, style, peculiar use of language, and the stamp of the time that the author lived in, involves a human limitation that cannot be overcome.[51] Human thoughts cannot contain divine revelation or do justice to God's essence. Barth quotes Augustine, who said that even though John experienced community with the Son of God, he could only speak as he was able. He could do nothing else than a human could with human concepts available to describe unspeakable and indescribable charismatic mysteries. Although the Spirit inspired the authors, they were still human beings. If they were not inspired, they would have had nothing to say, but inspiration enabled them to speak of God understandably. However, they did and could not talk about the whole, but only told what a human being could about God.[52]

---

51. Runia, *Karl Barth's Doctrine of Holy Scripture*, 67.
52. Barth, *Church Dogmatics* I.2, 508.

The Bible bears the character of a witness; God's revelation to human beings comes to them through the witness of human eye- and ear-witnesses. However, being a human always imposes certain restrictions. Witnesses can and will only speak about those aspects of what they perceived as brokered through their personal experience and knowledge. Their vantage point determines what witnesses remember about their experiences. In the words of Ridderbos, the Bible's witness accounts are the "fruit of an apperception" that is finite because they represent reproductions. No one can ever exceed the limits of their comprehension and memory.[53] For this reason, for example, not everything experienced by the apostles was written down, and there is uncertainty about the sequence of events and the exact words Jesus had spoken. God's words are transforming, but they remain bound to the limitations of human language.[54]

The Bible does not have authority as such, but its authority lies in the Spirit using the Bible to reveal God to contemporary believers. When that happens, the specific biblical word becomes authoritative for them.[55] Furthermore, the Bible's authority becomes self-evident when believers find that the text relates to and coincides with their experiences.[56] For that reason, God's voice is not limited to the Bible but also heard in anointed sermons, teachings, exhortations, testimonial narratives, and other charismatic words, including the operation of the *charismata*.[57]

In conclusion, the Pentecostal hermeneutics of experience that Pentecostal scholarship has been developing surpasses the hermeneutics applied by seemingly most Pentecostals. They apply a quasi-fundamentalist, biblicist, literalist, and limiting way of reading the Bible sympathetic to the Bible-reading practices of some conservative evangelicals. The new Pentecostal hermeneutics provides surprising ways of interpretation because it listens for the heartbeat of God in the text rather than rigidly applying texts that originated in another world and addressed a different culture to the contemporary situation.

When Pentecostals think about the challenges that theodicy poses, they necessarily use the Bible. In reading the Bible, their interpretation is limited by their hermeneutical angle. Most Pentecostals support the

---

53. Ridderbos, *Heilsgeschiedenis en Heilige Schrift*, 126.

54. See also further discussion of the limitation of language in speaking of God's essence in chapter 5.

55. Land, *Pentecostal Spirituality*, 100, 106.

56. Lewis, "Towards a Pentecostal Epistemology," 111.

57. Albrecht, *Rites in the Spirit*, 229.

viewpoints found in the Bible that suffering is due to retributive justice in response to human sin, a continuation of original sin, and serves as testing and discipline as a part of the divine plan for forming and developing believers' character. However, the new Pentecostal hermeneutics starts with God's character (essence) and the revelation of salvation (energies), reading the Bible in terms of their experience of God's presence. For that reason, their theodicy can present fascinating new ways of thinking about God's role in human and other sufferings, as will hopefully becomes apparent in the last two chapters.

Design of Book

The first chapter defined theodicy and discussed Pentecostal hermeneutics in terms of its historical development over the century of the movement's existence. The emphasis is on the new hermeneutics that developed in Pentecostal scholarship since the 1990s. In the following chapters, the argument unfolds as follows. First, it discusses the answers that philosophy and theology developed in engaging with the challenges that suffering poses to human beings. Then the responses of biblical authors of the Old and New Testament are investigated to complete the picture of theodicy in ecclesiastical thinking. Next, it attempts to paint a picture of current thinking among Pentecostals about theodicy. Because they did not publish much about theodicy as such since their practice disqualifies them from such a philosophico-theological undertaking, their teaching and practice of divine healing are investigated to develop a possible theodicy. In the last two chapters, a reflection on theodicy from the new Pentecostal hermeneutics is provided in contrast to the reigning view, referring to how Pentecostals depict God, think about evil, the afterlife, and their charismatic practice of living with suffering. Then a reflection of evil from a psycho-theological perspective is developed in the last chapter to complete the picture of theodicy.

2

Philosophical-Theological Answers to the Challenges of Theodicy

Introduction

THE FIRST CHAPTER DEFINES the two questions that theodicy presupposes: Why does a powerful God not prevent evil in the created world? And why does a loving God not prevent innocent suffering in the lives of people, in particular believers' lives? Why are some people born with severe physical or mental challenges? For instance, why does the young mother of children get cancer that costs her her life? Why do accidents occur where innocent victims are injured? Why do natural catastrophes wreak havoc, wiping out people and their possessions? Theologians and philosophers have provided several answers or solutions to the challenges that theodicy poses to believers.

Theology recently experienced a renewed interest in the debate, especially in the light of the challenges that New Atheism poses. That the Bible gives adequate expression to the problem of theodicy is evident from John Barton's[1] interpretation of the Old Testament in terms of four interlocking themes, an understanding that is also valid for the New Testament. The Bible is concerned, he writes, with issues related to creation and monotheism, covenant and redemption, ethics, and theodicy. The other three issues are related to theodicy and provide perspectives on the challenges and possible reasons for suffering. In the next chapter, biblical evidence is investigated. In this chapter, some of the leading solutions

---

1. Barton and Muddiman, *Oxford Bible Commentary*, 9–10.

presented by theologians are discussed. In the next chapter, a comparison will be made between the theological responses to theodicy described in this chapter and the evidence found in the Bible regarding the subject.

Not much attention is given to philosophical solutions, since it is irrelevant to evaluate how Pentecostals apply solutions to theodicy's challenges; a short summary will suffice to provide the necessary background information for further theological discussions presenting all proponents of the different perspectives.

In considering the possible philosophical answers, researchers developed several typologies that can be summarized in terms of the following.[2]

Suffering Is Due to Retributive Justice

A popular theodicy among believers is that suffering must result from the sins committed by those who suffer. Suffering is a deserved calamity; God employs it to punish wickedness. Punishment theodicy sees pain as a divine discipline.[3] God uses pain and suffering as ways to rehabilitate, deter, retribute, or protect human beings.[4]

Parts of Eastern philosophy have a similar view of human suffering, looking at it through the lenses of karma and reincarnation. Karma implies a moral law of cause and effect. If one suffers, the law of karma means that one deserves it. It is probably not possible and not even necessary to know what one did wrong. Reincarnation implies that the universe recycles human beings' lives over multiple lifetimes, making it likely that one experiences the effects of karma for something done in a previous life.[5]

The perspective argues that while the wicked suffer from their wickedness, the righteous prosper for being honest and upright (Prov 10:16, 24–25, 27–29).[6] It is not difficult to find evidence in the Bible to support this viewpoint. Reward and punishment happen in the form of prosperity or poverty, happiness or suffering, and long life or illness and death. John 9 defines it as the perspective Jesus' disciples used when they asked Jesus if the blindness of the man who was born blind was due to

---

2. See, e.g., Vicchio, *Book of Job*, 92, who provides nine such causes.
3. Murray, "Theodicy," 360–62.
4. Murray, "Theodicy," 360–61.
5. Orr-Ewing, *Where Is God in All the Suffering?*, 13.
6. Perkins, "Just Desert or Just Deserts?," 182.

his sin or that of his parents (John 9:2–3). Most of the Hebrew prophets also used it, as the Deuteronomist Historian also did, interpreting Israel's suffering at the hands of other nations, such as the Egyptians, Assyrians, and Babylonians due to their disloyalty and disobedience to YHWH. The modern-day prosperity gospel, attractive to so many, uses the same perspective. Much so-called religious elite within the prosperity movement also uses it to get people to conform with what they want, which is their monetary contributions to the ministry. By acting and speaking in the right way, one unlocks heaven, God's blessings, prosperity, and welfare.

The implication is that one is in control of one's fate amidst an otherwise uncontrollable life. One "controls" the amount of God's blessing in life by repenting from sin, praying in faith, doing good things, and avoiding sin. Life is fair; you get what you deserve. God is an impartial and unbiased judge and punishes the wicked and the bad. Although punishment for sin includes suffering, it also reveals the underlying goodness and justice of the cosmic order.

Another, extended version of this perspective is eschatological in essence, projecting the blessings and benefits for living good lives into the future of the afterlife. Believers are encouraged to live up to the requirements to gain entrance into heaven; failing to comply implies that one is heading towards hell and punishment. Such an eschatological expectation prevents people from asking questions about the unfairness of their situation when their expectations of blessings and prosperity do not realize.[7]

The problem is that not all suffering results from wrongdoing; punishment theodicy does not exhaust all possible explanations for evil.[8] When the proof is used in cases that do not deserve it, it leads to further suffering because the victims of suffering now also experience disproportionately excessive, unnecessary, and undeserved guilt. Punishment theodicy does not provide hope, although it may in some cases be true. Unfortunately, this answer is the default of many Christians, also through the ages, given the biblical support, especially by the Deuteronomist Historian (as discussed in more detail in the next chapter).

---

7. Perkins, "Just Desert or Just Deserts?," 182.
8. Scott, *Pathways in Theodicy*, 6.

Suffering Is Due to Free Will

The purpose of theodicy is to deflect blame from God by justifying God and by redirecting blame elsewhere. There are two main ways to explain theodicy: viewing it as the causal and moral responsibility for evil and suffering. The one is to put the "blame" for suffering on God; God punishes those who do evil. This is the theodicy of retributive justice discussed above. The other way to explain theodicy is to blame humankind. Then suffering is caused by one's own free choices. It argues that all or at least most evils can be traced back to sinful free actions of human beings or other creatures, such as angels, created by God. God created human beings essentially free; free action is of great value, and it is logically incompatible with divine causal control of humans' activities. The implication is that the fact that God is not intervening is necessary for the good of human creation. Their resultant sins are, however, not good to them or creation as such. Human freedom then serves as a morally sufficient reason for God's not preventing sins.[9]

John Calvin expressed this idea in several sermons, and countless other Christians, many Muslims, and Jews followed suit. However, Augustine (354–430 CE), Bishop of Hippo and the most influential church father in the West in ancient times, exemplifies this perspective, as does Alvin Plantinga (1932–), American analytic philosopher and Emeritus Professor of Philosophy at the University of Notre Dame, in modern times.[10] It seems that the idea of the two *yetzerim*, "imaginations" or "inclinations," the *yetzer ha-ra* and the *yetzer ha-tob*, support this explanation.

For instance, Plantinga's theory, a defense rather than theodicy,[11] states that a significantly free world contains creatures that can freely perform good and evil actions. A world where they perform more good actions is more valuable. God can create free human beings but cannot cause or determine them to do only what is right. If God determines what people decide, they would not be free. To be able for creatures to be free to do moral good, they must be able to perform evil. In their freedom, they can perform evil, and God is not able to prevent them. In creating creatures free, something went wrong in their exercise of freedom, which

---

9. Audi, "Theodicy," 910.

10. For more information about Augustine, see Evans, *Augustine on Evil*, and for more information about Plantinga, see Geivett, "Augustine and the Problem of Evil."

11. Santrac, *Evaluation of Alvin Plantinga's Free Will Defense*, 14.

also became the source and cause of moral evil. That free creatures sometimes perform evil counts nothing against God's power or might "for he could have forestalled the occurrence of moral evil only by exercising the possibility of moral good."[12]

From where does evil come? The answer to that question helps in the search for the question of who is culpable, linking causal and moral responsibility. If God is the almighty creator and maintainer of the universe, the logical solution to where evil comes from is that it cannot exist without God's will and intention. If human beings are the cause of evil, then the logical answer is that human beings are guilty. At the same time, theology asserts that whatever exists must ultimately derive from God, who created everything good (Gen 1:25). Where did evil then originate? Free-will theodicy finds the answer in Genesis 3 that recounts how Adam and Eve sinned shortly after being created, losing their privileged place in paradise.[13] Their sin represented original sin, whereby Adam and Eve biologically transmit "sin and death" to all generations to come. Thus, due to the first couple's sin, all people are totally depraved, without the ability not to sin, and all people are lost sinners in God's eyes. God elects only some to inherit eternal life, while the rest are destined for hell.[14]

This perspective builds upon a mythological view of creation without trying to correlate it with contemporary scientific theories.[15] Instead, its theological assumptions that determine how it reads the Genesis narratives identify the serpent with Satan, make Eve culpable for primordial sin, associate Eve's sin with sexuality, and establish the notion that "original" sin affects future generations of humanity biologically through this sexual connotation.[16] The reason why the first couple in the garden of Eden sinned was due to the exercise of their free will. The theory transfers moral blame for evil from God to human beings by attributing its origin to the misuse of free will. God permits evil because of human freedom; to be able to exercise meaningful agency requires the possibility of evil.[17] Only by creating automata would God have been able to have

---

12. Quoted in Santrac, *Evaluation of Alvin Plantinga's* Free Will Defence, 16.

13. Augustine, *City of God* XII.24.

14. In some Christian traditions, it even implies that innocent babies who die are also lost.

15. Scott, *Pathways in Theodicy*, 72.

16. In chapter 6, the discussion returns to the identity of the snake in Gen 3.

17. Scott, *Pathways in Theodicy*, 73.

created human beings who never sinned or strayed. In time, this became the majority view in Christianity to make sense of suffering.[18]

The prelapsarian Adam and Eve represent the Christian ideal awaiting them in the eschatological future, depicted in images of immortality and perfection. Only Jesus Christ can unlock that future that was lost for all humankind when the first couple sinned. Evil will also end with the coming of the eschatological future, with the final judgment and its accompanying reward and punishment for believers and unbelievers. Then the destruction of the devil, demons, the wicked, and sin will happen, and evil will cease to exist. The judgment will vindicate God's justice that is glaringly absent in this dispensation.

A positive feature of the theory is that it promotes ethical empowerment by accenting human responsibility and accountability.[19] However, free-will theodicy cannot explain the connection between sin and the suffering experienced by other life forms on earth as well as the suffering of innocent people, except to describe it as part of the brokenness attributed to original sin. The theodicy also does not adequately explain the origin of evil because an unqualifiedly good creature that sins is self-contradictory and unintelligible.[20] Its literal interpretation of the prehistorical Genesis narratives cannot be reconciled with contemporary science because it utilizes an outmoded cosmology.[21] Its depiction of God's actions in the narrative that recounts sin and the fall and the outcome of creation, in a final judgment as arbitrary and punitive, seems disproportional to the crime. Lastly, it asserts that genuine freedom requires the ability to sin, while in heaven, human beings will be free and not able to sin, consisting of a logical fallacy. The argument is, if God can give us that kind of freedom in heaven, why not from the start?

Suffering Is Due to Testing

For many centuries, the idea was accepted that suffering is due to human free will. Leibniz proposed in 1710 in his work, *Theodicy*, such comprehensive theodicy based on the view that God had adequate reason to bring into existence the actual world, despite all the evils that characterize

---

18. Hick, *Evil and the God of Love*, 36.
19. Scott, *Pathways in Theodicy*, 89.
20. Hick, *Evil and the God of Love*, 62–63.
21. Hick, *Evil and the God of Love*, 245–53.

it, because it represents the best of all possible worlds. His reasoning and basis for asserting it as the best possible world are that all evils are essential ingredients necessary to form the world. Omitting any of them would spoil the design of the whole.[22] The argument is based on the assertion that the end justifies the means, requiring one to ask whether the cost of consequent suffering due to evil is not much too high.

In 1966, the contours of the debate changed with the publication of John Hick's *Evil and the God of Love*. Hick was a British philosopher of religion. He designed a new paradigm in explicit and direct contradistinction to the "creation-fall myth" that underlies the theory of free will as the cause for suffering. Hick criticizes Augustine's view because it relies on ancient mythology and cosmology that conflicts with contemporary science and intellectual sensibilities. He describes the depiction of its view of God's punishment for the first couple's sin that applies to all people as excessive and cruel and asks the question, How could evil arise in a perfect paradise?[23] "The notion that man was at first spiritually and morally good, orientated in love towards his Maker, and free to express his flawless nature without even the hindrance of contrary temptations, and yet that he preferred to be evil and miserable, cannot be saved from the charge of self-contradiction and absurdity."[24]

In contrast to the theory of free will, Hick explains that he uses the ideas of Irenaeus (ca. 130–200 CE), an influential second-century bishop and apologist in the East.[25] Irenaeus argued that God uses evil and suffering to test people's moral character, especially in the lives of believers. Some of Job's friends also refer to this view.

In Hick's anthropology, based on evolutionary science, people begin life as children, not fully formed and morally mature adults. People represent works in progress, with perfection lying in the future. Evil came on the scene, not through the sin of the (what he calls "ahistorical primordial") first couple but through missteps and mistakes humans necessarily make in their transition from biological life (*Bios*) to spiritual life (*Zoe*). Humans exist to transcend biology into higher forms of reality; sin is self-centeredness, and perfection implies other-centeredness, exemplified in

---

22. Audi, "Theodicy," 910.
23. Scott, *Pathways in Theodicy*, 97.
24. Hick, *Evil and the God of Love*, 69.
25. Scott, *Pathways in Theodicy*, 99, argues validly that Origen would better fit as patron saint of Hick's theodicy.

Christ.²⁶ Evil originated in the struggle of life to evolve over the ages; it is not a transhistorical, spiritual force, like Satan, but consists of humans failing to realize their divine likeness.²⁷ God's purpose with evil in a good creation is concerned with the purpose and goal of creation, to facilitate human intellectual, moral, and spiritual development and growth. Suffering is thus necessary to facilitate and promote human moral, intellectual, and spiritual development. Without suffering, people are unable to realize their potential for divine likeness. He admits that a "surplus" of evil exists; he refers to it as the "dysteleological evil" of senseless, soulless, excessive, and meaningless suffering. However, even this suffering serves to contribute to the process of soul-making, since it cultivates compassion and elicits sympathy for those who suffer unfairly, and since it causes us to strive for the good for its own sake.²⁸ Its view of God is positive; God is a parent who guides humanity in its journey through the rigors of spiritual transformation. The parent has the best interests of human beings in mind. All suffering represents a phase in fulfilling God's good purpose, and all suffering will eventually be redeemed. It serves the soteriological function of creating the conditions for spiritual growth, which is the universe's purpose.

Hick believes an afterlife is crucial for theodicy but follows the Roman Catholic doctrine of an intermediate state where people continue their journey to the divine likeness through purgatorial experiences to perfection. It implies that all people will eventually reach this state and reach heaven (universalism), an optimistic view that contains hope for all human beings.

An earlier exponent of the thesis that suffering serves God's interest in the moral development of human beings is John Wesley (1703–91), a leader of a revival movement within the Anglican Church known as Methodism, who saw in theodicy a necessary test of God's ability "to extract good out of evil."²⁹ In attempting to theologize about evil and suffering, Wesley asked where evil comes from and why. Wesley's intention in doing this was to "justify the ways of God to man," especially to the philosophers of his day.³⁰ Wesley taught that the benevolent and loving God created

---

26. Hick, *Evil and the God of Love*, 257.
27. Scott, *Pathways in Theodicy*, 104.
28. Scott, *Pathways in Theodicy*, 108.
29. Wesley, "Sermon 56."
30. Bryant, "John Wesley: On the Origin of Evil," 112.

everything well according to its "kind."[31] Originally creation had no flaw or defect. "It was good in the highest degree whereof it was capable, and without any mixture of evil."[32] Sin was not a part of the created order in any way, shape, or form. Evil did not form part of creation's original state. The grandeur of God's works on earth reflects the primal creation without evil in any form. Then human beings introduced sin in their rebelliousness and disobedience to God. Adam and Eve's fall led to a distorted creation and humanity. Evil was introduced into the created order.

The implication is clear: God was not the author of evil. As some of Wesley's contemporaries argue, God did not create the best possible, perfect, or defectless world. Wesley said that such an argument ignores the biblical account in Genesis 1–3, which clearly distinguishes between the "before" and "after" states of creation and does not adequately provide for the power of sin in the world. If evil did not arise from creation, however, whence does evil come? Wesley's answer is found in a personal letter to his father. He stated that the concept of free will could only be true if humanity's endowed power to choose was not hindered in any way. He concluded that if freedom is unhindered, it implies that the possibility exists that such power can be abused. Wesley explained that God could have hindered free choice by not creating any being free at all (that would not comprise freedom of will). Or God could have restricted free choice by overruling God's power by way of constraining human beings to choose right (that would have comprised a contradiction of the divine self). Or God could have placed free beings in a world where no temptation could have led them to abuse that freedom. However, Wesley argued that temptations are necessary because they serve to exhibit human beings' God-given freedom to choose to do right. The implication is that evil is essential for such freedom to exist.[33]

Suppose evil entered into the ideal and perfect world by freedom, and God is the author of that freedom. In that case, God is responsible, and the question remains, How does one reconcile a personal and loving God with the suffering of people in their daily lives? Wesley's answer is found in the distinction of evil into natural and moral evil. He responded to the earthquake in Lisbon in 1755. He rejected the argument that natural disasters resulted from natural causes because creation is flawed, and

---

31. Sanchez, "John Wesley," 140.
32. Wesley, "Sermon 56."
33. John Wesley, *A Letter to His Father*.

God had nothing to do with such natural causes. According to Wesley, the hand of God is behind everything that exists and happens in the cosmos. However, God is exempted from evil and suffering because God created everything without flaws. God never intended the natural order to be blemished by the fall. The implication, that the fall of the first human beings contributed to the occurence natural catastrophes, is clear. Although God's salvation plan includes restoring creation to its original state, such changes will only occur when God's reign of peace is introduced with Christ's second coming.

In Wesley's view, evil can always be traced back to sin and immorality, representing moral evil. Therefore, his emphasis is on morality, holiness, and salvation. He addressed the existential problem of moral evil in terms of prayer, love of God, and love of people. Wesley's "means of grace" is the theological foundation to empower Christian believers to offset evil by avoiding evil and doing good deeds.[34]

Wesley's theology empowered Christians to accept their moral responsibility toward God and others at all times, especially during seasons of suffering. His theological genius created practical support for those directly tangled with evil and suffering and established practical support and help for them. He writes that morality needs to become a way of life to assist in God's salvific plan for creation radically.[35] Wesley provided an existential and pastoral challenge to believers to respond to their own suffering and those of others by using it as a pastoral entry point to help the pain and suffering of friend and foe alike. As Henry Nouwen stated, "Sorrow is an unwelcome companion and . . . anyone who willingly enters into the pain of a stranger is truly a remarkable person."[36]

However, the view of suffering, as due to testing and moral forming, downplays the destructive reality of evil and leans too heavily on eschatology. At the same time, Christ does not play a central role. Instead, he exemplifies "redemptive suffering" as an example of human suffering.[37] Lastly, in Hick's case, its universalism cannot be reconciled with Scripture or Christian tradition and threatens the freedom and rights of human beings, since all will be saved, regardless of their wishes.[38]

---

34. Yrigoyen, *John Wesley: Holiness of Heart and Life*, 41, 52–53.
35. Sanchez, "John Wesley," 148.
36. Quoted in Sanchez, "John Wesley," 149.
37. Scott, *Pathways in Theodicy*, 116.
38. Scott, *Pathways in Theodicy*, 117.

A more popular view among Christians is that God can use suffering if God pleases. A good case is that of Joni Tada, who is in a wheelchair after breaking her neck after a spinal cord injury and experiences devastating pain continuously. She writes about the meaning of suffering for her and asserts that suffering can turn someone from continuing in a dangerous direction. She refers to Psalm 119, which states that before the poet was humbled s/he went astray, but now s/he keeps God's word (v. 67). "It is good for me that I was humbled, so that I might learn your statutes" (v. 71). In other cases, suffering reminds the afflicted where their true strength lies, that God reveals God's strength in weakness. As Paul explains in 1 Corinthians 12:9, the LORD tells him when he pleads for deliverance from his affliction, "My grace is sufficient for you, for power is made perfect in weakness." For that reason, he will boast all the more gladly of his weaknesses so that the power of Christ may dwell in him (v. 10). Suffering can also restore the beauty of Christ that a believer lost, Tada argues, through careless ease, empty pride, earthly preoccupations, and too much prosperity. It can heighten the thirst for Christ, bringing believers back to Christ, the fountain of life. Suffering can increase their fruitfulness.[39] Lastly, suffering can teach believers the secret to be content with what they have and trust in Jesus, not to bless them but to save and use them.

"Contentment is realizing that God has already given her everything she needs for her present happiness. It is the wise person who doesn't grieve for the things he doesn't have, but rejoices over the things he does have."[40] In the last chapter of his letter, Paul explains why he writes to the Philippians. He was in jail, they provided for his needs, and he thanks them for their support. He acknowledges that he was in need but adds, "I have learned to be content with whatever I have. I know what it is to have little, and I know what it is to have plenty. In any and all circumstances I have learned the secret of being well fed and of going hungry, of having plenty and of being in need. I can do all things through him who strengthens me. In any case, it was kind of you to share my distress" (Phil 4:11–13).[41]

Tullian Tchividjian argues that there is a disorienting possibility that our suffering is actually ordained, implying that God is directly involved

---

39. Tada, *Place of Healing*, 80–92.

40. Tada, *Place of Healing*, 200.

41. The NRSV is used without regendering its language in terms of God, like in the rest of the text.

in it.[42] He refers to several ways that suffering can realize God's intentions with the lives of believers. First, suffering is often the process of being stripped of the things we worship, be it one's children, spouse, ambition, or dream of financial or career success. Second, suffering brings one to the end of oneself.[43] Finally, it confronts one with the reality that God-sent afflictions can be merciful intrusions designed to serve as wake-up calls to believers and break the chains of slavery to self-reliance.[44]

John MacArthur agrees with this view. He refers to 1 Peter's argument that believers may experience joy amidst their suffering because they have confidence in their protected inheritance "that is imperishable, undefiled, and unfading, kept in heaven for you, who are being protected by the power of God through faith for a salvation ready to be revealed in the last time" (vv. 4–5).[45] The "joy" refers, according to MacArthur, in the original language to something more robust than the usual word and means to be superabundantly happy in the richest sense. The New Testament uses the term for the spiritual joy that results from a relationship with God, never from other relationships. He suggests that Peter also emphasizes that trials and sufferings prove the genuineness of believers' faith, resulting "in praise and glory and honor when Jesus Christ is revealed" (v. 7).[46] MacArthur also mentions that suffering enhances future glory and yields greater wisdom and true humility as some of the suffering outcomes.

Suffering Is Caused by God's Lack of Omnipotence

Another philosophical response to theodicy utilizes the cosmology of process philosophy. Alfred North Whitehead (1861–1947) is the founder and figurehead of process thought, and Charles Hartshorne (1897–2000) extended his cosmology. David Ray Griffin (1939–) filtered it into a theodicy.[47] Process philosophy begins by rejecting Aristotelian metaphysics, outlined in Aristotle's book *Categories*, which influenced Western philosophy for centuries. Aristotle conceived of reality as static substances

---

42. Tchividjian, *Glorious Ruin*, 159.
43. Tchividjian, *Glorious Ruin*, 159.
44. Tchividjian, *Glorious Ruin*, 159.
45. MacArthur, *Power of Suffering*, 141.
46. MacArthur, *Power of Suffering*, 143.
47. Scott, *Pathways in Theodicy*, 119.

that can be categorized in metaphysical categories. Process philosophy denies that reality can be divided into organic and inorganic matter or human and nonhuman life. People and things do not consist of distinct, independent, static, ontological "stuff" or "thingness."

Reality has an evolving nature that functions ontologically interdependently. It starts with the pre-Socratic Hellenistic philosopher Heraclitus's observation that "all things flow." He asserts that it is impossible to step twice into the same river because different and again different waters flow there: "We step and we do not step into the same rivers."[48] Process philosophy describes reality in terms of "relatedness" rather than "quality" and "flow" rather than "permanence." Reality is a series of "actual occasions of experience" from biological to subatomic levels.[49] Likewise, the life of a human being consists of a series of distinct occasions of experience. All reality is interrelated; everything is related to what surrounds it. We perceive reality as unified and static as humans while it is actually fragmentary, incomplete, and fluid. All existence flows together at the atomic and subatomic levels.

The theodicy explains that the existence of evil is because God cannot banish evil from the creation. After all, God is not omnipotent, though God is a good God. Although this theodicy does not enjoy the support of many theologians, it was prevalent from ancient times, and it still influences some philosophers. Thus, God is causally unable to prevent evil from occurring while pursuing sufficiently great goods, although God is not logically unable. A current exponent of the view is found in process theology, inspired by Whitehead and based on a complex metaphysical theory about the nature of causal relationships.[50]

David R. Griffin, an American philosopher of religion and founder of the Center for Process Studies at the Claremont School of Theology, developed process theology in his most significant publications: *God, Power, and Evil: A Process Theodicy* (1976) and *Evil Revisited: Responses and Reconsiderations* (1991). He does not accept traditional theism with its ideas of God's omnipotence. God is instead the ground of the cosmos who directs it towards its highest possible actualization. God is the principle of concretion, the basis of creativity that does not exist apart from creation. God creates creation, and creation makes God. Creation

---

48. Heraclitus, *Readings in Ancient Greek Philosophy*, 30.
49. Keller, "Process Theism and Theodicies for the Problems of Evil," 345.
50. Audi, "Theodicy," 910.

embodies God, and God inhabits creation. God is its co-creator and husbandman, working in the world's garden where the weeds frustrate God. The future of the world is open, filled with peril and possibility.

God characterizes the occurrence of creativity with perfect love.[51] God directs creation but does not determine it. God does not stand outside creation as the "absolute controller." God creates the world, not *ex nihilo*, but out of primeval chaos, that is, unrealized potentialities.[52] God does not exert complete control over the cosmos; evil resists God's will. God does not want disease, death, and destruction, but God does not have the power to eliminate them. Thus, God cannot control or determine any events in the universe.

God creates by persuading the world to create and develop itself. God lures and guides creation towards higher states of actuality through evocative power. "God has gradually brought forth those increasingly complex forms of order that we call atoms, molecules, macromolecules, procaryotic cells, organelles, eucaryotic cells, plants, animals, animals with central nervous systems, animals with conscious souls, and animals with self-conscious souls."[53] Now God persuades and inspires human beings to advance in freedom, creativity, and harmony.

God loves human beings, not through feeling but action that involves sympathy with others, hurting with others, griefing with the bereaved, and rejoicing with those who are glad. God unites with and absorbs human suffering at an ontological level. God is not an individual with rational consciousness apart from creation. God is not the totally other but a principle. God is the process that lures creation, including human beings, forward to higher states of existence. Reality constitutes God's existence.

Because God is not personal or omnipotent, God cannot prevent evil and injustice. Evil originates from the chaos that God shapes into order, the chaos that continuously resists all God's efforts. Process theology accepts that God does not create *ex nihilo* and creation is not perfect. The resistant cosmic material that forms part of the order intrudes in several harmful ways to thwart God's intentions. Because it denies that God is omnipotent, it leaves room for the existence of evil. God cannot prevent evil, and for that reason, God cannot be held guilty for its

---

51. Griffin, *Evil Revisited*, 23.
52. See discussion in next chapter on the Old Testament and the theme of chaos.
53. Griffin, *Evil Revisited*, 23.

existence. God is not in control of the events of the world and does not determine it, leaving room for evil to interfere with God's benevolence toward creation.

Human beings are responsible for persistent evil. In contrast to the theory of free will that relates evil to human freedom and the so-called "fall" of Adam and Eve, process theology views God as the one who assists human beings to realize their freedom in limited terms. Thus, God is vindicated from moral guilt, culpability, and blame for evil. Although God is responsible for evil in metaphysical terms, God is not morally culpable.

What is the end of evil? The future is open because God does not determine how it will unfold, implying that what will eventually happen to evil remains an open question. The eschatological end of human life consists in the absorption of all life into the collective consciousness of the universe. The end is the interconnectedness that already characterizes creation that marks the collectivity of existence. Pierre Teilhard de Chardin elaborates on such a vision of the end. He views all of life as moving consistently toward what he calls the "Omega Point of history": realizing the maximal potential of complexity and consciousness. The end is marked by a union, with human life becoming engulfed in Being. Then everything will consist of an ocean where each drop remains conscious of itself. According to De Chardin, absolute evil will be overcome because of God's responsive love. There is no heaven with individual existence.[54]

The most critical remark in evaluating process theology's response to evil is that it uses the Bible sparingly and selectively. One does not find any christological emphasis or other mainstream beliefs that most Christian believers share. It does not deal with human sin and divine redemption. Its God, an impersonal force or characteristic of creation, is not attractive for people living with existential challenges seeking divine help. Its belief in an afterlife and eradicating evil, suffering, and death is also rather bankrupt and does not justify divine justice. However, an essential insight of process theology is that it is the supernaturalistic doctrine of divine omnipotence that created the insoluble problem of evil.[55] Without it, new possibilities for theodicy are opened up, and it leads to shifting theological metaphors. Process theology sees God as a fellow-sufferer who comforts those who suffer and lures human beings into

---

54. Cobb Jr. and Griffin, *Process Theology*, 123.
55. Cobb Jr. and Griffin, *Process Theology*, 140.

actualizing their potentialities, a theme continued in a theodicy where the cross of Christ stands central. Such theology is discussed next.

Suffering Is Due to Evil Forces, Representing Primeval Chaos

Many Pentecostals, especially in Africa and other parts of the Global South, view sickness as the result of the interference of Satan and his diabolical forces in God's good creation.[56] They believe that the purpose of evil forces is to undermine God's work among human beings. In the case of Christians who become sick, their illness is attributed to their succumbing to temptations, lax morality, and the result of divine punishment.[57] Therefore, the diagnosis and treatment of such illness should be expressed as being of both God and Satan, representing a combination of theodicy with diabology. They are defined as symptomatic of evil acts or words, and the victim's illness is the sign of its harsh assessment by God.

The devil's main task is to attempt to drive a wedge between God and human beings.[58] People's evil ideas and practices derive from and should be attributed directly to the devil. As God's opponent and adversary, he causes people to commit evil acts that are crimes against God. The devil's goal is that Christians should drift away from God, eventually following him away from God. Satan is everywhere globally; many traditional Africans assert that spirit beings directly influence their circumstances and require them to be appeased. To survive and successfully exist as human beings, it is crucial to mediate and appropriate these forces. African Pentecostal spirituality links directly with the New Testament's enchanted worldview which views events in the visible world as determined by what happens in the invisible world, where good and evil and God and Satan clash regularly.[59] All misfortune or sickness is ascribed to the work of Satan, and it requires much effort and spiritual warfare for Christians to resist diabolic interferences.

---

56. As is the case of God's lack of gender, the same is true of "Satan" and the various other designations of evil powers.

57. Zheng, Wang, and Wang, "Rural Christians' View of Sickness Treatment Behavior," 123.

58. Boyd, *God at War*, 19.

59. Nel, *Prosperity Gospel in Africa*, 21.

Believers are thus responsible for their own suffering. To solve the problem, they need to repent and pray for forgiveness of their sins. In addition, illness serves to warn them of the dangers of succumbing to temptation and strengthen their faith.[60]

Evil and Cruciform Theology

The twentieth century's two world wars led to the deaths of respectively 20 million people (with a further 21 million wounded) and 75 million people. The century also experienced deliberate genocides, massacres, mass-bombings, disease, and starvation. It led to new theological endeavors to justify God's involvement and intervention in such carnage. One answer was given by Dietrich Bonhoeffer, a German Lutheran pastor, theologian, anti-Nazi dissident, and key founding member of the Confessing Church (*Bekennende Kirche*). The Nazis martyred him for his involvement in an attempt on the life of Adolf Hitler. Bonhoeffer wrote, "Only the suffering God can help."[61] Jürgen Moltmann continued embellishing on the concept of divine suffering (passibility) in his influential publication, *The Crucified God*.[62] Christ's suffering and passion on the cross serve as the angle of incidence, ending a life in which Jesus shared in the entire spectrum of human suffering. He experienced the economic exploitation that characterized Galileans who were poor, social ostracism by the establishment and church, betrayal by his closest friends, and his own family's rejection, except for his mother, who supported him. His prayer in the garden of Gethsemane betrays his intense psychological distress. He interpreted his death as the means to carry the guilt of people's sins in order to restore their relationship with God. He knew human frailty; in the words of the author of the sermon of the book of Hebrews, Jesus is a Christian's high priest, sympathizes with their weaknesses because he was tested as they are, without giving in to sin. Later, the Nicene Creed (325 CE) would explain the early church's perception of Jesus as consubstantial (*homoousios*) with the Father, implying that he had to humble himself when he became a human himself. Jesus was in the form of God, explains Philippians 2:6–10, and did not regard equality

---

60. Zheng, Wang, and Wang, "Rural Christians' View of Sickness Treatment Behavior," 123.
61. Bonhoeffer, *Letters and Papers from Prison*, 8:479.
62. Moltmann, *Crucified God*.

with God as something to be exploited. Yet, he emptied himself by becoming a human being and served people like a slave. He humbled himself further by becoming obedient to the Father's will by being willing to die on a cross, leading to his eventual exaltation by God. The incarnation entails God's intimate familiarity with human suffering.[63] God internalizes human suffering on the cross.[64]

In contrast, traditional theology presupposed divine impassibility, based on the idea that the omnipotent Creator would not be able to suffer in an attempt to protect God's perfection. Today most contemporary theology rejects this doctrine to a greater or lesser extent.

That God is involved with the creation and human beings does not imply that God absorbs the imperfections that characterize creation, argues Moltmann.[65] However, the perfect love of the triune God means that God immerses the human condition to transform it. That God connects with human beings does not imply God's similarity to them. For instance, James 1:17 states that there is no variation or shadow with the Father of lights due to change or variation. God does not turn around.

The compassion and love God has for human beings are not characterized by feelings but actions. That is the reason why God suffers for, with, and from humanity. "A God who cannot suffer cannot love either."[66] Love always entails some form of suffering, implying that God does not stand above creation. God's love is the source of cruciform theology; the cross is the exemplification of divine love. "Love creates space in the self for the other, and that entails the internalization of the delight and despair of the other. If creation suffers, God suffers."[67]

---

63. Scott, *Pathways in Theodicy*, 147.

64. In response to cruciform theodicy, an African theologian Ngong ("Protesting the Cross," 17), argues that African Pentecostal soteriology is a protest against the idea of suffering for which the cross seems to stand. The author emphasizes that salvation does not reside only in the cross or suffering of Christ, as cruciform theodicy argues. It is rather found in the life, death, resurrection, and ascension of Christ. The cross does not validate suffering as such but rather demonstrates that suffering is an aberration. In contrast, Green ("Crucified God and the Groaning Spirit") writes that Moltmann's *theologia crucis*, and its pneumatological and ecclesiological implications, can help Pentecostals to clarify an account of suffering that is grounded in a genuinely Pentecostal theology of the cross.

65. In Weinandy, *Does God Suffer?*, 145.

66. Moltmann, *Trinity and the Kingdom*, 38.

67. Scott, *Pathways in Theodicy*, 152.

Luther's *theologia crucis* was the foundation for his assertion at the Heidelberg disputation on April 26, 1518, that the theologian of glory and the theologian of the cross should be distinguished from each other. "One deserves to be called a theologian, however, who comprehends the visible and manifest things of God seen through suffering and the cross" (Thesis 20); "A theologian of glory calls evil good and good evil. A theologian of the cross calls the thing what it actually is" (Thesis 21).[68] Luther's "God hidden in suffering" led to Moltmann's statement that the theologian of glory uses the impassibility of God to justify the theology. In contrast, the theologian of the cross uses passibility.

God is not pretending that God suffers, as Gnosticism teaches, nor does God suffer only to substitute sinful humanity. The Son suffers dying; the Father suffers the death of the Son, and the pain of the Father corresponds to the pain experienced on the cross by the Son. When Jesus died, the Father and Son were separated from each other, involving God's self-alienation and abandonment. "The Son suffers in his love being forsaken by the Father as he dies. The Father suffers in his love the grief of the death of the Son."[69]

In Moltmann's opinion, the only prospects for theology after Auschwitz is with a cruciform theology that can relate its propositions to the experiences of the victims.[70] Its God is the suffering God in the suffering of Christ who identifies with the suffering and cries out with the godforsaken God, "My God, why have you forsaken me?"[71]

Because Christ's suffering redeems humanity, it also redeems suffering. For that reason, human suffering can also have redemptive value when such suffering is intentionally aligned with Christ's. "My bold contention will be that the Christian approach to evil through redemptive suffering affords a distinctive solution to the problem of evil, for believers and unbelievers as well."[72]

It might seem that suffering does not necessarily lead to any advantages for its victim or have any redemptive outcomes. Cruciform theodicy then looks to the afterlife with its beatific vision of God, representing

---

68. Jackson, "Luther's Theologian of the Cross and Theologian of Glory Distinction Reconsidered," 352.
69. Moltmann, *Crucified God*, 245.
70. Moltmann, *Crucified God*, 277–78.
71. Moltmann, *Crucified God*, 227.
72. Adams, "Redemptive Suffering," 170.

intimacy that will engulf the evils that one experienced in life.[73] In other words, only the mystery of God answers the challenge that evil poses to faith. "For Christians as for others in this life, the fact of evil is a mystery. The answer is a more wonderful mystery—God himself."[74] No Christian theologian would disagree that the cross is of central significance for the New Testament and theodicy message. On the cross, the Father suffered with the Son and died paradoxically. From biblical evidence, it is unclear whether God suffers impassibly, like Cyril of Alexandria asserted, or whether God suffered passibly, as Jürgen Moltmann writes. Mark Scott argues that the cross means that God internalizes the suffering of the incarnation and identifies with human suffering as well, implying that God stands in solidarity with human suffering.[75] The cross also means that God redeems believers through Christ's crucifixion, death, and resurrection, enabling human beings to find redemptive possibilities of human suffering that provide a possible solution to the challenges of theodicy. It recasts the role of evil when God's solidarity with human suffering and human identification with the redemptive are combined. The belief that God does not distance the divine self from human suffering but experiences it with and through believers' experiences brings comfort to the suffering victims. Their spirituality obtains a sacred dimension that serves to make it more meaningful. Marilyn Adams refers to the classic *Revelations of Divine Love* of Julian of Norwich, which explains some of the mystical possibilities when Christians use this perspective to reflect on their experiences of suffering. Julian of Norwich expresses the hope of seeing God hereafter and describes the joy it will elicit.[76]

Cruciform theology reminds us that God does not only experience suffering on the cross as the crucified God but also redeems suffering and transforms its meaning. Human beings are not only redeemed through Christ's death, but the meaning and essence of their suffering on earth are changed and transformed when they interpret it in terms of Christ's passion that included the agony of Gethsemane and Golgotha, death, and resurrection. The redemptive power of suffering is illustrated by the martyrs of all centuries willing to sacrifice their lives for their belief in God. When they suffer in solidarity with Christ, believers see their suffering

---

73. Adams, "Horrendous Evils and the Goodness of God," 167.
74. Adams, "Redemptive Suffering," 187.
75. Scott, *Pathways in Theodicy*, 167.
76. Adams, "Horrendous Evils and the Goodness of God," 162–63, 219.

in a new light. They participate in Christ's suffering by suffering; it does not signify that God has rejected them but rather that God is with them in their suffering.

Cruciform theology also emphasizes that Christ's resurrection signifies the divine transmutation of suffering that promises its eventual elimination in the eschatological future.[77] The guarantee that evil will end is found in the divine love demonstrated when Jesus, as the innocent one, died on the cross for guilty sinners. That Christ suffers for people on the cross implies God's suffering in solidarity with people who suffer. Moltmann refers to the cross as the superlative manifestation and expression of divine love and the locus of divine revelation. Understanding suffering requires that one start at the cross. Moltmann adds that the theology of the cross was relevant only within the framework of human misery and salvation.

Not all agree that cruciform theology gives an acceptable version of the biblical message or successfully answers theodicy's challenges. They refer to its inability to address some of the central questions about evil's origin, nature, problem, reason, and end. For example, instead of explaining why a good God allows evil to sow destruction across God's creation, it presents God's actions about evil. However, by emphasizing God's solidarity with the suffering and the redemptive meaning that it assigns to human suffering, cruciform theology contributes in a remarkable way to the theodicy debate.

The question that should be addressed is whether cruciform theology's depiction of God is correct. Is its emphasis on God's immanence not implying that God's transcendence and perfection are coopted? Its doctrine of divine passibility may also suggest that it explains God in an anthropomorphic way in terms of human experiences, limiting divine love to human affects and implying that human experience is projected onto God. It should rather be acknowledged that human knowledge about the mystery called "God" is limited, including the extent and scope of God's love for humanity and what suffering on the cross implies for the way the Father, Son, and Spirit co-exist. What human beings can understand is God's revelation to human beings, which includes the vital knowledge that God loves human beings to such an extent that God was willing to sacrifice God's Son to restore the relationship with human beings that was broken by sin.

---

77. Scott, *Pathways in Theodicy*, 168.

The Impossibility of Explaining Evil, and Constructive Proposals to Deal with It

Two forms of anti-theodicy that accept the impossibility of explaining evil exist, both characterized by their rejection of theodicy but from different perspectives. Atheistic theodicy rejects it on moral and intellectual grounds, leading to rejection and denial of theism. It will not be discussed since it is not relevant to the present study. In contrast, theistic theodicy rejects theodicy but accepts theism. It argues that theodicy fails to solve the problems posed by the occurrence of evil and fails to explain radical, horrendous, or dysteleological evil. In the process, it contributes to evil and becomes evil itself when it justifies evil by shifting blame from God to humans.[78]

In thinking about the rationality of theodicy, Kenneth Surin provides three "socio-historical" reasons why it fails.[79] First, he argues that the Enlightenment's worldviews undercut classic theodicies. In the second place, the excessive intellectualization of the logical problem of evil that theodicy utilizes fails in his opinion to explain the social, historical, and existential dimensions of the problem. "Theodicy might be first and foremost a form of rational discourse about the phenomenon of evil, but the theodicist cannot afford to overlook the fact that rationality itself has social roots, and that occurrences of evil and suffering, and human responses to these occurrences, are likewise located in quite specific historical and material configurations."[80] Surin's third reason is found in the failure of theodicy because of the impossibility to explain the problem of evil intellectually.[81] No one knows how and why evil originated.

In considering these challenges, Surin accepts belief in God and God's goodness but argues for a shift from theory to praxis, the abstract to the concrete, the conceptual to the historical, and the description to direct participation. In other words, he rejects theodicy's tendency to provide theorized and ahistorical theories that are not connected directly to praxis. His theistic anti-theodicy is a critique of traditional approaches to theodicy.

---

78. Scott, *Pathways in Theodicy*, 184.
79. Surin, *Theology and the Problem of Evil*, 39–46.
80. Surin, *Theology and the Problem of Evil*, 48.
81. Surin, *Theology and the Problem of Evil*, 52–54.

D. Z. Phillips also rejects theodicy while still accepting theism.[82] Theodicy, in his opinion, fails to explain the empirical reality of evil and suffering.[83] In trying to reconcile theodicy with theism, theodicy minimizes evil, undermining the basic tenets of theism. He refers to Wittgenstein's allegory of bees. The relation between the bee's honey and its sting serves as an analogy for good and evil human experiences. There are ten "bee stings," or defects in theodicy. Without discussing the detail of his argument or listing the defects, Mark Scott summarizes it into three objections.[84] Traditional theodicy inherently justifies evil by instrumentalizing suffering, shifts the blame from God to victims of suffering, and minimizes earthly suffering, obscuring the problem rather than solving it by appealing to mystery and eschatology. Phillips concludes that theodicy should be rejected rather than revised.[85] What is vital for Phillips is that suffering is incomprehensible and that theodicy is unable to explain why evil exists in the world in profusion.[86] Although he finds cruciform theology attractive for its discussion of the meaning of redemptive suffering, he steers away from providing any reason for and consequent justification of suffering. The moment theism provides a theodicy, it becomes like a spider's web. "In that tangled web I never cease to marvel at a miracle: that theism survives theodicy."[87]

Another exponent is Sarah Katherine Pinnock.[88] She expresses her dissatisfaction with theodicy for political and existential philosophical reasons; it failed to address the horrors of the Holocaust in an acceptable manner. "After Auschwitz, theodicy is exposed as perpetrating amoral justifications of evil and rationalistic caricatures of practical faith struggles."[89] It fails by justifying evil as necessary for God to realize God's providential designs and focusing on the global at the cost of personal and corporate suffering.[90] She argues that theodicy needs epistemic humility, moral sensitivity, religious practice, and narrative memory before

---

82. Phillips, "Theism without Theodicy," 145–61.
83. Phillips, "Theism without Theodicy," 147.
84. Scott, *Pathways in Theodicy*, 168.
85. Phillips, "Theism without Theodicy," 152.
86. Phillips, "Theism without Theodicy," 156–60.
87. Phillips, "Theism without Theodicy," 161.
88. Pinnock, *Beyond Theodicy*, xi.
89. Pinnock, *Beyond Theodicy*, xi.
90. Pinnock, *Beyond Theodicy*, 7.

anyone will listen to its voice.[91] Instead of explaining why God permits evil by categorical explanations, it should be modest in theological and philosophical terms and resist excessive abstraction and systematization by engaging with concrete experiences of suffering and addressing their social, economic, and political causes.[92] Its focus should be personal stories of heartache and how religion engages with grief.[93]

The shift that these antitheodicies advocate is from theory to practice and the global to the personal. Instead of attempting to justify and condone evil, it should condemn it and constructively address its causes. Instead of finding its locus in philosophy and systematic theology, theodicy should exist in the existential world of practical and pastoral theology, empathizing with the suffering and marginalized.[94]

Although the present study does not accept anti-theodicy as an option, it seems imperative that Pentecostals support the viewpoint that theodicy should not function only in abstract theological arguments. Instead, it needs to "happen" where people suffer by accepting responsibility for their pastoral care.

New directions in which theodicy has been evolving are ethical theodicies, contextual theodicies, and pastoral theodicies. Ethical theodicies concern themselves with identifying social, economic, and political structures that result in suffering in order to recommend and apply effective ways to alleviate suffering. Contextual theodicies look at the problem of evil from the perspective of the disenfranchised and marginalized to offer constructive solutions to the oppressed's plight. Pastoral theodicies respond to suffering experienced by individual persons by supporting them pastorally. Anti-theodicy adds that when traditional theodicies justify and rationalize evil and silence the sufferer's voice, they become evil themselves.[95] Instead of attempting to answer why suffering occurs, the emphasis shifts to what religion and the church can do about it. How can it be prevented, and how can sufferers be supported in constructive ways? These perspectives are essential and will be applied when an alternative Pentecostal theodicy that is true to the Pentecostal ethos and hermeneutics is discussed in the last two chapters.

91. Pinnock, *Beyond Theodicy*, 139.
92. Pinnock, *Beyond Theodicy*, 140–41.
93. Pinnock, *Beyond Theodicy*, 141–44.
94. Scott, *Pathways in Theodicy*, 168.
95. Swinton, *Raging with Compassion*, 17.

Conclusion

This chapter discussed several theoretical solutions that philosophers and theologians have proposed to the challenges posed by theodicy and referred to some theological responses to it before looking at evidence for a biblical discussion of theodicy in the next chapter. The short discussion included the proposal that suffering can be justified due to retributive justice, free will, testing and forming of character, and that evil is one of the outflows of primeval chaos. Another way of looking at evil is through the lens of cruciform theology that finds redemptive meaning in suffering; this perspective is partly employed in the last two chapters. Lastly, antitheodicy was discussed, arguing that it is impossible to explain suffering but that philosophy and theology should instead respond to its profusion by engaging in constructive ways to combat it and support its victims.

Traditionally, theodicy was situated primarily within the field of philosophy. Even the term "theodicy" itself was developed by a philosopher. To find information about its discussion, one would have to consult books and courses on philosophy, the philosophy of religion, and philosophical theology.[96] Theodicy is discussed in theological terms in the present work, and only secondary reference is made to philosophy. The reason is apparent. It appears that questions about God's goodness and justice are essentially theological and existential questions. The submission is that theology may never abdicate its responsibility to struggle with the challenges posed by theodicy and that such theology should be based on existential and pastoral concerns for the suffering. In other words, it should cooperate with philosophy in thinking through existing theories but should also address the daily existential struggles that believers experience who live with suffering in its diverse forms. Theology should reclaim theodicy for itself by shaping the discourse with its distinctive methodologies and theories. Philosophy should be involved in all discussions about theodicy, but theology should join the conversation, benefitting from the conceptual nuance and precision that philosophy brings to the question. The study of theodicy should be an interdisciplinary dialogue to be representative.[97]

The last two chapters will highlight these themes in terms of a responsible Pentecostal response to theodicy. While it accepts no one of

---

96. Scott, *Pathways in Theodicy*, 54.

97. This is Mark Scott's opinion as well. See discussion in van Woudenberg, "A Brief History of Theodicy," 177–91.

these reasons for suffering, it argues that each individual case of suffering should be evaluated on its own and in terms of the victim's subjective existential experience. However, it rejects anti-theodicy; the argument is based on biblical information, as evidenced in the next chapter.

3

Biblical Answers to Theodicy

Introduction

IN THE PREVIOUS CHAPTER, some theological solutions to theodicy's challenges were discussed without reflecting on biblical texts related to these perspectives. In this chapter, biblical data concerning theodicy is summarized to compare with these theological solutions and provide the necessary background for evaluating Pentecostal solutions to the challenges that theodicy poses to contemporary people. It does not contain the broad scope of the debate that characterizes current theological endeavors in terms of these texts, since the purpose is to demonstrate the various possible solutions proposed by biblical authors. In the last two chapters, the need for differentiating between different theodicean responses is motivated partly in terms of the biblical precedent, and partly for existential reasons related to people's diverse, subjective experiences of suffering.

The Tetrateuch

In Genesis 18, Abraham reasons with YHWH about God's intended judgment of Sodom and asks, "Will you indeed sweep away the righteous with the wicked?" (v. 23). Abraham starts with a process to negotiate with God about the required number of righteous people for God to save the city and concludes by asking the rhetorical question, "Shall not the Judge of all the earth do what is just?" (v. 25b). The supposition is that the only possible answer is an emphatic affirmation.[1] The implication is clear: the correlation between divine judgment and human wickedness can seemingly be broken if enough righteous people can be found. The God of Genesis 18 is a just but also gracious God who does not act despotically or arbitrarily but is willing to abandon God's judgment in response to pleas and arguments for the sake of the righteous.[2]

The other portrayals of God presented in the Pentateuch do not conform to this image. Their God is a severe judge, although God is also portrayed as righteous. One gets the impression that God's dealings with Israel were not always transparent, and God could only be partially known. At the same time, every characterization of God is deficient, given God's incomparableness to anyone or anything else.[3]

Some of Israel's hardships are interpreted by biblical authors as God's ways to test what is in the people's hearts, whether they would keep God's commandments or not. For that reason, God subjected them to the hardship of hunger in the wilderness before providing manna for them to eat. God taught the people that human beings do not live on bread alone but on anything that YHWH decrees (Deut 8:2–3). What was crucial was that Israel should not forget who elected them, the one who freed them from oppression in Egypt and led them through the wilderness "to humble you and to test you, and in the end to do you good" (Deut 8:14–16). Their hardships served as trials and tests that YHWH arranged to reveal their true character and sincerity in following YHWH.

Many of the narratives about Israel's stay in the wilderness betrayed their lack of trust in YHWH (e.g., Exod 15:22–26). Thus, the pedagogical intents with certain events are not realized because of Israel's unfaithfulness to YHWH in times of hardship. For instance, the book of Exodus relates Israel's reaction to the lack of food. They raged against Moses and Aaron, wishing they had rather died from a disaster brought by YHWH in Egypt, where they had enough to eat. Then they would not have been in the wilderness where they were now dying from starvation. Verse 4 gives God's response to these complaints. YHWH states that bread from heaven would rain upon the people, and God commands them to each day go out and gather enough, but just for that day, except on the sixth day, when they are to collect double the amount to care for the needs of

---

1. Houtman, "Theodicy in the Pentateuch," 151.
2. Houtman, "Theodicy in the Pentateuch," 152.
3. Houtman, *Exodus*, 95–96.

the Sabbath. "In that way, I will test them, whether they will follow my instruction or not," demonstrating YHWH's pedagogical intents.

Exodus 20 relates how YHWH gave Moses the law, and Israel's response to the theophany is related in verses 18–20. When they witnessed the thunder and lightning, and the mountain smoking, they were afraid. So they told Moses, "You speak to us, and we will listen; but do not let God speak to us, or we will die." Then Moses replied, "Do not be afraid; for God has come only to test you and to put the fear of him upon you so that you do not sin." The testing was also not limited to Israel as a people only.

Individuals could also experience the "desert events" that marked Israel's visit to the wilderness. It might also seem as indeterminately long as the people's stay in the desert around Sinai. For instance, in Genesis 45, Joseph revealed his identity to his brothers after testing them by his rejection of their explanations for why they found themselves in Egypt. When he revealed himself, his brothers were confounded and afraid that Joseph would revenge himself for what they had done to them. So instead, he told them, "Do not be distressed, or angry with yourselves, because you sold me here; for God sent me before you to preserve life . . . God sent me before you to preserve for you a remnant on earth, and to keep alive for you many survivors" (vv. 5, 7).

The Pentateuch addresses whether God directed the behavior of evil people; it is clear that YHWH used such behavior in some cases to reach YHWH's purposes. For instance, one repeatedly reads that God made the pharaoh obstinate so that he did not respond to Israel's pleas for relief from their tribulation (e.g., in Exod 9:12; 10:20, 27; 11:10; 14:4, 8). Further, Exodus 9 relates how YHWH sent Moses to tell the pharaoh that plagues were to visit the country "so that you may know that there is no one like me in all the earth. For by now, I could have stretched out my hand and struck you and your people with pestilence, and you would have been cut off from the earth. But this is why I have let you live: to show you my power, and to make my name resound through all the earth" (vv. 14–16).

Israel's faith is monotheistic; it acknowledges only one God, leaving no room for a dualism between powers of good and evil. YHWH made Israel invincible when they entered the promised land, implying that strength lies entirely in YHWH's hands. The pharaoh was ultimately in YHWH's power, and his actions served YHWH's intentions without him knowing it. It does not leave room for any power that could counter God's power. Evil did not exist separately or independently from God.

However, that did not imply that human beings were not responsible for their evil actions. There was no room left for denial of one's guilt and blame, even if one's evil actions unknowingly served God's intentions and purposes. The pharaoh remained obstinate (e.g., Exod 7:13, 22; 8:15; 9:35) even though Israel's God caused his obstinateness, and in the end, the pharaoh paid the highest price for his obstinateness.

Exodus 4 contains a disturbing depiction of God. On his way to Egypt, Moses was attacked during the night by YHWH, who "tried to kill him" (v. 24). Eventually, his life was saved, and YHWH left him alone when his wife took a flint, cut off her son's foreskin, and touched Moses's feet with it with the words, "Truly you are a bridegroom of blood to me!" (v. 25). It might be that the context suggests Moses's symbolical circumcision was in effect his consecration to his commission to lead Israel out of Egypt to the promised land. However, the cost of such benefits is high in terms of the specific way the author describes YHWH's actions.

The same is true of Genesis 11, which relates to the story of the tower of Babel. What was the nature of the people's iniquity that led to such harsh measures against them? It seems that their iniquity was in staying together: "Let us make a name for ourselves; otherwise we shall be scattered abroad upon the face of the whole earth" (v. 4). Their enterprise was visited by YHWH, who, in anthropomorphic terms, had to come down to be able to see their high tower, illustrating God's highness in terms of human hubris. YHWH then judged, "This is only the beginning of what they will do; nothing that they propose to do will now be impossible for them" (v. 6). YHWH decided to confuse their language with the purpose of scattering them abroad. This rather primitive image of God as an arbitrary judge contrasts with other Pentateuch traditions' view of God as the lofty and righteous judge.[4] The different depictions of God have implications for theodicean explanations for Israel's suffering; the feature that the descriptions share is that good and evil come from God's hand. It did not leave room for any power that could challenge God's rule.

Deuteronomic History

One of the philosophical-theological "solutions" to theodicy discussed in the previous chapter explained that suffering is due to retributive justice. The widespread belief among Pentecostals that supports this view

---

4. Houtman, "Theodicy in the Pentateuch," 181.

is based primarily upon some parts of the Old Testament, following the Deuteronomist's attempt to explain Israel's history of disobedience and punishment and eventual exile by way of this principle. Thus, the challenge of theodicy is to reconcile the justice and power of a good God in the face of suffering, especially innocent suffering. Ronald M. Green investigates the Deuteronomic History (Deut—Josh—Judg—Sam—Kgs) and distinguishes five different forms of theodicy in its monotheistic context.[5] These include the free-will theodicy, based on the idea of retribution that people who do not obey the will and commandments of God are punished while those who remain loyal to God are blessed. This option that overshadows the History's theodicean discussions is discussed in detail below.[6]

Second, Green writes that one finds an educative theodicy, which emphasizes that modest suffering can enrich the sufferer's life by giving them a deeper understanding of life. Hence, it argues that the Judeans in exile enjoyed a closer relationship with YHWH than those who had not experienced the removal themselves, indicating that their suffering benefitted the first group.[7] Third, in the Deuteronomic History, one also finds an eschatological or recompense theodicy, implying that a full reward for the faithful will follow human life that ends in death. However, there are only vague references to this theme since it only developed fully since the intertestamental period.

Fourth, a theodicy that refers to the deferral or mystery of suffering plays a minor role, and the history of Josiah refers mainly to it. This will be discussed at the end of the section. Josiah fulfilled the Deuteronomic ideal for kingship that David established. Nevertheless, he lost his life at a critical juncture in Judah's history during the battle of Megiddo. For the Deuteronomic History, with its theodicy of retribution-and-punishment, this event was incomprehensible. Finally, one finds some intimations of the presence of a communion theodicy in the History that eventually led to further developments in other traditions and emphasized that suffering provides the occasion for a deeper relationship with God. However, it is only fully developed in the Psalms, the book of Job, and Isaiah 53.

One of the most popular solutions in the Old and New Testament to the challenge of suffering is to explain it as punishment in response to sin,

---

5. Green, "Theodicy," 430–41.
6. See also Thompson, *"Where Is the God of Justice?,"* 8.
7. Laato, "Theodicy in the Deuteronomic History," 184.

either of the group or individual. The idea is developed in several passages in the books from Deuteronomy to 2 Kings, except for Ruth. The Deuteronomic History has since Martin Noth's proposals been regarded as a single literary presentation of the history of Israel.[8]

The need to have a holy book did not exist in Israel's history until the Babylonian exile (598/97–587/86–530 BCE) of Judah and Benjamin, the two tribes of the southern kingdom. Since the forty-year stay in the desert, Israelite religion was focused on a sanctuary, first in the tabernacle and then in Solomon's temple and the temple in Samaria as well after the parting of ways of the two kingdoms. The northern kingdom, consisting of the ten tribes of Israel or Ephraim, eventually perished as a distinct people during the Assyrian exile (722 BCE). During the Babylonian exile, the people of Judah lost their king and the accompanying political independence, and Jerusalem, its capital, with the most significant element of their religion.[9] The temple was razed to the ground. Judah did not have any replacement for the presence and involvement of God among them when the Babylonians destroyed the temple. In a foreign country, chances were good that they would also have lost their identity as a separate people, like their sisters and brothers of the ten tribes. Then some wise person or group, probably from the priestly class, realized that writing down the people's religious and cultural traditions would preserve their memory and serve to substitute the role the temple had formerly played.

During the exile, a vital contributor to the project was the Deuteronomic Historian, a group or person responsible for preserving the people's ancient history but from a specific viewpoint.[10] The History represents several historical traditions, their modifications, and redaction in the present form of the text. Some of the traditions may go back to the reign of Josiah, as A. Kuenen already asserted.[11] The last date that

---

8. Noth, *Überlieferungsgeschichtlichen Studien*.

9. Albertz (*Israel in Exile*, 90–91) estimates that the population of Judah at the end of the seventh century BCE and the beginning of the sixth was approximately eighty thousand; about twenty thousand people were deported by the Babylonians from Judah. Perhaps as any as another twenty thousand Judahites perished in the war, were executed by the Babylonians, or emigrated to Egypt. It implies that the Judahite population in Judah was reduced to forty thousand, giving a ratio of about two to one for the number of people remaining in Judah and the number in the Babylonian *golah*.

10. As Albertz (*Israel in Exile*, 203) explains, the Deuteronomistic History was the first continuous historical work of Israelite history written, embracing Israel's history from the entrance into Canaan to the exile.

11. Kuenen, *Historisch-kritische Einleitung*, 88–100.

is recorded in the History is in 567 BCE, found in the events related in 2 Kings 25, which recounts how King Nebuchadnezzar of Babylon destroyed Jerusalem and took the king and elite in exile. Underlying the different traditions are key theological ideals, one of which is an attempt to demonstrate the importance of the Deuteronomic ideals of loyalty and obedience to YHWH and YHWH's commandments. The Historian uses Israel's disobedience and disloyalty to YHWH as the determining factor in the historical events that led to the eventual exile of both kingdoms. The historical traditions are adopted, adapted, and, where necessary, modified to form paradigmatic examples of how the covenant between YHWH and Israel functioned.[12]

The perspective that determined the way the history was interpreted was that both exiles of the two Israelite kingdoms resulted from Israel's disobedience to their God. The historian started the narrative with Moses, who retold how the Israelites were saved from slavery in Israel and accompanied by YHWH to the promised land in the book of Deuteronomy. The rest of the narrative tells how they conquered and eventually lost the land due to their disloyalty to the God who promised and gave them the land.

Vital in understanding the Deuteronomic ideal of loyalty and obedience is to note that the Deuteronomic History begins with an explication of the law that YHWH gave to Moses, a duplication of the narrative found in Exodus 20. The law explicitly states what God expected of the people God had elected as the divine own. The speech of Moses ends in Deuteronomy 28 with the explicit assertion, in the form of a formula, that human obedience always leads to divine reward, while disobedience results in punishment.

The Historian interpreted Israel's history by way of a strict scheme that states in black-and-white terms that when people obey YHWH, they would always experience YHWH's blessings in the form of good health and longevity of the king and his people, victory over all their enemies, a bountiful and fruitful land providing excellent crops, the absence of drought and threats of pests that might threaten agriculture, healthy domesticated animals, and prosperity for the inhabitants. To illustrate by mentioning only one example, the Deuteronomist writes: "If you will only obey the LORD your God, by diligently observing all his commandments that I am commanding you today, the LORD your God will set you

---

12. Laato, "Theodicy in the Deuteronomic History," 189.

high above all the nations of the earth; all these blessings shall come upon you and overtake you, if you obey the Lord your God . . . But if you will not obey the Lord your God by diligently observing all his commandments and decrees, which I am commanding you today, then all these curses shall come upon you and overtake you" (Deut 28:1–2, 15).

For that reason, it was important for the people to pledge their loyalty exclusively to God at the cost of the idols that surrounding nations worshiped and that served as a constant temptation for the people of Israel. The religion of the surrounding nations was characterized by a cult that promoted the fruitfulness of all biological life and nature, in a cult of temple prostitution based on the supposition that by arousing the sexual lust of the gods and goddesses, the earth would benefit in fruitfulness. The principle is illustrated by Deuteronomy 5:32–33, which warns Israel to be careful to do as YHWH had commanded them and follow exactly YHWH's path, "so that you may live, and that it may go well with you, and that you may live long in the land that you are to possess." The choice for the Israelites was clear. If they heeded every commandment of YHWH, to stay loyal to YHWH and serve YHWH faithfully, they would be blessed (Deut 11:13). What was important was not to be seduced into serving other gods and worshiping them, because that would result in punishment (vv. 16–17).

Especially in the book of Kings (in the Christian Bible found in two books but combined in one book in Hebrew Scriptures), one finds the application of this principle in how the reigns of the individual kings were evaluated. The principle forms the leitmotif as a prevailing theme in the book. The first two kings receive a good report, although their human failures are mentioned honestly and prominently. However, after the reigns of David and Solomon, with the severance of the kingdom into two, the Deuteronomist characterized only a few kings in a positive light. Not one of the kings of the northern kingdom succeeded in the test, and only two in the southern kingdom. One of them is Hezekiah, son of King Ahaz of Judah, who did what was right in the sight of YHWH just as his ancestor David had done by removing the high places where idols were worshipped, broke down their pillars, and cut down their sacred pole (2 Kgs 18:3–4). Because he trusted in YHWH, the author judges that there was no one like him among all the kings of Judah after him or among those who were before him because he held fast to YHWH and kept YHWH's commandments (vv. 5–6).

The other king who qualified, according to the Deuteronomist's evaluation, is Josiah of Judah. He was still a child, only eight years old, when he became the king. 2 Kings 22:2 states that he did what was right in YHWH's sight and walked in all the ways of his father, David. He ordered that the Jerusalem temple be repaired and reformed the temple cult, based on discovering the "law" in the house of YHWH. 2 Kings 23 explains the extent of the reform. He brought all the vessels made for Baal, Asherah, and the host of heaven out of the temple and burned them outside Jerusalem. He deposed the priests of the idols, took down the image of Asherah from the temple, and burned it at the Kidron wadi. He broke down the houses of the male temple prostitutes in the vicinity of the temple. He defiled the high places where the priests had made offerings, including Tophet, the valley where people made a son or a daughter pass through fire as an offering to Molech. And he burned the images of horses and chariots dedicated to the sun at the entrance to the temple. The description provides an idea of the extent of Judah's adherence to the Canaanite cult, at the expense of their election by YHWH. He removed the shrines of the high places in the towns and slaughtered their priests. The extent of Josiah's reform was necessary to address the defilement of the temple cult, thanks to the reigns of faithless Manasseh, Amon, and their like. Josiah also commanded that all people keep the Passover and put away the mediums, wizards, teraphim, and idols. The Historian concludes the discussion of the life of Josiah by stating: "Before him there was no king like him, who turned to the Lord with all his heart, with all his soul, and with all his might, according to all the law of Moses; nor did any like him arise after him" (v. 25). The principle the Historian used to measure the worth of a king was his perceived faithfulness to YHWH.

And still, Josiah died in battle at a comparatively early age, which was inconceivable for the Historian because it did not fit the principle of retribution. When Pharaoh Neco of Egypt went to Assyria to attack its king, Josiah tried to subvert his mission, but the Egyptian forces killed him in the ensuing battle (2 Kgs 23:28–30). It confronted the author with the challenge of explaining the validity of his theological schema where a good person always experiences the blessings of YHWH. In contrast, a bad person meets a terrible fate. Josiah probably attacked the Egyptian king to show his loyalty to the king of Assyria, who was ruling over Judah.

Or perhaps he wanted to alliance with the pharoah against his Assyrian overlord.[13] The discussion is continued below.

It has been explained that the Deuteronomist retold Judah's history to save them from the same fate as their sisters and brothers of the northern kingdom, of extinction as a separate people, by designing a religious identity apart from the temple cult. Israel's history is subjected to a theological evaluation in terms of two categories, those who showed their loyalty to YHWH by their obedience to the Mosaic laws and those who were disobedient. The History also explained the Assyrian exile of the northern kingdom and Babylonian exile of the Judahites in this manner. The History serves to provide the people with an explanation for their suffering. For example, 2 Kings 17 states that this occurred "because the people of Israel had sinned against the Lord their God, who had brought them up out of the land of Egypt from under the hand of Pharaoh, king of Egypt. They had worshiped other gods and walked in the customs of the nations whom the Lord drove out before the people of Israel, and in the customs that the kings of Israel had introduced" (vv. 7–8).

The principle is that faithfulness to God leads to a successful life, while sinfulness leads to disaster, as demonstrated by the Deuteronomic History of the exile.[14] It represents historiography that expresses a particular theologically-colored perspective of Israel's history, viewed through the lens of covenant conditions. In the process, the Historian used only the historical facts that served their interests. The purpose was to explain to exilic Judeans why they were in exile and what the Deuteronomists saw as the potential hope for a future of the people.

Who the Deuteronomist(s) was/were is not known. Perhaps it was a priestly or politically motivated group or individual that represented a theodicy of Israel's suffering that explained the calamities that befell Judah as the result of their sinfulness and unfaithfulness to YHWH.

The book of Lamentations captures something of the emotional experiences of Judeans. They had lost their temple and temple cult, with its sacrificial system, king, independence, capital, and country, and now lived in a foreign country where people spoke an unknown language. The book consists of five lamentations. In chapters 1, 2, and 4, every verse begins with another letter of the Hebrew alphabet to explain the totality of what can be stated about the suffering of exile entails. In chapter

---

13. Miller and Hayes, *History of Ancient Israel*, 167–72.
14. Thompson, *"Where Is the God of Justice?,"* 10.

3, every three verses start with another letter of the alphabet. Judah felt abandoned and betrayed by their God, and in line with the Deuteronomic schema, their desolation is explained in terms of their disobedience to YHWH. In the words of Lamentations 1, "Jerusalem remembers, in the days of her affliction and wandering, all the precious things that were hers in days of old . . . Jerusalem sinned grievously, so she has become a mockery" (vv. 7–8). It is clear that the Deuteronomist's theodicy also informs Lamentations. Here, however, one also finds expressions of hope, as in Lamentations 3: "This I call to mind, and therefore I have hope: The steadfast love of the LORD never ceases, his mercies never come to an end . . For the LORD will not reject forever . . . I called on your name, O LORD, from the depths of the pit; you heard my plea, 'Do not close your ear to my cry for help, but give me relief!'" (vv. 21–22, 31, 55–56). For the most part, Lamentations is a lament portraying the distress of an exilic people who expressed their desired vengeance on Jerusalem's enemies.

Josiah based his temple reform on the laws of Deuteronomy. He made a covenant between YHWH and Israel (2 Kgs 23:2–4; in line with Deut 5:8; 29:1, 9) and eliminated idol worship (2 Kgs 23:4–7; in line with Deut 13). He destroyed the astral cult (2 Kgs 23:5, 11–12; in line with Deut 17:3) and eliminated cult prostitution (2 Kgs 23:7; in line with Deut 23:17–18). He centralized the cult in the temple (2 Kgs 23:8–9, 19; in line with Deut 12), prohibited the sacrifice of children (2 Kgs 23:10; in line with Deut 18:10), and eliminated illegal divination (2 Kgs 23:24; in line with Deut 18:11–14).[15]

Josiah should have merited blessings from YHWH, according to Deuteronomy 28–29's prescriptions. The Deuteronomist leaves out the formula that he uses with all the other kings that evaluate their reign in terms of their faithfulness to the ideals of loyalty and obedience in the case of Josiah. Instead, one finds a reference to all the evil Judah did during the reign of Manasseh, noting that YHWH did not turn from the fierceness of YHWH's great wrath because Manasseh had provoked YHWH. Eventually, this leads to the judgment, "I will remove Judah also out of my sight, as I have removed Israel; and I will reject this city that I have chosen, Jerusalem, and the house of which I said, My name shall be there" (2 Kgs 23:26–27).

In other words, the author emphasizes that Josiah was not responsible for the destruction of the city and, by implication, his own death; the

---

15. Laato, "Theodicy in the Deuteronomic History," 218.

responsibility for the catastrophe is laid squarely upon King Manasseh. Clearly, the retribution theology of the Deuteronomist is incomprehensible in this case, and the reign of Josiah contains a mysterious aspect that challenges the theodicy, leading to the hermeneutic explanations in 2 Kings 22–23, Psalm 89, and the book of Jeremiah.[16] The Deuteronomist shifts responsibility for the catastrophe at Megiddo onto Manasseh's shoulders. In Psalm 89, the psalmist laments the demise of the royal house and might suggest the events at Megiddo in 609 BCE (or else the catastrophe of 587 BCE). Why did YHWH reject the anointed king that remained loyal to YHWH? Josiah is portrayed as a *typos* of the righteous Davidite who was rejected by YHWH.[17] Jeremiah's critical attitude toward Josiah's reform initiatives (Jer 3:6–13) indicates that although Josiah was a righteous king and his reforms served God's purposes, the people did not turn in loyalty to God. It implies that the prophet's disappointed expectations are connected to the people's disloyalty to God. Isaiah 53 contains the concept of the vicarious death of a figure that is associated with YHWH, a servant who serves as a symbol for the righteous Israelites who are to suffer on behalf of other people. A symbol invites thought, in Paul Ricoeur's words. Antti Laato suggests that the suffering servant might be linked to the lamentations over the fate of Josiah at Megiddo, explaining another interpretation of the challenge it posed to Deuteronomist theodicy.[18] He explains that Isaiah 53's inversion of the standard portrayal of the deceased by using lamentations shows that the servant's fate is being hyperbolized, reflecting the sorrow and disappointment that Israel felt with the death of Josiah.

That the death of Josiah as a significant national trauma for Judah is also evident from Jeremiah 22:10–15, which states that Judah should not weep for King Josiah, as 2 Chronicles 35:24–25 states, but rather for Shallum, son of King Josiah of Judah. The latter succeeded his father Josiah, and his reign was characterized by unrighteousness and injustice. Shallum was deported three years after the Megiddo catastrophe, where his father had died.

In conclusion, the Deuteronomist Historian's work contains, *inter alia*, a free-will theodicy to explain the catastrophe of the destruction of Jerusalem and the temple and the exile of the people and their king in

---

16. Laato, "Theodicy in the Deuteronomic History," 219.
17. Laato, "Theodicy in the Deuteronomic History," 228.
18. Laato, *Servant of YHWH and Cyrus*.

terms of the reward-and-punishment scheme.[19] Certain features in the History imply that the people's suffering had an educative purpose. Still, for the most part, the suffering experienced by people and individuals is explained in terms of the choices they made in serving and staying faithful to God's commandments. Josiah's death posed a challenge to this formulaic theodicy and produced lamentations that spawned a communion theodicy during the time of the Babylonian exile.

Chronicles—Ezra—Nehemiah

Another view of Israel's history is presented by the Chronicler, responsible for the books of Chronicles and Ezra-Nehemiah. Again, the exile forms the background for the history of Israel, the people associated with YHWH. The books represent late historiography.[20]

For the author of Chronicles, God as just and righteous forms one of the most fundamental aspects of God's image. The prophets' message that the Chronicler records is that the people's sins would eventually lead to exile; God in divine justice judged them righteously. Beginning with Adam (1 Chron 1:1) and continuing until the new beginning for Israel, in Cyrus's proclamation that they may return to their own country, the book is concerned with Israel's history.

Now is the restoration time, from the first year of Cyrus (Ezra 1:1) to the second term of Nehemiah's office (Neh 13:6–7). The narrative records the events of this period from a historical perspective. But the perspective reaches beyond the present of post-exilic Jews to the nation's past. As in many other traditions in the Hebrew Bible, the Chronicler describes and interprets the present in terms of the past. The past is painted not primarily historically, but as salvation history, in terms of God's revelation to Israel. The rhetorical passages of confessions, prayers, and dialogues appeal to this past that links past and present events in a formula for cause and effect. The past is the root of the present and the origin and cause of its circumstances.[21]

---

19. Other Judean cities affected by the destruction with which the Babylonian reacted to Judah's rebellion were Ramath Rachel, Lachish, Gezer, Tell el-Hesi, Arad, and Tel Masos, as evidenced by archaeological excavation (Albertz, *Israel in Exile*, 72). In Benjamite territory, cities like Tell en-Nasbeh, Gibeon, and Bethel escaped destruction and remained inhabited well into the Persian period (Albertz, *Israel in Exile*, 73).

20. Japhet, "Theodicy in Ezra-Nehemiah and Chronicles," 429.

21. Japhet, "Theodicy in Ezra-Nehemiah and Chronicles," 430.

The narrative in Ezra-Nehemiah presents a two-sided view of God's attributes. While God's justice is the decisive factor in Israel's past, God's mercy determines their present. This perspective makes the Chronicler's work a unique contribution to the Old Testament. The work provides the answers to the problem of retribution created by this perspective. It explains how Ezra-Nehemiah explains the hardship and troubles that the Jews still encountered in the restoration period, like the many enemies that threatened them, the widespread poverty, and the state of disrepair in which they found Jerusalem and the other towns. Are they signs of God's punishment? Nowhere does a reader find any reference that explains their hardships in terms of their sins. It does not explain the matter of hardships and difficulties in terms of theodicy. The Jews are depicted as pious and God-fearing, and there is no threat of future punishment for either the ruling class, priests, or common people.

How did God then react to the people's sins in this period? Several descriptions refer to these sins; the most prominent is undoubtedly the phenomenon of mixed marriages that still occurred between Jews and people of the surrounding culture (Ezra 9–10). However, nowhere does one find that the people's hardships are explained in terms of this transgression or any other sin. Even the profanement of the Sabbath (Neh 13:15–22) and neglect of the temple and priests (Neh 13:10–14) do not serve to arouse God's wrath. Ezra-Nehemiah's narrative also does not refer to any reward that God granted the pious Jews for their faithfulness. The familiar schema of good deeds-reward and evil-punishment of the Deuteronomist Historian does not feature in this work at all. Even though Nehemiah reminded God that God should remember what Nehemiah did for God's people, it does not view any of his achievements as the reward for his good deeds. They were all due to God's favor and divine benevolence that rested on Nehemiah.

Especially the rhetorical passages emphasize the mercy and compassion of God as having been the means of Israel's survival amid the complex challenges that the post-exilic country posed to them. The Persian rulers' positive attitude towards the returning Jews, permitting them to rebuild the city and temple, was due to God's favor resting on the Jews. For that reason, Ezra 5:5 explains that the eye of their God was upon the elders of the Jews, and the Persian governor did not stop the work in repairing the temple, despite the complaints of their enemies. And Ezra 6:22 explains that the Assyrian king's heart was inclined toward the Jews due to the influence of YHWH.

In conclusion, the narrative in Ezra-Nehemiah does not apply the principle of God's justice to the current historical situation. It does not view their history within the conceptual framework of theodicy.[22] The Jews' hardships are not interpreted as their due for sinning against God, and their achievements are not viewed as due to their piousness and faithfulness to God. In their prayers, they appeal to God's compassion, loyalty, and faithfulness to cause them to prosper.

The Chronicler depicts God in terms of God's rule over the whole world, God's justice, compassion, and providence, in line with Ezra-Nehemiah. However, the way the book of Chronicles applies these themes to the historical description differs in several ways from Ezra-Nehemiah.

In contrast to Ezra-Nehemiah, Chronicles is interested in theodicy from the vantage point of God's justice. Israel's calamities are explained as the result of their transgressions against God (1 Chron 5:25–26; 10:13–14; 13:10; 2 Chron 12:2; 20:37; 21:10; 21:12–15; 24:24; 25:27; 28:19). The good things Israel experienced are explained as the reward for their righteousness and faithfulness (e.g., 1 Chron 4:10; 5:20; 13:18; 14:6; 15:15; 17:3–5; 26:5; 27:6). At times, God averts the deserved punishment, as shown in 2 Chronicles 12:7–8; 19:2; 32:25–26. Reward and punishment as God's response to Israel's faithfulness and sins form the main tenet of Chronicles's theodicy.

Another element is the history presented as a chain of cause and effect, of a deed and its retribution, as illustrated in 1 Chronicles 14:16–17; 2 Chronicles 17:6–10; 28:1–5; 33:10; 33:32–34. Chronicles's definition of God's justice consists of the view that retribution is meted to those who earned it, allowing for no exceptions. In contrast to the Deuteronomist's view that retribution is transferable from one generation to another and cumulative, Chronicles states that the person who sins shall die, in line with Ezekiel 18:20. The book of Chronicles applies the principle, however, not only to individuals but the people at large. Thus, God's justice excludes the possibility that a sinful generation's retribution may affect the next generation. Hence, according to 2 Chronicles 25, Amaziah, a servant of YHWH, killed his servants who had murdered his father the king but did not put their children to death, according to what is written in the law, "Parents shall not be put to death for the children, nor shall children be put to death for their parents; only for their own crimes may people be put to death" (Deut 24:16).

---

22. Japhet, "Theodicy in Ezra-Nehemiah and Chronicles," 444.

The book of Chronicles also emphasizes the element of warning within the system of God's justice, consisting of a verbal address to the potential sinner, stating what the deliberate and intentional sin is. The Chronicler does not show that unintentional sin *per se* is ever punished. The author also distinguishes between corporate punishment and the sin of the reigning class. A feature of the Chronicler's history is that the national leaders are apportioned the more significant part of the blame for the people's sinfulness. Gerhard von Rad has already noted that each generation stood and fell with their anointed king.[23] The principle remains the same, as expressed in Proverbs 11:6: "The righteousness of the upright saves them, but the treacherous are taken captive by their schemes." The black-and-white interpretation of historical events has a moral purpose, to encourage listeners to follow the injunctions of the teacher to obey YHWH faithfully. For that reason, listeners were faced with the choice to walk on the road to wisdom with wealth and prosperity as a result or to folly with poverty and hardship as a result. The rewards of wisdom include happiness, fulfillment, and longevity.[24]

Israel's restoration would remain incomplete until they repented and converted to the God of Israel. For instance, 2 Chronicles 15 explains that the Spirit of God came upon Azariah, son of Oded, and he told Asa, the king of Judah, that YHWH was only with them while they were with YHWH. "If you seek him, he will be found by you, but if you abandon him, he will abandon you" (v. 2). Asa responded by destroying the idols in Judah and Benjamin and repairing the altar of YHWH.

The author of Chronicles interprets the division of the kingdom after the death of Solomon and the catastrophe of Jerusalem's destruction in terms of the concept of God's justice. He does not blame Manasseh for this catastrophe; in fact, Chronicles's Manasseh is not even a "great sinner," as depicted by 2 Kings 21. Manasseh was punished for his own sins (2 Chron 33:11), then acknowledged God and repented (33:14), and was rewarded by prosperity (33:15–17).[25]

The destruction of Israel's land and capital had to do with the deliberate and wilful nature of Israel's sins by rejecting God's clear warning of an impending catastrophe. For this reason, God visited them with a terrible punishment. The blame of their sin fell on them and their generation;

---

23. Von Rad, *Old Testament Theology*, 1, 349.
24. Dell, "Get Wisdom, Get Insight," 18–20.
25. Japhet, "Theodicy in Ezra-Nehemiah and Chronicles," 465.

no sin was postponed or transferred. The actual perpetrators received their due; the wilful and deliberate sinner deserved the just punishment.

In terms of Ezra-Nehemiah's emphasis on God's mercy and compassion, what place does it have in the Chronicles's view? There are only three references to God's love and compassion in Chronicles (1 Chron 21:13 / 2 Sam 24:24; 2 Chron 30:8-9; 36:15). God's mercy functions within the concept of God's justice, in contrast to Ezra-Nehemiah. For that reason, the emphasis is on the many opportunities that God gave the people for repentance. Should they have turned in time, they would have been forgiven, despite the severity of their sins (as in the case of Rehabeam in 2 Chron 12:12 and Manasseh in 15:8-15; 17:7-10; 24:2-14, 29-31).

Theodicy in Prophetic Literature

The Former Prophets developed a monumental theodicy[26] and ascribed suffering to retributive justice. The exile represented a deserved calamity for Judah.[27] The book of Isaiah begins with an explanation: "Your country lies desolate, your cities are burned with fire; in your very presence aliens devour your land; it is desolate, as overthrown by foreigners . . . When you stretch out your hands, I will hide my eyes from you; even though you make many prayers, I will not listen; your hands are full of blood" (Isa 1:7, 15). What is the reason? Because the people sinned against YHWH. The solution to their problem lies in repentance: "Wash yourselves; make yourselves clean; remove the evil of your doings from before my eyes; cease to do evil, learn to do good; seek justice, rescue the oppressed, defend the orphan, plead for the widow" (vv. 16-17).

The prophets' interpretation of the exile and restoration in the land resulting from an inoperative temple cult provides liturgical readings of these historical events. A good example is in Amos 4:6-12; Crenshaw suggests that it represents a popular liturgy that celebrated specific victories believed to demonstrate divine favor.[28] YHWH brought famine ("cleanness of teeth in your cities," v. 6); drought ("I also withheld the rain from you when there were still three months to the harvest; I would send rain on one city, and send no rain on another city; one field would be rained upon, and the field on which it did not rain withered," v. 7); fungi,

---

26. In the words of Crenshaw, "Theodicy and Prophetic Literature," 238.
27. Thompson, *"Where Is the God of Justice?,"* 14.
28. Crenshaw, "Theodicy and Prophetic Literature," 251.

locusts, and pestilence ("I struck you with blight and mildew; I laid waste your gardens and your vineyards; the locust devoured your fig trees and your olive trees," v. 8); warfare ("I killed your young men with the sword; I carried away your horses; and I made the stench of your camp go up into your nostrils," v. 10); and earthquakes. The refrain used five times to describe the people's response to God's initiative is, "yet you did not return to me." That these calamities and catastrophes were God's initiative showed that God chastened God's people, disciplining them to save them from further punishment. However, that the misfortunes continued and would end in meeting their God in judgment (v. 12b) was not the deity's fault but that of the people who were wasting the opportunity to repair their relationship with God.

Deutero-Isaiah (40–55) provides hope for the people of God, but still, the author(s) used the principle of suffering as a deserved calamity. The exile would soon end because Judah paid double for all their sins (40:2). Trito-Isaiah (56–66) relates how (some of) the Jews returned from exile. Still, already they were sinning again against YHWH so that the prophet confesses: "For our transgressions before you are many, and our sins testify against us. Our transgressions indeed are with us, and we know our iniquities: transgressing, and denying the Lord, and turning away from following our God, talking oppression and revolt, conceiving lying words and uttering them from the heart" (Isa 59:12–13). And the principle is explained in verse 18: "According to their deeds, so will he repay; wrath to his adversaries, requital to his enemies; to the coastlands he will render requital." The same is true in the books of Jeremiah and Ezekiel. For example, in Jeremiah 9:12, the prophet asks, "Why is the land ruined and laid waste like a wilderness, so that no one passes through?" The answer he receives from YHWH is: "Because they have forsaken my law that I set before them, and have not obeyed my voice, or walked in accordance with it, but have stubbornly followed their own hearts and have gone after the Baals, as their ancestors taught them" (vv. 13–14).

Unique to the book of Jeremiah is a series of passages, called the "Confessions" of Jeremiah, although they do not contain confessions of sin or faith. The Confessions comprise 11:18–23; 12:1–6; 15:15–21; 17:14–18; 18:19–23; and 20:7–18. They are rather akin to the psalms of individual lament that demand answers from God as to why suffering should be a lot of those who attempt to live faithfully before God, in contrast to the godless people who disregard God and experience prosperity. Kathleen O'Connor defends the scholarly use of "Confessions" for these passages, arguing that they are confessions of faith because the prophet clings fiercely to God amid profound and incomprehensible suffering, even though the speaker, on the verge of despair, accuses God of not listening to his pleas.[29] The author prayed, even though he stumbled in finding words to express faith in God. He expressed his very personal suffering and anguish, praying for retribution on the people of Anathoth, the people of his own village, who persecuted him. Jeremiah 11:21 explains their motivation: "The people of Anathoth, who seek your life... say, 'You shall not prophesy in the name of the Lord, or you will die by our hand.'" Jeremiah prays in verse 20, "Let me see your retribution upon them, for to you I have committed my cause." In the next Confession, Jeremiah lays a specific charge against YHWH: "You will be in the right, O Lord, when I lay charges against you; but let me put my case to you. Why does the way of the guilty prosper? Why do all who are treacherous thrive?" According to Jeremiah 15:18, Jeremiah accuses YHWH: "You are to me like a deceitful brook, like waters that fail." YHWH is erratic in divine care of the prophet.[30] According to Jeremiah 20:7, YHWH deceived the prophet: "O Lord, you have enticed me, and I was enticed; you have overpowered me, and you have prevailed. I have become a laughingstock all day long; everyone mocks me."

In the individual psalms of lament, the psalmist comes to an expression of confidence in many cases.[31] In the Confession in Jeremiah 20, it seems as if the prophet also expresses his confidence in verse 13, "Sing to the Lord; praise the Lord! For he has delivered the life of the needy from the hands of evildoers." But the prophet immediately continues to state in verse 18: "Why did I come forth from the womb to see toil and sorrow, and spend my days in shame?"

Ezekiel used as a point of departure the knowledge of the irrevocable nature of the catastrophe, the fall of Jerusalem, and in trying to justify the divine decision of judgment on Israel, he searched Israel's history from its beginnings as a witness of YHWH to divine faithlessness (Ezek 16; 20; 23). History shows that Israel's adulterous faithlessness became a hereditary burden for generations, with Israel having an Amorite for a father and a Hittite for a mother (16:23). The result was the stony heart that Israel's

---

29. O'Connor, "Lamenting Back to Life."

30. Thompson, "Where Is the God of Justice?," 45.

31. As, e.g., in the case of Pss 5:7, 11–12; 7:10, 17; 55:19–23; etc. See also discussion at the end of chapter 5 that reconsiders lament as one strategy that Pentecostals can use to survive suffering.

traitorous disloyalty to YHWH demonstrated (3:7; 11:13; 36:16–36). While Hosea and Jeremiah attribute Israel's faithlessness and the resultant judgment of God to the influence and temptation of the Canaanite vegetation and fertility cults, Ezekiel differs by finding Israel's faithlessness in their being bastard children of heathens. The other prophets view Israel's stay in the desert for forty years as a testimony of their moral quality and intimate relationship with YHWH, despite the different picture depicted in the Pentateuch. Ezekiel radicalized the *Torah* traditions of a morally exemplary generation in the desert and found Israel's sins going back to the nation's founding. Like Hosea and Jeremiah, Ezekiel painted Israel's faithlessness in terms of erotic images, showing the influence of the fertility rites. To be able to introduce a new beginning in Ezekiel 34, Ezekiel used another image, that of the traditional caring shepherd.[32]

In contrast to his determinism when naming the roots of Israel's faithlessness, Ezekiel emphasized individualistic ethics where each person and generation were responsible for their own deeds. Thus, the present generation did not need to do penance for the sins of their ancestors. Instead, it implies that each individual can strike a new beginning, despite their own history of faithlessness. With his theology of forgiveness and personal responsibility, Ezekiel provided the exile generation hope amidst the profound despair they experienced and contributed to what Benjamin Uffenheimer calls the "renaissance" that had its beginnings in the Babylonian exile and culminated in the prophecies of Deutero-Isaiah.[33]

Ezekiel's new ethics also led to an eschatology that created room for God to replace the stony heart with one of flesh, when God would revive the dead and pour out God's Spirit upon Israel (11:19; 36:16–36; 37–39). God renewed God's kingdom in the form of a new Israel. The prophet's eschatological interest was not motivated by pity for Israel, but rather to protect the interests of God's name in Israel. Ezekiel 40–48 depicts the future Jerusalem and its rebuilt temple as the present utopian fulfillment of these hopes.[34] The vision motivated the remainder of Israel to dream about their return to the promised land and rebuild their independent lives, apart from the experience of exile.

---

32. Uffenheimer, "Theodicy and Ethics in the Prophecy of Ezekiel," 224.
33. Uffenheimer, "Theodicy and Ethics in the Prophecy of Ezekiel," 225.
34. Uffenheimer, "Theodicy and Ethics in the Prophecy of Ezekiel," 226.

After the return of some exiles, they did not rebuild the temple immediately, given the sad state of what was left of Jerusalem and the surrounding country. The prophet Haggai then explained to the exiles that what they were experiencing was due to their disobedience of rebuilding the temple. They experienced a drought that led to crop failures and hardship from their enemies because YHWH ordained it as a response to their sinfulness and faithlessness (1:7–11). What they should do to turn the situation around is explained in verse 8: "Go up to the hills and bring wood and build the house, so that I may take pleasure in it and be honored, says the Lord." The principle is that sin leads to suffering while righteousness leads to prosperity.[35] What people sow is what they reap.

The early death of King Josiah is mentioned along with the author's silence about any explanation (2 Kgs 23:28–30) in what is called "a conspiracy of silence."[36] Why would the thirty-nine-year-old king end his life in battle when the Deuteronomist was interpreting history such that those who walked in God's ways would enjoy longevity and prosperity? The historian judges the king's contribution in glowing terms: "Before him there was no king like him, who turned to the Lord with all his heart, with all his soul, and with all his might, according to all the law of Moses; nor did any like him arise after him" (v. 25). However, that did not result in a change of heart in YHWH about Judah's punishment: "Still the Lord did not turn from the fierceness of his great wrath, by which his anger was kindled against Judah, because of all the provocations with which Manasseh had provoked him" (v. 26).

What should also be considered is that later generations sometimes had to pay for the sins of their forebears and that the measure of punishment might be out of proportion to the people's sins. And when a large group of people was punished, there would always be innocent ones among them who did not earn suffering in any deserved way.

Like the Joseph Novella (Gen 37–50), the book of Habakkuk touches upon issues of suffering, coming to a kind of resolution. In the case of Joseph, his suffering was set loose by family favoritism, family violence, and guilt, being played out against the background of famine and starvation. In his case, his suffering had a beneficial outcome; he justified his suffering in terms of realizing a greater goal. In the prophecy of Habakkuk, the prophet asks why various apparently negative and challenging things

---

35. See also Pss 1; 15; 106; Neh 9:6–37; Dan 9:4–19; Exod 34:6–7; Num 14:18; Ezra 9:6–15.

36. Frost, "Death of Josiah," 369.

happen to Israel.[37] During Habakkuk's lifetime, the Assyrians, the foreign nation called the "Chaldeans," oppressed Israel and threatened their survival. The other prophets explained the attacks by foreign enemies by stating that they were God's agents who effected divine judgments upon the people of Israel and Judah for their evils. Habakkuk had a problem with the issue of divine justice, questioning the standard explanation of evil provided in the Old Testament as being entirely due to human sinfulness. The book consists of a dialogue between the prophet and his God, consisting of chapters 1:1–25; 2:6–20 describing a series of woe oracles, and 3:1–19 with the prayer of Habakkuk. There are four players that the book introduces, the prophet, YHWH, the Chaldeans, and the Jews.

1:1	Title of book
1:2–4	Prophet's first prayer to YHWH
1:5–11	YHWH's first response to Habakkuk
1:12–17	Habakkuk's second prayer to YHWH
2:1	The prophet waits for YHWH's response
2:2–20	YHWH's second response, to Habakkuk (2:2–5) and the Chaldeans (2:6–20)
3:1–19	Habakkuk's third prayer to YHWH, comprising a vision (3:2–15), the prophet waiting prayerfully (3:16), and the expression of the prophet's confident hope (3:17–19).

The oracle that Habakkuk saw (1:1) is called a "burden" (*massā*). It is the same word used for a burden that a human being or donkey carries and is not to be borne on the Sabbath day. The prophet's use of the word acquired the meaning of a prophetical oracle concerning foreign nations, frequently prophesying disaster and destruction for these enemies of Israel. Michael Thompson speculates that the use of the word at the beginning of the book might suggest that the Chaldeans were facing imminent disaster, solving the prophet's theodicy question, at least to some extent.[38]

---

37. Thompson, "Where Is the God of Justice?," 62–63.
38. Thompson, "Where Is the God of Justice?," 65.

In referring to the Chaldeans, the prophet asks YHWH in Habakkuk 1:13: "Your eyes are too pure to behold evil, and you cannot look on wrongdoing; why do you look on the treacherous, and are silent when the wicked swallow those more righteous than they?" The prophet protests against what is going on and asks God for a reason. He does not accept the traditional explanation of the prophets of the suffering wrought on Israel by the Chaldeans. In 2:1, the prophet declares his willingness to wait on YHWH's response to his complaint: "I will stand at my watchpost, and station myself on the rampart; I will keep watch to see what he will say to me, and what he will answer concerning my complaint." It is strange to note that the prophet states that he will keep watch to *see* what YHWH will *say* to him. One finds the combination of seeing and hearing in terms of the "word" of YHWH also in Isaiah 2:1, Amos 1:1, and Micah 1:1.

YHWH's response consists of two parts. In the first part (2:2–5), God sets out the attitudes and inner qualities that the people of God should embrace. The second part concerns the Chaldeans, relating the dreadful fate that awaits them in God's judgment. Habakkuk 2:4 is a crucial verse, referring to two different ways of life: the proud people's lifestyle whose spirit is not correct or upright in them, and the righteous, those who live by faithfulness to God.[39] The proud ones have a most ephemeral, temporal, and tenuous hold on life. "Look at the proud! Their spirit is not right in them, but the righteous live by their faith (or faithfulness)."

Habakkuk ends with the third prayer of the prophet. It is in the style of a biblical psalm; its title declares it a "prayer," as also found in Psalms 17; 86; 90; 102; and 142. It bears the expression, "according to *Shigionoth*," also found in Psalm 7. The tone of the prayer differs in various respects from the rest of the book, possibly explaining why the chapter is missing in the commentary on Habakkuk found at Qumran. In the prayer, the display of divine power is to affect judgment on the Chaldeans but also to bring salvation for the people besieged by the Chaldean tyrant. In verse 16, the prophet states, "I wait quietly for the day of calamity to come upon the people who attack us." The next verse expresses confidence for the present and the future, using the imagery of even greater suffering. Like the psalms of lament, the description of troubles is followed by a change of mood with thanks and praise when the trouble appears to be over. The book ends with the expression of quiet and hopeful confidence in God. The prophet expresses hope and confidence despite what the future may

---

39. Thompson, "*Where Is the God of Justice?*," 71.

hold for the people. The reason for his hope and faith is found in the confession, "God, the Lord, is my strength; he makes my feet like the feet of a deer, and makes me tread upon the heights (v. 19)."

In the prophet's theological evaluation of his situation, he links with the two extensive speeches of YHWH in the book of Job (38:1–40:2; 40:6–41:34). While the book of Job emphasizes God's greatness and otherness and Habakkuk emphasizes YHWH's power to defeat the enemy, both books are concerned with the sufferings experienced by believers and human perception of the divine rule on earth in the context of God's care for faithful people.[40]

The book of Habakkuk cannot be called a proper theodicy but represents instead a religious strategy to be embraced in a time of suffering and the witnessing of the suffering of others.

The last book of the Latter Prophets, Malachi, wrestles with the question of why the wicked are seemingly prosperous and without care while the righteous suffer hardships and poverty. The author accuses the Judge of the world guilty of dereliction of duty, resulting in evildoers who are encouraged in their ways. YHWH responds to these accusations and shows the prophet what the end of the argument of evildoers implies. They assert that it is vain to serve YHWH because no one profits by keeping YHWH's commands. For that reason, they count the arrogant happy. They prosper, and when they challenge God ("they put God to the test"), nothing happens to them (Mal 3:13–15). The remark shows how pragmatically prosperous people argue about the usefulness of religious alliance.[41] Religion is viewed as barter, and they operate on a principle of giving in order to receive. They gave and did not receive; they conclude that YHWH is not faithful to what YHWH promises (see Mal 3:8–18 how they also argue about tithes for God). Their conclusion is, "It is vain to serve God" (v. 14).

James Crenshaw explains that this is where every effort to provide a theodicy fails, because mortals lack a global perspective. Thus, it is not possible to justify divine activity until the temporal and spatial limitations are lifted, and human beings are not more limited by the weaknesses of their intellect, moral insight, and worldviews.[42]

---

40. Thompson, "Where Is the God of Justice?," 75.
41. Crenshaw, "Theodicy and Prophetic Literature," 238–39.
42. Crenshaw, "Theodicy and Prophetic Literature," 239.

Jesus seemingly supports the view that suffering results from personal sin when he tells the invalid, after healing him according to John 5:14, that he should not sin anymore, lest something worse happens to him. It suggests a direct link between the man's physical and spiritual condition, associating punishment of sins with suffering. It is not denied that such a connection may exist in individual cases; it is essential to remember that God deals with individuals in their unique situations. When such an answer is applied to all cases "because the Bible says so," people are subjected to formulas that do not necessarily work in each individual case.

It was argued in the previous chapter that most Pentecostals seemingly view suffering in the same terms as punishment of sin. They believe that godly people would experience blessings. However, it is clearly not the experience of all believers. Not all of them are healed when illness befalls them. Some of them lose their jobs and cannot find other employment. They are victims of natural catastrophes and crime, and sometimes their children are also born with physical or mental disabilities.[43] The principle of deserved calamity and retributive justice does not apply in all cases. Theodicy cannot render a single adequate answer to the questions posed by suffering. When one becomes involved as a believer in circumstances that represent suffering in one form or another, one may find that it defies a systematization of understanding according to reward and retribution in terms of one's own human choices.

Theodicy in the Psalms

In the Bible, suffering is never the theme of philosophical or theoretical considerations. The book of Psalms clarifies the many socio-historical contexts of individuals and groups of people who are suffering.[44] The discussion occurs in terms and for the sake of existential interests. The psalmists ask the question, What is the role of God in suffering? How does God engage with evil? What does God do to overcome it?[45] Several of the psalms relate the psalmists' experiences of the absence of God in

---

43. It would represent an interesting experiment to test empirically the extent of believers' experiences of suffering in relation to those of "unbelievers." Most probably the conclusion would be that there do not exist any differences.

44. Lindström, "Theodicy in the Psalms," 258.

45. Surin, *Theology and the Problem of Evil*, 60, 130.

times of suffering and the irrationality of evil that they experience. They do not try to justify God; instead, they accuse God of culpability in the calamities they experience and blame God for innocent suffering, as the main character in the book of Job also does. The God of the lament psalms is clearly not portrayed as omnipotent, omnipresent, and omniscient.[46]

Themes related to human sin, guilt, remission, and forgiveness are not prominent in individual complaint psalms. The psalmists do not connect their distress to punishment for their sins. Instead, God is held accountable for the situation the psalmist finds themselves in and accused of negligence of God's faithful servants.

Another characteristic is that although God is viewed and accused as responsible for the psalmist's dire straits because God does not act to save God's children, another reality exists that functions apart from God. Evil opposes the petitioner as well as God and is often connected with the forces of evil, not only in a metaphorical sense. Chaos consists of the brokenness that characterizes reality, ending with death, which is often personified. The evil that confronts believers is not always the result of human choices but is often interpreted as primeval chaos. The perspective of suffering is determined by a dualist view, at least in some of the psalms.

The psalms' Jerusalem temple theology, which forms the tradition-historical background of the book, also characterizes many of the psalms' interpretations of YHWH's role in suffering.[47] The Zion psalms (Pss 46; 48; 76) and YHWH-kingship psalms (Pss 47; 93; 96–99) view YHWH as the king and the temple as God's palace and fortress. God's battle is against the chaos that threatens God's reign. YHWH must defend God's kingship, land, and people. One finds the same theme in some of the individual psalms, e.g., Psalm 125, which states confidentially that those who trust in YHWH are like Mount Zion, "which cannot be moved, but abides forever." YHWH surrounds God's people as the mountains surround Jerusalem. The implication is that the scepter of wickedness shall not rule over the righteous (Ps 125:1–3).

The individual complaint psalms represent those who protest and complain. They are not lamenting but attempt to change a situation of misery and injustice for the better. They refer to times of great danger and include Psalms 3; 5; 6; 7; 13; 17; 22; 26; 27; 28; 31; 35; 40; 41–43; 54–57; 59; 61; 63–64; 70–71; 86; 88; 102; 109; 120; and 140–43. They testify to

---

46. See discussion in chapter 5 about these concepts from a Pentecostal hermeneutical perspective.

47. Lindström, "Theodicy in the Psalms," 258.

God's absence during their suffering. God is hiding from their cries and pleas. They agree that YHWH is the king of glory who reigns on the mount of Zion, and the honor it brings to God tempers their complaints and accusations.

The psalms do not link God's hiding to their sin in terms of retributive justice. That YHWH is hiding has no cause that they know of, and for that reason, God's hiding is the reason for their suffering. YHWH's hiding is not interpreted as punishment and God's wrath for their sins. The motif of wrath is dominant in Psalms 6; 27; 38; 42–43; 88; and 102 and does not function as a rational explanation of the problem of why God has abandoned the believer. In contrast, divine wrath is part of the problem, not the reason for its solution.[48] For that reason, the psalmist does not view sin as the reason for the problematic situation. Sickness and suffering are not connected as a consequence of sin. This differs from the Deuteronomist's view, which is prevalent in large parts of Old Testament traditions.

Psalms 38; 40–41; and 68 specifically refer to human sin and guilt within the context of the psalmists attempting to interpret sickness in a causal context. The sufferers, however, express the belief in their innocence, also emphasized in Psalms 5; 7; 17; and 26. Because the sufferer is innocent, it leads to the plea that evildoers should be expulsed from their presence.

The individual thanksgiving psalms respond to YHWH's answer to the prayers and complaints of the individual complaint psalms, thanking God for a specific act of deliverance that the psalmist has experienced. Psalms 30; 116; and 138 belong to this group. The psalms of confidence found in Psalms 23 and 27 presumably follow the individual complaint psalms, demonstrating that it is only possible to pray to someone one trusts. Psalm 23 shows the confidence of a believer who lives in the shadow of death and the temple.

The hymns of praise comprise Psalms 8; 19; 29; 33; 65–66; 68; 103–105; 111; 113–114; 117; 135–136; and 145–150 and praise God's greatness and goodness in creation and the sustaining of the world, and the mighty acts of God in the history of Israel. Evil is connected to the chaotic forces that threaten life and YHWH's order. YHWH is, however, a God who fights, one who is mighty in battle (Ps 24:8). It relates to the

---

48. See remark by Fretheim, *Suffering of God*, 63–64, about the kind of God who is portrayed in the Old Testament, interpreted by some as a God of judgment and wrath whose fatherhood "smacks of a certain remoteness and coldness, even ruthlessness."

divine speeches found in Job 38–41, finding a causal connection between the individual's suffering and the construction of the world in which the chaotic finds room to function.

The Psalms do not consider evil and the fate of the believer in eschatological terms. The only exception is Psalm 73. Here the psalmist honestly confesses that although they realize that God is good to the upright, their feet had almost stumbled because they were envious of the prosperity of the wicked. They state that the wicked have no pain, and they are not in trouble as others are. For that reason, pride is the necklace of the evil ones, and violence covers them like a garment. They do not even regard God but set their mouths against heaven. And people react to their wealth and influence by praising them, finding no fault in them. They reason, "How can God know? Is there knowledge in the Most High?" The psalmist complains that it was all in vain that they kept their heart clean and washed their hands in innocence. To consider the matter of the prosperity of the wicked was a tedious task, "until I went into the sanctuary of God; then I perceived their end. Truly you set them in slippery places; you make them fall to ruin" (vv. 17–18). The psalmist realizes that when the prosperity of the wicked embittered them, "I was stupid and ignorant; I was like a brute beast toward you" (v. 22). The argument concludes that those who are far from God will perish because God will put an end to them (v. 27), but "for me it is good to be near God" (v. 28).

The catastrophe of the Babylonian exile that followed the destruction of Jerusalem, the temple, the monarchy, and the economy of Israel in 587 BCE led to a revision of the way believers saw God's engagement with evil. This led to the national complaint psalms found in Psalm 44; 60; 74; 79–80; 93; 85; 89; and 102. YHWH is present in history even without the base of the temple as God's place of residence. Evil is an experienced reality. Suffering is incomprehensible and irrational and largely left uninterpreted. The catastrophe is ascribed to YHWH's absence, and God is accused of being responsible for the affliction. In several of the psalms, the psalmist refuses to accept the sin-punishment idea as an explanation for the misfortune. Only in some cases are the specific political enemies identified; the "enemy" rather serves as the symbol of the power(s) that threatens Judah's survival.

The youngest addition to the book of Psalms is wisdom poetry, which is often found along with devotion to the law. In this tradition, evil is reduced to moral evil. The threat against God's rule comes from human sin. Life's adversities can be explained in terms of the dogma of individual and corporate retribution.[49]

The diversity of views concerning evil and divine justice is demonstrated by the discussion of the various genres found in the book of Psalms that represent different historical and social contexts and religious traditions, providing an overview of the multiple perspectives about theodicy found in the Old Testament.

Theodicy in *Qohelet*

In *Qohelet* (Ecclesiastes), theodicy is the most critical point on the agenda. At the same time, the book poses the most problems of all biblical books for the theologian, exegete, and educator.[50] For the author of *Qohelet*, the world in which human beings live is full of absurdities: everything is *hebel*, that is, absurd.[51] "Absurd" refers to a "disparity between two phenomena which are thought to be linked by a bond of harmony or causality but which are actually disjunct or even conflicting."[52] When the two undeniable realities are contradictory, it leads to absurdity. One observes the absurdity when one sees that one's ideas and convictions do not tally with reality as it is experienced. While human reason attempts to discover order in the world, observing absurdity in all of its reality leads to despair. Although wisdom is better than folly, it is absurd when one observes that the wise and the fool end up at the same destination (2:12–14). Working hard to earn a good living is also absurd when one observes that other people who are not necessarily deserving end up with one's possessions (2:18–23).

A remarkable fact of the book is that the name of Israel's God, YHWH, is never mentioned. However, God does function in the author's philosophy; the author refers to *Elohim* (God) not less than forty times, making it a central theme in the book. Seven times the verb "to do, make" and the adjective "good" is used with God as a subject (3:11, 14; 7:14, 29; 11:5); the references seem to be alluding to the creation narrative in Genesis 1. However, *hebel* ("absurd") does not apply to creation but only to human life and its events. The conclusion is that "good" does not refer, as

---

49. Lindström, "Theodicy in the Psalms," 295.
50. Carny, "Theodicy in the Book of *Qohelet*," 71.
51. Schoors, "Theodicy in *Qohelet*," 375.
52. Schoors, "Theodicy in *Qohelet*," 375.

in Genesis 1, to the acknowledgment and admiration of the way God created everything but to "appropriate" since it is bound with "in its time," which refers to the appropriate times of all things described in 3:1–8. "God made everything good for its appropriate time" (3:11).

The pessimistic tone of the book results in *Qohelet* not being interested in offering any rationally acceptable solution to the challenges of theodicy. Instead, the author is interested in providing a phenomenal description of life's challenges from a philosophical perspective that views everything that happens in human lives as absurd and without meaning. *Qohelet* offers no theoretical solution, and for that reason, it does not provide a coherent theodicy.[53] In *Qohelet*'s theology, God makes everything under the sun for its appointed time. God has fixed this whole system and is in control of all that happens on earth. God gives everybody their allotted lifetime; wealth and pleasure is a gift of God, clearly not given to all people, as are intelligence and wisdom. However, the righteous, identified with the wise and the wicked, placed with the foolish, receive the same treatment and reward in life, making life on its ground absurd.

What about *Qohelet* 8:12–13, which states that it will be well with those who fear God but not with the wicked? It seems that these verses collide with the mood of the rest of the book, and some researchers regard it as a gloss. Another preferred solution is to consider *Qohelet* 8:12–13 as a restatement of traditional wisdom; the author responds by explaining that their observations instead led to the opposite conclusion. For that reason, 8:14 states, "There is a vanity that takes place on earth, that there are righteous people who are treated according to the conduct of the wicked, and there are wicked people who are treated according to the conduct of the righteous. I said that this also is vanity."

The view is repeated in *Qohelet* 9:1–3, that the deeds of the righteous and the wise are in the hand of God, showing a form of determinism. However, everything that confronts the righteous and wise is vanity, since the same fate comes to both. Michael Thompson's proposal is worth some consideration: that "vanity" should be translated as a superlative, as "worthless, ephemeral, transitory, futile, even absurd."[54] There is no distinction between the righteous and the wicked, the good and the evil, the clean and the unclean, and those who sacrifice and those who do not sacrifice. The same fate comes to every one of them, and for the *Qohelet*,

---

53. Schoors, "Theodicy in *Qohelet*," 403.
54. Thompson, *"Where Is the God of Justice?,"* 23.

this is an evil state of affairs. At the same time, *Qohelet* concludes that people's hearts are full of evil and madness, whether righteous or wicked. And when they die, all go to the world where the dead are kept.

Pin'has Carny argues that a biblical theodicy would typically consist of the ideas of a just presupposition that presupposes the belief in human freedom to choose between good and evil, a question that is highlighted in laments and prayers. A notable example of the consensus of wisdom is the dialogue between Job and his friends.[55] In Job 5:9–11, Eliphaz vocalizes that God does great things and unsearchable, marvelous things without number. He gives rain on the earth and sends waters on the fields; he sets on high those who are lowly, and those who mourn are lifted to safety.

For *Qohelet*, God is the creator of the phenomena in nature and human life. God has made everything beautiful; everything has its season, and there is a proper time for every happening, states *Qohelet*. The periodic occurrence of good and evil happens each at its time as a firm order of events, and this is something that no human being will ever be able to understand. The free will of God cannot be disputed; there is no divine providence that is just. Success or failure in human acting is arbitrarily determined, and its enactment is arbitrary. These views of God as creator, the negation of a ruling providence that combines just retribution to a just judge and human free will are determined for *Qohelet*. Neither in this life (6:8; 8:10, 14), nor after death (5:14–16; 6:6; 9:5–6; 10; 11:8) does just retribution figure. In any case, there is no life after death and hence no eschatological expectation that can solve life's injustices (3:19–20; 6:4). *Qohelet* motivates his advice to his readers by referring to the matter in *Qohelet* 9:9–10: "Enjoy life with the wife whom you love, all the days of your vain life that are given you under the sun, because that is your portion in life and in your toil at which you toil under the sun. Whatever your hand finds to do, do with your might; for there is no work or thought or knowledge or wisdom in *Sheol*, to which you are going." The human being is finite without any existence beyond the grave. Death is finality. To strife is without any meaning.[56]

Qohelet seemingly also comments on the deity's distance from the world and its people. The deity is not only inscrutable and beyond challenging but also absent. God is transcendent but not immanent at the same time, in *Qohelet*'s estimation. For instance, in *Qohelet* 5:2 (5:1 in

---

55. Carny, "Theodicy in the Book of *Qohelet*," 72.
56. Thompson, *"Where Is the God of Justice?,"* 29.

Heb), the author advises readers: "Never be rash with your mouth, nor let your heart be quick to utter a word before God, for God is in heaven, and you upon earth; therefore let your words be few." Deuteronomy 4:39 contains Moses's instructions to Israel and gives the same idea: "So acknowledge today and take to heart that the LORD is God in heaven above and on the earth beneath; there is no other." Remarkable is that both authors use the same words, but *Qohelet* leaves out the name of YHWH, confining himself to "God" (*'elohim*). *Qohelet* consistently restricts himself to use only "God" to refer to the deity in forty instances in the book, as stated above, implying that the author is serious about the deity. Still, the way he refers to God betrays what God he is speaking about. The Deuteronomist states that YHWH is God in heaven above and on the earth beneath, while *Qohelet* restricts God's presence to heaven, reserving the earth as the abode of human beings. For *Qohelet*, God is conspicuous by God's absence upon the earth; God is transcendent but not immanent.[57]

God's role in the *Qohelet*'s world is as unlimited power, but the one who asserts this power without any trace of justice, mercy, or wisdom.[58] *Qohelet* does not argue with or accuse God because *Qohelet* views God as unfathomable, and trying to understand what happens under the sun only leads to unhappiness (1:13). No human being can ever grasp what God does or understand God's works (3:10–11). Human beings should remember that God is in heaven and they are on earth, and while God makes everything happen and has total control over everything, humans have no rational access to God's works or mind. The only human response to this observation is agnosticism or "erkenntnistheoretischen Skeptizismus."[59] God is not for *Qohelet* the problem; the problem is instead the shortcomings of all human rational discourse about God. An omnipotent God has determined all creatures and their mutual relations entirely; the human being cannot influence God in any way, freeing God from human disposal and calculability. *Qohelet* recognizes God's existence and presence, but it is not a salutary divine presence in the *Qohelet*'s view. The solution to the theodicy problem is found in the unfathomable mystery of God, the maker of a problematic world determined by a *Deus absconditus* (hidden God).[60]

57. Thompson, "*Where Is the God of Justice?*," 27–28.

58. Pfeiffer, "Peculiar Scepticism of Ecclesiastes," 101–02. See also Gericke, "Comprehensive Typology of Philosophical Perspectives on *Qohelet*."

59. Michel, "Ein Skeptischer Philosoph," 25.

60. Schoors, "Theodicy in *Qohelet*," 409.

Qohelet also rejects the idea of a hypostasis of evil. By such a belief, it becomes possible to explain theodicy. For *Qohelet*, God remains the only cause of all that exists in the cosmic and human realm, as the oldest tradition in the Old Testament also asserts. Only in the time of Isaiah (45:5–7) did the idea of evil as a separate realm apart from God originate, a notion supported by the Chronicler (compare, e.g., 2 Sam 24:1 with 1 Chron 21:2). For *Qohelet*, it is impossible to justify God's actions in terms of the occurrence of evil because a vindication of God cannot take place in an eschatological future.[61]

Theodicy in Lamentations

Lamentations shares in the view that YHWH is Israel's only God and the only power in the universe that matters, implying that bad things also come from God.[62] In the words of the rhetorical question in Lamentations 3:38, "Is it not from the mouth of the Most High that good and bad come?" However, that does not mean that people are not to be considered evil for their bad behavior, although it is God who allows evil; otherwise, it could not happen. Theodicy is the justification of God's actions, especially when it seems as if God is standing aloof from human suffering.

In Lamentations, one does not find many references to such a justification of God, but the book consists of heart-rending descriptions of human suffering. Moreover, the book raises the question of the relationship between this suffering and God, specifically in the context that the people who suffer had been elected by God and viewed themselves as God's people.

The book originated during the fall of Judah and Jerusalem in 587 BCE when the people were exiled to Babylonia. King Nebuchadnezzar (605–562 BCE) reigned over the New Babylonian Empire and besieged Jerusalem for eighteen months before the city fell to his forces. He took the king, ruling class, officials, and a significant portion of the population in exile to the foreign country. The songs found in Lamentations describe the suffering of these people and can be ascribed to the temple singers who had remained behind. Their songs verbalized their pain and despair, and underlying the songs is the question of how to harmonize the catastrophe with their faith in their God.

---

61. Carny, "Theodicy in the Book of *Qohelet*," 80–81.
62. Renkema, "Theodicy in Lamentations?," 410.

The experience of the catastrophe stood in radical contrast to Israel's faith in God, a faith that was based on their perception of God's involvement with the elect people. Some of the cultic prophets preached in the face of the threat of the Babylonian siege that Israel's God would never allow the people to be taken from their country since they were living in the country that God had promised their ancestors. The songs of trust that the temple singers used in the temple cult, like Psalms 46 and 48, underlined their trust in the faithfulness of their God to save them from their enemies. A part of their belief that they shared with the surrounding nations was that the country and the presence of their God were directly linked to each other, symbolized by God's temple in its midst. Now that the temple was destroyed and Judah lost its independence and control of its own country, Judahites were confronted with the question of whether their God was also taken in custody and exiled to a land that belonged to other gods. "Their entire religious constellation had reached its visible end in the destruction of the temple (Lam 1:4; 2:6–7) and the imprisonment and deportation of the Davidic kin (Lam 4:20; 2:9)."[63]

The five songs of Lamentations contain the theological reflections of those who had remained faithful to YHWH. In contrast, many of their fellow Judahites had probably turned their back on the God of their ancestors who had not saved them as God's people. Some aspects in the songs appear to justify YHWH's punishing of Israel, as in 1:5: "YHWH has made her suffer for the multitude of her transgressions." The context of this statement, in verses 4–6, indicates that these sins must have been immense, given the portrayal of Zion's suffering: "The roads to Zion mourn . . . all her gates are desolate, her priests groan . . . her foes have become the masters . . . her children have gone away, captives before the foe. From daughter Zion has departed all her majesty."

Why did the catastrophe occur that might have ended Judah's existence, as happened to the people of the northern kingdom who were taken into exile by the Assyrians in 721 CE? Lamentations 1:18 provides the answer: "YHWH is in the right, for I have rebelled against YHWH's word . . . my young women and young men have gone into captivity." Yet, despite this acknowledgment, the notion of God's justice receives scant attention while the suffering is portrayed in all its stark reality.

The songs did not consider God responsible for the disaster of the destruction of Jerusalem and the temple. The reason for Israel's suffering

---

63. Renkema, "Theodicy in Lamentations?," 414.

should instead be sought in their sinful behavior and rebellious performance towards their God. However, the extent of their suffering was so great that it was difficult, even impossible, for them to square it with their belief in the God who revealed the divine self in their history. The references to infants and babies that faint in the streets of the city (Lam 2:11), children who faint for hunger at the head of every street (Lam 2:19), and hands of compassionate women who boiled their own children to get some food (Lam 4:10) demonstrate the colossal pain of the suffering.

Where did God fit in? The song in Lamentations 3 explains that the sufferers called and cried to God for help, but God shut out their prayers, blocked their ways with hewn stones, and made their paths crooked (vv. 7–9). That what happened to God's people influenced God directly is clear from Lamentations 3:33, which states that YHWH "does not willingly afflict or grieve anyone." This observation gives the sufferers hope that YHWH would not reject them forever. Thus, although God caused grief, God would have compassion according to the abundance of God's steadfast love (vv. 31–32).

The extent of their material, physical, and spiritual suffering disqualified the singers from providing explanations for God's behavior and is exceeded by the laments and questions of the songs, culminating in Lamentations 5:20, "Why have you forgotten us completely? Why have you forsaken us these many days?" Thus, it is impossible to detect any divine rationale in the catastrophe. However, that is not what is essential. All that mattered was to experience God's nearness again, as expressed in the following verse: "Restore us to yourself, YHWH, that we may be restored; renew our days as of old" (v. 21). Their expectation did not, however, exclude the possibility that their rejection by God might be permanent, as the final words of the book express: "unless you have utterly rejected us, and are angry with us beyond measure" (v. 22).[64]

Theodicy in Job

The book of Job is discussed in more detail in terms of a Pentecostal hermeneutical perspective of theodicy in chapter 5. As the main character in the book, Job is concerned with the absence of the God of justice in his suffering. For instance, Job states in 16:11–17 that God has given him up

---

64. At the end of chapter 5, the discussion returns to laments as a possible means and strategy to develop a practice that supports a practical Pentecostal theodicy.

to the ungodly and cast him into the hands of the wicked. God seized him by the neck and dashed him to pieces, making Job his target. He slashed open his kidneys and poured out his gall on the ground. Now Job has laid his strength in the dust, and his face is red with weeping. He experiences this suffering although he asserts that there is no violence in his hands, and his prayer is pure.

In the opening scene (Job 1:1—2:13), God is depicted as somewhat capricious, allowing the suffering to Job to proceed so that God can be proved correct in God's assessment of the faithfulness of God. God seems to be making a bet with Satan to prove Job's loyalty. Thus, the prologue sets the tone for the book, that it is a folk tale. It can be evaluated in two ways: as a story that is used to set the scene for the debate about suffering that will follow and that does not intend to set out a theodicy; an alternative view is that it represents a possible theodicy that brings suffering in connection with a God characterized by capriciousness.[65] The last argument is not accepted because it does not represent the portrayal of God found elsewhere in the Hebrew Bible.

The following scenes portray the suffering of Job and his family, with one catastrophe following the other. Job's faithful response in each case is, "Naked I came from my mother's womb, and naked shall I return there; the LORD gave, and the LORD has taken away; blessed be the name of the LORD" (v. 21). The next verse states that in all this, Job did not sin or charge God with wrongdoing. His wife's reaction is, "Do you still persist in your integrity? Curse God, and die" (2:9). Job's response to his wife's advice is to ask whether they should not receive the bad from the hand of God like they received the good from the hand of God. "In all this Job did not sin with his lips" (2:10).

His three friends who came to sympathize with his suffering do represent a theodicy that the cause of suffering in the world, including Job's, is human sinfulness. A fourth friend, Elihu, makes a new point, that suffering may serve as a divine discipline. Eliphaz refers to it in 5:17–18, that the one whom God reproves is happy, and for that reason, Job should not despise the discipline of the Almighty.

In YHWH's speeches that conclude the book, Job receives no immediate answers to his complaints and questions. What it does is explain that God does come to the faithful people who belong to God. God does not present any justification for Job's suffering or about divine

---

65. Thompson, *"Where Is the God of Justice?,"* 153.

involvement in the suffering. Theology turns here into theophany; God appears, and the human being bows in worship and praise. The theophany also confirms that God is aware of God's children and their suffering. There may be evil in the world, yet at the same time, YHWH does keep that evil, and its associated tendencies to chaos, under control. In Michael Thompson's evaluation, it does not represent a theodicy but rather explains theodicy's inevitable earthly limits.[66] From a Pentecostal perspective, the encounter with God leads to a deep trust in God amidst difficult circumstances, even though the theophany did not provide any explanations for the circumstances.

The epilogue (42:7-17) contains the divine judgment of Job's friends and the restoration of Job's fortunes and wealth. It is clear that the theodicy in the book does not include any reference to the afterlife and the judgment of good and evil people, with the retribution of divine bliss or punishment. In such a world, scholars argue, there had to be a happy ending of some sort to unlock the enigma of suffering to make sense of the suffering in the present world.

In the revelation of God to human beings, the challenges and questions of theodicy give way to worship that strengthens believers' trust in God despite suffering. "I had heard of you by the hearing of the ear, but now my eye sees you; therefore, I despise myself, and repent in dust and ashes" (42:5-6). H. H. Rowley describes the contribution of the book's theology to the discussion of theodicy in the same terms, that it represents the profit one person experiences from the suffering through the enrichment of his fellowship with God. He agrees that the book's author was interested in this encounter with God, leading the reader to this climax.[67] And Robert Gordis writes that the poet's message is not only "we do not know" (*ignoramus*) but "we may never know" (*ignorabimus*). Therefore, the message calls and empowers readers to rejoice because the dark mystery of suffering that encloses believers contains a bright and shining miracle.[68]

---

66. Thompson, "Where Is the God of Justice?," 154.

67. Rowley, "Book of Job and Its Meaning," 183.

68. Gordis, *Book of God and Man*, 134. In chapter 5, the book of Job receives further attention.

Theodicy in Daniel

Daniel is the only book that contains a fully developed apocalyptic, in its second part (7–12), following on the proto-apocalyptic found in Isaiah 24–27; 34; Joel; and Zechariah 12–14. The main features of apocalyptic include numerical symbolism, obscure language, a doctrine of angels, the expectation of a coming time of salvation, a division of history into periods, and the expectation of life after death with its accompanying redressing of unjust suffering and retribution of just and unjust people, in terms of an eternal destination.[69] It is accepted that the book dates from the second century BCE, during the time of the Seleucid (ca. 201–142 BCE) oppression of Jews in their own country, and especially in the period when Antiochus IV Epiphanes (175–64 BCE) reigned over them. His prohibition of the temple cult in all its forms and eventual defilement and contamination of the temple and its altar in response to Jewish rebelliousness and refusal to submit to his arrangements and the martyrdom of those who did not subject them to the prohibition inevitably led to believers asking the question, "Where is the God of justice when their God's temple is defiled and they are forced to denounce their loyalty to God?"[70]

The book's first six chapters contain narratives that underline the belief that YHWH, the God of Israel, is the one with the real power; earthly powers are temporary, and those who oppress other people cannot last. They only act at the behest and with the consent of God. YHWH determines what happens with such rulers and uses them to serve God's purposes for the benefit of God's people. It also emphasizes that God's kingdom shall never be destroyed, and God's dominion has no end (6:26). The theodicy of this author is that God's ways are just and would be made manifest in the world in the fullness of time, although it does not look at an afterlife. God's actions are limited to the earthly world.

The visions in the second part accept that suffering will not continue forever but that believers may know that it will last only a limited time. Daniel 10–12 forms a unit and contains a kind of world history. It understands everything that happens in the world in terms of a great conflict between worldly and divine powers. The purpose of the historical recall is

---

69. Thompson, *"Where Is the God of Justice?,"* 158.

70. The many unanswered questions that the book poses are not discussed here because they do not have any relevance. For one such discussion, see Nel, "Aktualisering van die Apokaliptiese Openbarings," and Nel, "Teologies-Hermeneutiese Ondersoek."

to demonstrate that tyrants and their evil have a limited time to run; their doom is determined by God (7:25; 9:27; 12:7).

Daniel 12 presents a new theodicy, with a time dawning when "Michael, the great prince, the protector of your people, shall arise. There shall be a time of anguish, such as has never occurred since nations first came into existence" (v. 1). At that time, those Jews found written in the book would be delivered and *many* of those who sleep in the dust of the earth would awake, some to everlasting life, and some to shame and everlasting contempt. The reference is clearly to the resurrection of some individuals; the text does not explain why *all* people are not included. Now there is a division of people, with the faithful going to everlasting life while the destination of the rest contains shame and contempt that will last everlastingly. The author breaks the silence of the grave that marks the rest of the Old Testament in terms of an expectation of retribution at the end of the world, with an afterlife and the righteous enjoying their rewards while the unrighteous suffer their punishment for at least a long time.[71] Although the doctrine of divine retribution that characterizes the rest of the Old Testament still occurs here, it is now applied to an eternal judgment.

What should be remembered is that Daniel 12 originated during the Antiochene crisis of the second century BCE. The book assured its readers, who were suffering during the oppression of a foreign ruler, that it was only a matter of time before the situation would change for the better. The evil leader's time was limited, and God had already delivered his judgment. Then God would hand over the power to a person of God's choosing, who would exercise that power in a way that would benefit Israel. Whether a "son of a man" refers to a human or divine individual personality is not clear. Still, the text assures readers that the time of his appointment will surely come, and he would change Israel's situation for the better. The one who will deliver them is on his way. There would be a life after death for the faithful, the wise people, a belief also found in Isaiah 24–27.[72] While the present may include suffering for believers, they are encouraged by the reference to real hope for the future that extends beyond earthly life.

Before turning to the New Testament, the discussion about theodicy in the Old Testament can be summarized with the following remarks:

71. See discussion of "eternity" in the Hebrew world in Chapter 5.

72. Although the reference in Isaiah may rather refer to a "resurrection" of exiled Israel to become a mighty nation once more, as the prophet presumed was the case in David's time.

The Old Testament does not deny that people do suffer, the righteous as well as sinners (however, these terms are defined by different traditions in the Hebrew Bible). The better part of the Old Testament accepts that there is only one God and that all things in creation owe YHWH their existence, including evil and evil powers. To explain suffering and justify divine justice in the face of it, the Old Testament presents several theodicies, the most extensive of which is the theodicy of deserved calamity or retribution. The exception is the book of Job, which rejects this explanation as applicable to all experiences of suffering. However, it does not explicitly deny that it might be the cause of some person's suffering. Another popular theodicy that receives somewhat less attention is the idea that suffering is necessary because it profits the sufferer's soul. Elihu, in the book of Job, expounds this the best. Suffering may also be a part of faithful service; such faithfulness may realize in and through suffering. Isaiah is an exponent of this idea. Isaiah 53 may also contain a reference to life after death as a way of redressing what people have suffered on earth. The book of Daniel accepts that some evil in the world may result from an evil regime's political ambitions and activities. In this book, one finds perhaps the first reference to resurrection (for some) and a future redressing of unjust suffering. These attempts do not provide theodicies in the technical sense of the term because they do not explain why suffering takes place. Michael Thompson is correct when he thinks that it is rather a strategy to deal with the reality of suffering.[73] The questions are not answered, but the presence of God in suffering is emphasized to encourage believers to trust in and endure suffering.

Theodicy in the New Testament

Remarkably, recent theological discussions of theodicy and its challenges are characterized by an interest in the death of Jesus Christ on the cross, providing apposite material for elaborating the so-called "suffering of God" theodicy.[74] The theme of the suffering of God has become the central practical approach to discuss the challenges that suffering poses to faith. In this development, the cross serves, as in traditional terms, to explain the vicarious suffering of Christ in place of sinners but also as an

---

73. Thompson, "Where Is the God of Justice?," 194.

74. See Holmén, "Theodicean Motifs in the New Testament," 605, for a short bibliography of relevant resources.

expression of God's empathy with those who suffer along with creation. It shows that God suffers in solidarity with sufferers.

The death of Jesus on the cross now becomes the new way of looking at suffering next to other perspectives developed in the New Testament, such as the Deuteronomist's retribution theology (Deut 28; Dan 12:1–3; 2 Macc 7; found in, e.g., Matt 5:3–12), the perception of suffering as testing by God to form the believer's character (Job 1; found in 1 Cor 10:13; Jas 1:2–4), or as disciplining (Prov 3:11–12; Wis 11:9–10; found in Heb 12:5–11). This way of interpreting the cross stands in contrast to the way people living in Jesus' time viewed the crucifixion of habitual criminals as repulsive and reprehensible, and skeptics' evaluation of the death and resurrection of the Son of God as impossible, ridiculous, and superstitious. Amy Orr-Ewing refers to a cartoon found on a wall in the ruins of ancient Rome. It demonstrates what people of the time thought of the Christian message. It contains a caricature of Jesus' crucifixion, showing a man's body hanging on a cross with a donkey's head. Next to the cross is the figure of a young man with a hand raised as if in worship. Underneath is the inscription, "Alexamenos worships his god!"[75] The cross and the empty grave are the central motifs in the early church's proclamation. Finding that the cross was viewed as a shameful death for anyone, early Christians spent much attention to explaining the reasons for their Savior's scandalous fate.

In scrutinizing the discussions of New Testament authors that refer to Jesus' cross, one does not find a unanimous perspective. Even Paul, presumably the author of 28 percent of the New Testament, did not present a systemic whole, but his discussion consists of various motifs and expressions. Tom Holmén provides a sensible and helpful way of categorizing these different perspectives.[76] He describes, in the first place, the cross's soteriological interpretations as vicarious satisfaction of people's sins leading to redemption through Jesus' sacrifice and victory over the dominion of evil. Second, there are interpretations based on identification with the rejected messenger of God, interpretations based on the suffering servant of Isaiah, the righteous sufferer, the heavenly high priest, and the new Adam. Lastly, there are interpretations with a social function, as Christians' participation in the death of Jesus, as an example, a new way of knowing, and a revelation of God's love for humanity.

75. Orr-Ewing, *Where Is God in All the Suffering?*, 103.
76. Holmén, "Theodicean Motifs in the New Testament," 612–14.

Especially Holmén's last category of interpretations with a social function, in my opinion, helps define a theodicy compatible with thinking in the New Testament. For instance, Jesus' cross was viewed by the author of Romans 8 as a sign of and related to believers' suffering in the present world of the first century CE. By suffering for their belief in Jesus through martyrdom, discrimination, and rejection by society, Christians suffer with and like Christ. The end to their suffering would be marked by their glorification along with and in the same manner as Christ (v. 17). For that reason, the author argues, the present sufferings are not worth comparing with the glory that believers would share (v. 18). Until that time, they groan inwardly while awaiting the redemption of their bodies (v. 23). Even when their sufferings are abundant, they trust that their consolation would also be (2 Cor 1:5). In the interim, they realize that their affliction produces for them an eternal weight of glory (2 Cor 4:17). The only way to share in Jesus' resurrection is by sharing in his sufferings, writes the author of Philippians 3:10–11, and for that reason, oppressed Christians rejoice in their suffering (Col 1:24). The author's reminder of the cross serves as a consolation for suffering readers, proclaiming that suffering is temporary. However, one has to pass through it to share in the end in Christ's resurrected glory.

Even though some exegetes differ, I submit that the author does not imply that suffering is required from believers if they wish to enter Christ's glory. Instead, Paul argues that the suffering of some serves to testify to believers' hope to share in the glory, reminding them that to share in divine glory, they need to follow in the way Christ had to go to his eventual glorification. In suffering, Christians become fellow sufferers of Jesus, sharing in the agony that the cross produced for him. Jesus warned believers that they would suffer for their faithfulness to him because to be his follower implies that one should deny oneself and take up one's cross and follow in his footsteps. Those who want to save their lives will lose it, while those who pay the highest price for Christ's sake will find it (Matt 16:24–25).

Another element that Paul discusses in Romans 8 is that creation also shares in humanity's suffering. For that reason, creation waits with a longing that God would reveal who God's children are because it will also introduce the salvation of creation. Creation is also subjected to futility as human beings are but will also share in being freed from bondage to decay and experience the glory in which God's children will participate. Until then, creation groans as if with birth pangs (vv. 19–22).

Creation's suffering differs from those of humanity because its suffering was not earned in any way; it was subjected to futility by God (v. 20). The author assumes that Adam's disobedience implies that all men have sinned. Creation could not sin, however, and its suffering is innocent, although it will share in the freeing of suffering that Jesus's obedience as the new Adam brings. "Creation" signifies non-human nature, including animate and inanimate, that was supposed to be subjected to futility through Adam's sin. However, its situation was reversed through Christ's obedience on the cross, and it will be freed from its slavery to decay.

In other words, the author is not concerned with human suffering. He understands the brokenness that characterizes the created world in terms of Adam's fall and views the cross and resurrection as the means of the eventual restoration of creation, along with believers' redemption at the second coming of Christ.

Another observation of the author of Romans 8 is that nothing can separate believers from the love of God in Christ (v. 39), traditionally understood as representing concrete sufferings of individuals (vv. 35–38). What is important to note is that the author refers to believers alone, and the suffering is qualified as the eschatological distress of Christians who share in Jesus' suffering.[77] The hardship, distress, persecution, famine, nakedness, peril, and sword (v. 35) refer to the sufferings of this present time referred to in verse 18. The present suffering stands in contradistinction to the glory that is to be revealed to believers. Suffering cannot separate believers from Christ; sharing the sufferings of Christ belongs to believers and cannot set them apart from God's love in Christ.

Another perspective that Paul, as the supposed author of 2 Corinthians 12, develops is that God's power is made perfect in believers' weakness (v. 9). The context of the discussion is Paul's boasting of his spiritual experiences, but now the author also tells of his troubles, referring to the thorn in the flesh that God gave him. He interprets the thorn as necessary to keep him from boasting of his excellent and outstanding charismatic experiences. Even though he had called on God thrice to remove the thorn, God did not but instead explained to him that divine power is made perfect in and through Paul's weaknesses. His weaknesses are how Christ's power dwells in him (v. 9). For that reason, Paul rests in his fate that includes insults, hardships, persecutions, and calamities that constantly befall him because of his faithfulness to Christ. He has

---

77. Holmén, "Theodicean Motifs in the New Testament," 627.

found that whenever he is weak, then he is strong (v. 10). What this world deems as weak represents the power of God, he argues; what this world considers foolish is wisdom to God. That explains why the message about the cross is foolishness to those who are perishing, but to believers who are being saved, it is the power of God (1 Cor 1:18). Jews and Gentiles view the crucifixion of Christ as a stumbling block, but to believing Jews and Greeks, Christ is the power and wisdom of God. The author concludes the argument in 1 Corinthians 1 by reminding the readers that God's foolishness is wiser than human wisdom, and God's weakness is stronger than human strength (vv. 23–25).

Paul is teaching readers that he has learned to transform the experiences of distress, allowing him to delight in insults and persecutions by realizing that suffering for the sake of Christ (2 Cor 12:10), the result of his avowal and loyalty to Jesus, actualizes God's power abiding in him. Suffering gets another meaning than what other people would think; what they consider as foolishness, to suffer for one's loyalty to another man, is the wisdom of God.

Paul connects the mystery of the suffering of Christ to save the world with the mystery of God, allowing believers to suffer by viewing it in the perspective of the scandal and foolishness of the cross and connecting it to the idea that the fate of Christ's disciples will necessarily imply that they also suffer. Yet, like Christ, their suffering demonstrates that they enjoy the favor of God; that they are not afflicted can only be understood when viewed from the cross.

The letter of 1 Peter's perspective on the cross emphasizes that Christ's suffering serves as an example for believers, encouraging them to follow in his steps (1 Pet 2:21). The author refers to unjust suffering (v. 19) that gets God's approval (v. 20). Being reviled for faith in Christ implies that believers are blessed because the Spirit of glory rests on them (4:14). It is essential to understand that the author is not referring to suffering as such but qualifies it as suffering due to believers' commitment to Jesus. Clearly, the author intends to bring meaning to believers who suffer persecution and martyrdom for their faith by reminding them of Christ's suffering as an example that they should follow.

Despite the emphasis on the cross of Christ, his death does not provide a clear pathway to the problem of suffering in the world and human life in particular. In the New Testament, one finds only a few references that connect the two elements. The cross is not inherently prone to considerations about suffering and does not serve any theodicean function.[78] The cross, however, explains that suffering will not last forever but will end when the eschatological future dawns, and the cross attests to believers' suffering as communion with Christ, as a condition for sharing in his glory. Innocent suffering is a grace from God's hand as part of the calling of God. The cross teaches believers what the wisdom of God consists of, according to which suffering is the condition where God's power is made perfect, as demonstrated when God resurrected Jesus on the third day.

The New Testament's considerations of suffering are mainly concerned with believers who suffered persecution and martyrdom because they decided to stay loyal to Christ. It does not apply to contemporary believers who suffer as such, although it still applies to believers who suffer persecution for their faith. The New Testament also does not present Jesus as a fellow-sufferer; the opposite is rather accurate, that to be a follower of Christ necessitates that one is called to be his fellow-sufferer. That in Christ God undertook to suffer together with the suffering world may sound encouraging, but it does not seem to concur with any of the interpretations of the cross found in the New Testament.[79] Christ did not die because of the distressfulness of being a suffering human being but for the sinfulness of humankind. The New Testament is not concerned with justifying God in the face of suffering but with the justification of human beings before the righteous God that allows them to enter God's presence in Christ.

Theodicy in the Book of Revelation

The last book in the New Testament is also the most difficult to understand due to its purpose of providing a glimpse of the eschatological future awaiting believers. Much has been written about eschatology and apocalyptic in Christian theological circles, betraying widespread differences of definitions and content. "Eschatology" refers to the religious view of history as linear from its beginnings with the creation of the first human couple to its divine denouement and consummation, as opposed to the cyclic view of the universe, generally held by Indo-European religions in the first century CE, which views everything as recurring endlessly.

---

78. Holmén, "Theodicean Motifs in the New Testament," 646.
79. See discussion about the *theologia crucis* in chapter 6.

"Apocalyptic" refers to detailed predictions, images, and sequences of the expected end, characterized by strange visions and dreams, predictions, and images.

Previously, the view of Johannes Weiss and Albert Schweitzer of consequent eschatology determined the theological debate about eschatology. H. S. Reimarus explained that Jesus was a Jew who expected the eschatological earthly Jewish kingdom to come. However, his disciples misunderstood his message, leading to a gap between the historical Jesus and the early church. The disciples expected the imminent return of Christ (*parousia*) that introduces the end of the existing order and the coming of a new world. Within a few decades, Christians realized that the hope of the kingdom's immediate appearance that ends the world as it is known failed, leading to a re-evaluation of the faith. Either the New Testament had to be reinterpreted, or the conclusion had to be drawn that Jesus was mistaken. However, the New Testament does not provide any evidence to justify a consequent eschatology or an eschatological crisis due to the eschatological future that did not dawn imminently.

Early nineteenth- and twentieth-century New Testament theology evaluated apocalyptic in negative terms, as a decline of classical biblical prophecy into pessimistic predictions of an imminent end that represents speculation by some religious eccentricities.[80] During the last few decades, however, this view changed with a new interest in apocalyptic. Before the new interest, eschatology underwent a trans-historical reduction and reinterpretation when Karl Barth saw eschatology no longer as an actual event in the future but a linguistic and hermeneutical maxim to denote the Christ-event as God's self-revelation that takes place each time a human being encounters God.[81] He argued that eschatology refers to a state of consciousness, in other words, in the presence of eternity. Apocalyptic does not have any role to play in this view of eschatology.

Ernst Käsemann reacted to the devaluation and negative assessment of apocalyptic and explained that it is impossible to understand Christianity, or Christ, apart from apocalyptic. It is the mother of Christian theology.[82] Attempts to analyze apocalyptic, e.g., in terms of pseudonymity, vision, anachronistic historical surveys, pessimism, determinism, imminent expectation, etc., to distinguish it as a distinct genre, have been

---

80. Simojoki, "Book of Revelation," 662.
81. McDowell, "Karl Barth Having No-Thing to Hope For," 12.
82. Käsemann, *Exegetische Versuche und Besinnungen 2*, 105.

unsuccessful. The New Testament applied Jewish apocalyptic in a novel way by reinterpreting it in christological terms, giving it a new content with missiological, ecclesiological, and ethical relevance. Anssi Simojoki argues for viewing apocalyptic as a complex notion that is impossible to reduce to a single formula and for abandoning the dichotomy between eschatology and apocalyptic.[83]

The early church lived from the imminent expectation of the constant presence of Jesus in his kingdom, the church (*ekklesia*), and the future appearance in his glory. These two realities, of the kingdom that has already come and will come, do not exclude each other as different kinds of realized and future eschatologies but as sides of the same coin. They are held together christologically, with the coming King already in and with his children through his Spirit. While the Synoptic Gospels emphasize the future transcendence of Christ, the Gospel of John emphasizes the present immanence in the *ekklesia*. Because the early church interpreted the *parousia* christologically, they did not experience a crisis when Christ did not return within a generation (Mark 13:30; Matt 24:32–35; Luke 21:29–33). The book of Revelation uses both aspects, of the coming LORD (Rev 1:7; 3:11) and the present LORD of the church (Rev 1:13, 20). The most important solution that the New Testament proposes for the challenges of theodicy is the belief that Jesus' *parousia* is imminent.

John's Apocalypse is a prophecy in which prophets play a significant role. It is also an epistle containing a mixture of Hellenistic epistolary forms.[84] It includes an interpretation of the Old Testament in christological terms, reinterpreting several events in terms of Jesus' coming kingdom. The Old Testament is seen as Scriptures fulfilled in Christ's revelation of God. The question of why Christians must suffer before the second coming of Christ is answered in the same terms. Christians are participating in the eschatological-apocalyptic drama that will end in the *parousia*, and for that reason, they are encouraged to remain faithful even in times of persecution.

Revelation 10 contains the key to unlocking the book's message. The prophet refers to an angel standing on the sea and the land that raises his right hand to heaven and swears by the Creator that when the end comes, the mystery of God will be fulfilled, as God had announced to the divine servants the prophets (vv. 5–7). All God's words to God's prophets, written

---

83. Simojoki, *Apocalypse Interpreted*, 29–34.
84. Simojoki, "The Book of Revelation," 671.

down in the Old Testament, must first be fulfilled before the *parousia* will end believers' suffering at the hand of God's enemies. Revelation is not concerned with whether Christ failed to return as he promised. Instead, it encourages believers to continue in their faithfulness despite what cost it might hold because what God said will surely take place. What is written will be fulfilled. Christ will soon come, but first, all the words of God are to be fulfilled in history. The idea of such a conditional *parousia* also occurs in Matthew 23:39; 2 Thessalonians 2:3–4; 1 Corinthians 15:25–26; and Romans 11:25–27.

Conclusion

This chapter provided an overview of notions of theodicy represented by the different traditions that compose the Bible in broad terms. Especially within the Old Testament, one finds diverse views. Instead of choosing one at the cost of the others, it is probably best to use the broad spectrum of views to explain the variety of causes of suffering while admitting that, in many cases, it is not possible to find any solution from a human perspective.

One of the purposes of the chapter was to describe the responses of various biblical traditions to compare them with the theological responses described in the previous chapter. It seems that the theological responses that in many cases were qualified in terms of philosophical categories reflect, in most cases, the biblical evidence. What should be emphasized in theological evaluations is that the theory that suffering is directly related to retributive justice is the response provided by most biblical traditions. That biblical authors present various answers that differ and in some respects are mutually exclusive should also give rise to space for individuals to find meaning in their own suffering, using examples provided by biblical authors.

The next chapter attempts to describe the theodicy that influences Pentecostal thinking, at the hand of a doctrine emphasized by Pentecostals for many years, of divine healing and in terms of a specific denomination in Africa. The reason for investigating Pentecostal theodicy at the hand of a doctrine is the lack of relevant publications about theodicy. This theodicy will then be evaluated at the hand of biblical evidence, representing the second motivation for describing the biblical evidence.

4

Pentecostal Thinking about Theodicy

Introduction

INSTEAD OF ATTEMPTING TO provide an overview of the vast world of Pentecostal literature, consisting of scholarship, sermons, and popular works about theodicy, the discussion is limited to the Apostolic Faith Mission of South Africa, the most prominent classical Pentecostal church in South Africa and the biggest, with 1.2 million members.[1] This way of working localizes the discussion to the existential experiences within one main Pentecostal denomination.

It is asserted that Pentecostals traditionally did not engage with theodicy as a potential challenge to believers' faith because of their continuationist emphasis that God keeps on repeating the same kind of miracles and wonders that people in biblical times experienced and described. Chris Green starts his article about a Pentecostal *theologia crucis* with the remark that Pentecostals have not yet developed a theologically and pastorally adequate account of suffering, even though Pentecostal praxis is directed in its affective dimensions to providing a means of coping with pain and suffering.[2] Pentecostals expect God to save them from suffering, not to explain why suffering occurs. And B. Scott Lewis writes, "Historically Pentecostals have not reflected upon the traditional problem of evil from a philosophical perspective. In other words, no formal theology of the problem of evil exists from a Pentecostal perspective."[3]

---

1. Wikipedia, "Apostolic Faith Mission of South Africa."
2. Green, "Crucified God and the Groaning Spirit," 127.
3. Lewis, "Evil, Problem of," 186. The exceptions are McLean, "Pentecostal

Pamela Engelbert refers to the tension between their theology of victory and the experience of suffering as the Achilles' heel of Pentecostalism.[4]

Pentecostals did not invest much of their time in theological endeavors but instead concentrated on current encounters with the Spirit due to the restorationist and primitivist urge to continuate the experience of the earliest church and recreate what they perceive to be the revival climate of the New Testament church. "Instead what is found is a vast array of literature regarding the removal of suffering by way of healing."[5] Pentecostals did not accept suffering; they trusted God for its removal.

Pentecostals' continuationist perspective was born from the conviction that a worldwide outpouring of the Spirit, comparable to the early church's experience, would result in the restoration of miraculous power to motivate and empower the church in its mission. They believed that their mission would manifest in signs, wonder, healings, and miracles, along with the palpable presence of the Spirit, most notably witnessed in glossolalia.[6] Steven Fettke and Michael Dusing explain that Pentecostals lack an adequate response to evil and chronic and unrelieved suffering.[7] They keep on praying, repeating God's promises that God will provide, call on "prayer warriors" and famous preachers to pray and trust with them, and command demon spirits to leave them. They trust that if they have enough faith, God will provide and answer their prayer.[8] They view God as the "invisible Guarantor of social benefits," who is "present" to those who react in faith and claim their healing, deliverance, or other miracles. They "pray through" and "receive their victory" because they "claim the promises" and believe that "in Jesus' name" they are blessed, clarifying some of their unique scripts. If the miracle does not realize, it is because of a lack of faith, either with the victims or those who pray for them.[9] In reading through their literature, one finds many testimonies of divine healing and intervention, seemingly affirming and legitimating Pentecostal doctrines and practices.[10] Such testimonies punctuate

---

Perspective on Theodicy" and "Pentecostal Responses to the Problem of Evil," and Archer, *Gospel Revisited*, chapter 5.

4. Engelbert, *Who is Present in Absence?*
5. Torr, *Dramatic Pentecostal/Charismatic Anti-Theodicy*, 59.
6. Anderson, *To the Ends of the Earth*, 12.
7. Fettke and Dusing, "Practical Pentecostal Theodicy?," 160.
8. Fettke and Dusing, "Practical Pentecostal Theodicy?," 161.
9. Fettke and Dusing, "Practical Pentecostal Theodicy?," 161.
10. Fettke and Dusing, "Practical Pentecostal Theodicy?," 162.

many worship services, prayer meetings, and Bible studies. This practice is found in most Pentecostal churches. Its purpose is to build the present believers' faith to trust God for miracles in their own lives. Shane Clifton argues that healing has been so central to Pentecostal theology and practice that, alongside Spirit baptism, it has come to define the essence and being of the Pentecostal movement.[11]

Seldom does one find a scholarly engagement with theodicy among Pentecostals, although a significant scholarship has been developing since the 1970s. In the discussion about a hermeneutical perspective on theodicy, such contributions will be discussed.

To illustrate Pentecostal thinking about theodicy, this study focuses on the doctrine and practice of divine healing within the AFM of SA with the purpose of demonstrating the underlying theological concepts of God's continuationist interventions in believers' lives.

The AFM of SA and Theodicy

History of the AFM of SA

At the beginning of the twentieth century, South Africa was impoverished due to two wars with English overlords. The second was the Anglo-South African War of 1899–1902, which led to widespread devastation and poverty. The country was ripe for spiritual awakening. When John G. Lake and Thomas Hezmalhalch arrived in Johannesburg in 1908 as missionaries from the Azusa Street Revival in 312 Azusa Street, Los Angeles,[12] they found people with deep spiritual needs that required a religious revival.[13] Their services started in the church building of the Zionist assembly in Doornfontein on May 25, 1908. Most members of the Doornfontein congregation were Black, with only a few Whites.[14] Like the church in Azusa Street, Los Angeles, most of the members of the Doornfontein congregation were impoverished and marginalized, and most were Blacks.

---

11. Clifton, "Dark Side of Prayer for Healing," 205.
12. See discussion in Liardon, *Azusa Street Revival*.
13. Apostolic Faith Mission of South Africa, "History of the AFM."
14. Burger and Nel, *Fire Falls in Africa*, 55.

John G. Lake's Ministry of Divine Healing

In an article from 1925, Frank Bartleman described his reminiscences of the worship services he had attended at Azusa Street in Los Angeles since 1906: "Demons are being cast out, the sick healed, many blessedly saved, restored, and baptized with the Holy Ghost and power. Heroes are being developed, the weak made strong in the LORD. Men's hearts are being searched as with a lighted candle. It is a tremendous sifting time, not only of actions, but of inner, secret motives."[15] This was also the case with the ministry of John G. Lake; he emphasized divine healing and the miraculous as an integral element of his Pentecostal message, as Isak Burger, an official historian of the AFM of SA, has stated.[16]

Lake's healing ministry went back to his involvement with John Alexander Dowie of the Christian Catholic Apostolic Church in the city of Zion in Illinois. Dowie taught Lake in 1899 that divine healing was the key to the totality of the gospel.[17] He became convinced in 1907 of the necessity of Spirit baptism, an experience he shared while he was praying with Thom Hezmalhalch for a lady suffering from rheumatic inflammation. He wrote that he immediately experienced the work of the Spirit in revealing the characteristics of Jesus and God's power to heal.[18] "My nature became so sensitized that I could lay hands on any man or woman and tell what organ was diseased, and to what extent, and all about it."[19]

Lake attended some of the services at Azusa Street in 1907, contacted William Seymour, and kept contact with him while ministering in South Africa. Lake also met Charles Parham, an early pioneer of the Pentecostal movement, and they stayed friends until Parham died in 1929.[20]

---

15. Quoted in Bartleman, "How Pentecost came to Azusa Street," 40. Bartleman (in Bartleman, "Frank Bartleman and Azusa Street," xx) describes the five doctrines that characterized the theology of Azusa Street as justification by faith alone, sanctification as a definitive work of grace, baptism with the Spirit accompanied by the initial sign of speaking in tongues, divine healing, and belief in a personal premillennial rapture of believers at the second coming of Christ.

16. Burger, *Geskiedenis*, 115.

17. Reidt, *John G. Lake*, 18.

18. Lake, *John G. Lake Sermons*, 23, 27.

19. Lake, *John G. Lake Sermons*, 17. Lake (*John G. Lake Reader*, 63–69) tells how it came about that he dedicated his whole life and ministry to bring the message and reality of healing to all people.

20. Burger, *Geskiedenis*, 132; Lake, *Tune in for Adventures in Religion*, 12–15.

At the first meeting that Lake and Hezmalhalch held in Johannesburg, a Black employee of an influential family was healed, and this healing served as a trigger for many ill people to attend further meetings. Many of the church's first members testified that they joined the AFM of SA after being healed.[21] Lake wrote that within the first three years of the ministry in South Africa, 2,023 cases of healing were reported. He also referred to a meeting he had with the bishop of the Church of England, who invited him to meet with Anglican priests. Eventually, the church appointed a commission of inquiry into the healing ministry and invited Lake and Hezmalhalch to visit Britain to discuss divine healing further with church leaders.[22]

The AFM of SA from the start accepted Lake's theological principles that illness resulted from Satan and that God does not want anyone to be sick. Sickness does not honor God; healing brings glory to God's name. The Bible ascribes illness to Satan and his demonic powers. A second principle is that God wants to heal all believers. It is a promise God made, according to the Bible, that has not been revoked. And the third principle is that it emphasizes human faith. Unbelief is the most crucial reason why people are not healed when they pray for healing.[23]

Early in the history of the church, one already notices that the human element plays a role. The minutes of the Executive Council of the church notes on January 22, 1909, shortly after establishing the new church, why a Brother Schneidermann resigned as a church member. He writes that it is because "a great deal of very sad exaggerations in cases had been made, that messages had been given not by God, etc. and that the name of God was dishonoured thereby."[24] The Council decided that the letter contained much that was true. They resolved "in future to use the utmost caution, and to do all in our power with the help of God to eliminate from the work whatever was not of God; and to admit to the public that many mistakes had been made, even if such a confession cost humiliation." The AFM of SA was at that stage eight months old!

Lake left South Africa in February 1913 to cooperate with Cyrus B. Fockler in Milwaukee and eventually established "Divine Healing Rooms" in Spokane, where he administered divine healing daily to

21. Burger, *Geskiedenis*, 178.
22. Lake, "Does God Ever Heal?," 22.
23. Lake, *John G. Lake Sermons*, 125.
24. Executive Council of the AFM of SA, "Minutes," January 22, 1909.

clients. The main elements of his theology of healing were derived from his sermons and publications and consist of the following. He based his theology on an interpretation of biblical texts with all texts from the Old and New Testament, Gospels and letters, poetry of the Psalms, and narrative descriptions of the history of Israel placed on one level. He quoted long lists of texts with any statement to "prove" his views. Still, he never spent any energy looking for any text's historical and social context as a condition for interpreting it in terms of the author's original intention, as far as it is possible to find it, and the situation of the first listeners.

The Pentecostal movement in the United States used "faith healing," "prayer healing," and "divine healing" interchangeably. Still, Lake followed Dowie in using "divine healing" exclusively to emphasize that God is the healer.[25] Lake criticized the other two terms for their focus on the human factor, of faith and prayer, as though human performance contributes in any way to the divine action of healing. For Lake, it was essential to note that healing is exclusively God's work and choice, denying that God may choose to use any human medication in doing the healing work. The AFM still prefers the term "divine healing."

He defined "divine healing" as the removal of illness by the power of God, a process and act of God that repairs the damaged organ. He saw the human body as the temple of the Spirit and illness as a foreign invader that should be chased away. He defined "divine health" as constant contact with God, allowing the life of God to flow through one's body.[26]

Divine healing serves to prove to the world that Jesus Christ is the Son of God. Lake explained that it represented Jesus' answer to John's disciples whether he was the Messiah expected to come to Israel; Jesus referred to the signs of his ministry, among which healing played a prominent part (Matt 11:3–6).[27] For that reason, divine healing is a significant element in the church's evangelistic efforts. Signs and wonders attract people over great distances and demonstrate the power and reality of God's presence. Likewise, miracles affirm that God is present among people.[28] Lake defined miracles as the descent of God's kingdom to the

---

25. Hanekom, "Wonder of Vergissing?," iv–viii.
26. Lake, "Genade van Goddelike Genesing," 15.
27. Lake, *John G. Lake Sermons*, 122.
28. Reidt, *Jesus: God's Way*, 37.

human domain: "They are God intervening in the general order of things to meet a need by supernatural means or power."[29]

Illness is "incipient death," the result of sin that always results in death. For that reason, no illness is found in God or among the first people before the Fall (Gen 3), in Lake's opinion. The God-man turned into earth-man when the first couple rebelled against God, and sin is the parent of illness. Without sin, there would have been no illness.[30] Lake asserted that when one analyzes illness, one usually finds some element of sin behind it; not necessarily an act of sin or personal sin, but rather the laziness or passivity of the soul, failing to do Bible study or pray regularly, a lack of faith, prayer, love, or something similar.[31] For that reason, the approach to illness should be the same as to sin: it should be viewed as hateful, something that should be reprimanded, cast out, and destroyed.[32] It is clear that the blame for illness is placed upon the ill person.

Illness should be seen holistically and qualified in terms of disease in the body, soul, and spirit. The basic and primary illness is the illness of the spirit that requires conversion and restoration of the person's relationship with God. It necessarily leads to healing in the body as well: "The whole problem is cleaning up a man in his spirit."[33] Every physical change in the body can be traced to a spiritual state.[34]

Keeping up one's spiritual health requires that one regularly engage in three exercises, consisting of feeding on the word, continuous public confession of who the believer is and what Jesus means for them, and communion with Jesus through his Spirit. "As your spirit becomes strong and vigorous, there issues from it a faith that is triumphant and creative."[35]

Lake interprets "atonement" as "at-one-ness," implying a unification of body-soul-spirit with Christ, both in salvation and one's ministry in his service. Divine healing should always be seen in its relation to salvation. In healing people's bodies, God demonstrates to them that their sins are forgiven.[36] Healing is an essential element of the salvation that

---

29. Reidt, *Jesus: God's Way*, 1.
30. Reidt, *Lake: A Man without Compromise*, 108.
31. Lake, *John G. Lake Sermons*, 54.
32. Lake, *John G. Lake Sermons*, 167.
33. Lake, *John G. Lake Sermons*, 37.
34. Lake, *John G. Lake Sermons*, 37.
35. Lake, *New John G. Lake Sermons*, 39.
36. Lake, *John G. Lake Sermons*, 17.

God offers to human beings through Jesus Christ's work on the cross. The implication is clear, that divine healing should be seen in the same terms as forgiveness, as a gift guaranteed by God to the believer because it is based on the historical fact of the crucifixion of Jesus.

Lake correctly distinguishes between suffering or oppression that all believers will experience at times and sickness. Suffering can include temptations, false accusations, persecution, physical needs, tiredness, loss of possessions, and other difficult circumstances due to the believer's faithfulness to Christ.[37] Sickness is, however, in another category than suffering for the sake of the gospel and should be ascribed to its author, Satan. It is not God's will that the believer should suffer from illness. God will not always rescue the believer from suffering, but in the case of sickness, the believer may expect instant relief in answer to prayer. "Never did Jesus tell a person that he must remain sick."[38] Illness is not a cross that believers should bear for the sake of Christ; it is not God's will that the believer should suffer from illnesses.

Paul's thorn in the flesh falls in the first category of suffering, persecution for the sake of the gospel.[39] God did not promise to save Paul (or us) from wicked people's attempts to intimidate him to forsake his faith.[40] Christ also suffered at the hands of wicked and unscrupulous people and institutions. However, Christ promised to save us from illness. In Lake's opinion, God does not use sickness to teach and train believers. Lake refers to Christ, who never experienced illness in his body (something that cannot be ascertained from the New Testament); although he was the Son of God, he learned obedience through what he suffered (Heb 5:8).[41] Likewise, suffering due to the oppression and persecution of Christians at the Jews' and Romans' hands was part of God's school to form their characters and does not refer to illness. A good father will never punish his children with illness or accidents that crush their bodies. In the same way, God protects believers from such practices of suffering.[42]

---

37. Lake, *New John G. Lake Sermons*, 54–55.
38. Lake, *New John G. Lake Sermons*, 56.
39. Lake, *New John G. Lake Sermons*, 61.
40. Lake, *New John G. Lake Sermons*, 39.
41. Lake, *New John G. Lake Sermons*, 36.
42. Lake, *New John G. Lake Sermons*, 87.

According to Lake, to end the prayer for healing with the words, "if it be Thy will," is a sign of unbelief.[43] To pray in such a way is to believe that God does not necessarily want to heal in every case, which Lake denies.[44] He writes: "We believe that this attitude of mind and this character of reasoning is due to the ignorance of the plain Word and Will of God, as revealed through Jesus Christ. We contend further that it is not necessary for God to will the healing or non-healing of any individual. In His desire to bless mankind, He willed once and for all and forever that Man should be blessed and healed."[45] God's will is healing and health.[46] Lake suggests that one should instead pray: "I banish this illness from my body as something evil because it is not from you, LORD. I dominate it because it does not bring honor to you, Jesus."[47]

Lake also shared Dowie's reaction to medical science. He states in a sermon: "It is not my desire to degrade medical practice. It is man's best effort to lift himself out of the mess Adam brought upon the race by his high treason. I only wish to present God's better way."[48] He then explains that the better way consists of disciples, pastors, elders, and their gifts of healing, who minister in the power of God.[49] To entrust one's body to God to whom it belongs and then run to the doctor when one becomes ill reflects the sin of unbelief. "It is a violation of your consecration to God."[50]

Lake believed that the progress of medical science is not as positive as many people think.[51] In Lake's day, it must be remembered that medical science had not seen the advancement of modern times, as reflected in Lake's attitude. He was pessimistic about the use of medicine because trust in medicine undermined the believer's belief in God. God uses illness to bring believers to where they experience their utter dependency on God

43. Lake (*John G. Lake's Life and Diary*, 12–13) believed that Satan is the origin of illness, and therefore no healing can be attributed to him. In his day, some believers thought that medical healing was the work of the devil, serving as the reason for their resistance to any form of medical help.

44. Lake, *John G. Lake Sermons*, 131.

45. Lake, *John G. Lake Sermons*, 131.

46. Lake, *John G. Lake Sermons*, 46. Lake (*John G. Lake: His Life*, 173, 181) explains that God's will is always to heal in answer to the prayer of faith because the Son of God is a "redeemer even unto the uttermost for body and soul and spirit."

47. Lake, *New John G. Lake Sermons*, 118.

48. Lake, *New John G. Lake Sermons*, Preface.

49. Lake, "Vrae met Betrekking tot Genesing," 26.

50. Lake, *New John G. Lake Sermons*, 121.

51. Lake, *John G. Lake Sermons*, 135.

alone, Lake argued, requiring the believer's mortification. Many believers do not reach that stage because they had run to the hospital for help, implying that they trust the doctors instead of God. What is needed, is Lake's prescription, is that the Spirit of God should operate their hearts. By using the medicine, believers find themselves in the same place as spiritualists because they set themselves open for foreign powers to enter their lives and bodies.[52] They worship "the little medicine god behind the door."[53]

Israel did not put their trust in the doctors. "The Gentile world had her doctors and medicine, but the Covenant people of God . . . trusted God and God alone for four hundred fifty years."[54] Only in Solomon's time were non-Jewish doctors imported, along with Egyptian women and their idols.[55] The foreign doctors taught Israel to take their trust from God as the sole healer. Even Jesus refused to use the drugs of his day; the vinegar the soldiers offered him on the cross was mixed with gall, a pain reliever widely used in the first century CE.[56] "Drugs have always been the unbeliever's way of healing. God always was and is the real Christian's remedy."[57] Lake verbalizes his disapproval of medicine with the words, "Throw your medicine in the toilet, and then apologize to the toilet."[58]

Lake did not leave room for believers not to be healed. Those who keep on suffering were perceived as a kind of critique of the prevailing understanding of the healing and miracles doctrine, as Stephen Fettke and Michael Dusing explain. The only way to explain their suffering was to find some flaw in their faith.[59] In Stanley Hauerwas and Richard Bondi's terminology, they became a "dangerous memory" in the

---

52. Lake, *Tune in for Adventures in Religion*, 53.

53. Lake, *John G. Lake Sermons*, 42.

54. Lake, "Does God Ever Heal?," 11. Lake (*John G. Lake Reader*, 341) argues that healing by God, through faith and prayer, was already practised by the patriarchs. He refers to Gen 20:17 to support his assertion. God also made a covenant "of healing" with Israel that cannot be annulled, as the unchangeable God is one of the parties, with reference to Exod 15:26. See also discussion of God's immutability in chapter 5.

55. For Lake's statement that doctors were imported by Solomon, no biblical evidence exists. Thus, the assertions about the influence of the "Egyptian doctors" cannot be proven.

56. Lake, *New John G. Lake Sermons*, 47.

57. Lake, *John G. Lake Sermons*, 43.

58. Reidt, *Lake: A Man Without Compromise*, 53.

59. Fettke and Dusing, "Practical Pentecostal Theodicy?," 163.

community,[60] and they were marginalized, rejected, and ignored. Lake explained that his practice was to keep on praying for a sick person until the person testified to being healed. He claimed that his success rate in praying for the ill for healing was 75 percent.[61] "We always prayed for a person until we were satisfied that the healing was complete. There was no dependence on the arm of man. Go for ministry until you are well," is his advice for the sick.[62] He advises ministers of healing to settle down to minister to the individual again and again until it is a finished job.[63]

The last remark is Lake's emphasis that healing should be viewed in the correct perspective. The greatest manifestation in the life of a human being is not healing from an illness, even though that may be important for the person, especially in cases of a terminal illness. The greatest manifestation is not even conversion or Spirit baptism but the manifestation of love in and through the believer's life (1 Cor 13).

The discussion illustrates the (lack of) theodicean perspective found in the theology of John G. Lake. He believed that healing is believers' right, based on the atonement that Christ brought about by sacrificing his life on the cross. God would never punish someone with disease in any form. God's will for believers is that they should be well and prosperous in all respects. There are no exceptions to the rule. Belief in God protects the believer from all sickness.

Although Lake never discussed theodicy in any of his publications or sermons, his view is clear. He accepted that some believers would suffer persecution for their faith, like Paul, and they should view it as a privilege to share in Christ's humiliation in the world. Others suffer due to evil, and all the works of the evil one should be resisted in faith and prayer. Believers should not look for a possible reason for their suffering; they should look for the reason why they are not healed or delivered or why their prayer for provision is not answered. The implication is clear, that the blame for "unanswered prayers" should be placed on the shoulders of believers and those who pray for them.

---

60. Hauerwas and Bondi, "Memory, Community and the Reasons for Living," 439–52.

61. Burger, *Geskiedenis van die Apostoliese Geloof Sending van Suid-Afrika*, 144–45.

62. Lake, *New John G. Lake Sermons*, 117.

63. Bosman, "Teorieë vir 'n Genesingsbediening," 21.

The Early AFM of SA in the Time of Pieter L. Le Roux and Healing

Shortly after Lake departed for the United States, the AFM of SA elected Pieter Louis Le Roux as their leader, a position he held with distinction for thirty years (1913–43), leading the church in consolidation and balanced expansion.[64] In this time, the church expanded amidst the South African Rebellion (1914), the poverty crisis of White people that led to the Carnegie Report, and the involvement of some churches in helping solve the crisis. In addition, the country experienced large-scale urbanization due to thousands of people turning from farming to mining and related industries, leading to severe changes in the fiber of society.[65] Nevertheless, P. L. Le Roux led the AFM of SA for three decades of change and transition with calmness and security to unity, durability, and consolidation.[66] Bengt Sundkler opines that "It was largely due to his leadership as President of the Apostolic Faith Mission that the sound development of the White Pentecostal movement was due. All this goes to prove that P. L. Le Roux has a place in South African church history."[67]

Divine Healing and Medical Science

In Le Roux's time, most members of the AFM of SA accepted Lake's radical approach to medical science. For instance, Eva Stuart, one of the earliest women leaders of a Zionist congregation that joined the AFM when it was established in 1908, writes that God does not need any means to help in ministering healing in the same way as God does not require any means to save those who turn to God for their salvation.[68] In his dissertation, John Bosman refers to an older member of the church who reminisced in 1986 about the early days when the congregation members were immersed in mourning when they noticed the medical doctor's car standing in front of another member's house.[69] As late as 1933, some members still did not regard the medical treatment as one of the ways

---

64. Nel, "Leerstelling van Goddelike Genesing," 127.
65. Bosman, "Teorieë vir 'n Genesingsbediening," 48.
66. Burger, *Geskiedenis van die Apostoliese Geloof Sending van Suid-Afrika*, 227.
67. Sundkler, *Zulu Zion*, 67.
68. Stuart, "Gods Wil in Genezing," 6.
69. Bosman, "Teorieë vir 'n Genesingsbediening," 19.

that God uses to heal people or that medical work was reconcilable with faith in God as the healer.[70]

Bosman explains that the church's attitude towards medical treatment was codetermined by a lack of money due to the depression of the thirties and widespread drought in South Africa, the high tariffs doctors and hospitals charged for their services, and the relative ineffectiveness of medication during the early decades of the twentieth century.[71] However, the church's hermeneutics also played a significant role. When people read all texts in the Bible evenly and on the same level, and as though they were written for people living in contemporary times and culture, they found in the Bible the encouragement addressed to Israel to trust in God alone and not to lean on the arm of flesh. They concluded that God does not heal by any other means than the Spirit's power revealed in signs and wonders.[72] The "arm of the flesh" can refer to nothing else than medical help!

Le Roux held his own opinion about medical help, which differed somewhat from that of the church. He wrote as early as October 10, 1910, that "We do not hold that anybody will be excluded from heaven because of the use of medicine."[73]

The AFM of SA's attitude towards medical science led to several problems and challenges in the church. In Krugersdorp near Johannesburg, where Eva Stuart was the pastor, members of the congregation refused in 1917 that their ill child should receive any medicine. When the child died, they were charged with "wilful neglect of their child because they refused medical aid and refused to use medicines."[74] The court in Krugersdorp found the parents guilty of the charge, and the AFM of SA appealed the conviction, but the appeal did not succeed. The church responded by encouraging its members to sign a petition addressed to the government that requested an amendment of the Children's Protection Act to make provision for a conscience clause "granting exemption from use of medicine etc. to those who belong to a Recognised religious body against whose faith it is to use medicines."[75] In addition, it encouraged

---

70. Bosman, "Teorieë vir 'n Genesingsbediening," 18.
71. Bosman, "Teorieë vir 'n Genesingsbediening," 49.
72. Nel, "Leerstelling van Goddelike Genesing," 142.
73. Quoted by Sundkler, *Zulu Zion*, 23.
74. Executive Council of the AFM of SA, "Minutes," April 2, 1918.
75. Executive Council of the AFM of SA, "Minutes," April 2, 1918.

members to contribute to the costs of the appeal case that amounted to 150 pounds, and half the amount was collected in this way.

History repeated itself in 1931 when a couple from Port Elizabeth in the Eastern Cape were charged for refusing medical help for their sick child. They were also found guilty and fined ten pounds at their conviction.[76] Again, the AFM of SA requested the South African government to consider adding a conscience clause that would provide relief for people who, on religious grounds, objected to the use of medicine. A delegation of the church eventually met with the Minister of Justice to state the church's case, without any positive response from the government's side.

The question of the vaccination of children became controversial in the AFM of SA during the 1920s. South African law made it compulsory that all children be vaccinated against measles, mumps, and typhoid. Already in 1919, the AFM of SA decided "that our members and children be provided with a certificate of membership upon which be printed the attitude of the Mission on the question of vaccination, inoculation and the use of drugs and medicine."[77] At the same time, the church addressed a letter to the Minister of Home Affairs requesting an exemption for all its members from vaccination requirements; the letter explained the request by referring to Daniel's faithfulness to God that required of him not to use any of the king's food and wine. It stated that church members wish to stay faithful to the government, but they also need to obey God.[78] At the next meeting of the Executive Council, the minister's response was noted, which warned that no exemption from vaccination would be granted to anyone and for any reason and that the government would not recognize the certificate that the church issued to its members. However, the letter

---

76. A case with similar characteristics was reported in 2008 in the USA. A fifteen-month-old girl by the name of Ava Worthington died on March 2, 2008. She contracted bacterial bronchial pneumonia and a blood infection. Her parents, Carl and Raylene, refused any medical treatment because they believed in faith healing, including prayer, anointing with oil, and community vigils, as recommended in the letter of James. At the end of a three-week trial in July 2009, a jury convicted the father on a charge of criminal mistreatment, sentencing him to two months of jail time and five years' probation, on condition that the parents seek medical care for their five-year-old daughter and newborn baby (Oregon v. Worthington, Clackamas County Circuit Court, 08–0403 [2009]; Campbell, "What More in the Name of God?," 2).

77. Executive Council of the AFM of SA, "Minutes," October 18, 1919. See also Bosman, "Teorieë vir 'n Genesingsbediening," 18.

78. Executive Council of the AFM of SA, "Minutes," October 18, 1919.

closed with the assurance by stating that government would not use any coercive powers against conscientious objectors.[79]

At the meeting of the General Conference, on April 11, 1920, President P. L. Le Roux announced that members' refusal to vaccinate themselves and their children might lead to a conviction and even jail time, "but he exhorted all to be steadfast or if prosecuted and convicted and given the option of a fine to refuse to pay it and go to gaol rather."[80] The church also decided to support the Anti-Vaccination League and assisted it in establishing branches throughout the country.

The Executive Council announced in the monthly magazine in 1921 that the church's view of the Bible as the word of God does not allow believers to be vaccinated and injected or to use medicine in any form.[81] The church's stance was motivated by referring to Mark 16:18, which promises that the disciples would lay their hands on the sick and they would recover. In addition, James 5:14–15 instructs sick believers to call for the elders of the church and have them pray over them, anointing them with oil in the name of the Lord, and their prayer of faith will save the sick. At the General Conference in 1931, the church decided "that Divine Healing excludes the use of medicine and that we should take a strong stand against those who made a habit of the practice as described above." The minutes further noted that several members testified to the power of God in healing their bodies "because they put their entire trust in Him."[82] Later in the same year, the Executive Council of the church decided to withdraw the certificates of all workers who make them guilty of using any medicine, disqualifying them from working in a church congregation.

The implication of the church's attitude towards medical help was clear: all believers who trusted God for their healing would be healed. It did not allow for any exceptions. The church's response to those who did not get healed is discussed at the end of the section. But, first, it is necessary to look at the theological grounding for the AFM of SA's perspective on divine healing.

---

79. Executive Council of the AFM of SA, "Minutes," December 11, 1919.

80. Executive Council of the AFM of SA, "Minutes," April 11, 1920. The minute books were written by hand and at times the writing is almost unreadable. The ink of the fountain pen also started to get very dull in places, making it difficult to decipher it.

81. Quoted in Bosman, "Teorieë vir 'n Genesingsbediening," 18.

82. Executive Council of the AFM of SA, "Minutes," April 2, 1931.

Healing in the Atonement

In 1918, Scott Moffat stated in a sermon at the General Conference that "the origin of sickness in the Human race was the fall and the instigation of the fall was Satan . . . He then showed the remedy for sickness to be in the atonement of Christ."[83] Sin leads to the situation where a human being becomes separated from God, and the result of all sin is the curse of illness and death. People are born under the law of sin, disease, and death due to the sin of disobedience of Adam and Eve in the garden of Eden. In motivating the same viewpoint, Eva Stuart refers to Luke 13:16, Acts 10:38, Hebrews 2:14, and 1 John 3:8. She asks why illness continues to exist on earth and influences believers as well as unbelievers and answers that healing from illness can only be received in the same way as salvation, by searching for God and believing in God's power to heal.[84] J. A. Jamieson states it even more explicitly: "Where is the remedy for sickness found? In the atonement . . . If we go to Christ for the forgiveness of sin, why not go to Him also for healing, for both are found in the atonement . . . Jesus bore in His body on the cross the sickness that now afflicts you . . . As you believe this and accept the healing purchased by His precious blood, you are healed."[85]

Forgiveness of sins and healing are put on the same plane as related and integrated aspects of God's plan of salvation for humankind (see the discussion of the use of Isaiah 53 by the AFM later in the chapter). By believing in Christ, one receives both forgiveness and healing. Both are products of the same act of salvation on the cross as Christ's sacrifice for others' sins. The believer stands before the cross to receive forgiveness of sins, restoring the relationship with the Creator destroyed by sin. And for the same reason, the believer comes to the cross to receive healing. The implication is clear: as believers may believe that their sins are forgiven in Christ, they should believe they have received healing. Both forgiveness and healing are the results of the cross's sacrifice, and both are guaranteed because they are based on a historical given, the cross of Golgotha.

The equalization of forgiveness and healing leads to the pragmatic problem that when recovery is not realized in the believer's life, it implies that the believer's security that forgiveness took place might also be at

---

83. Executive Council of the AFM of SA, "Minutes," July 16, 1918.
84. Stuart, "Gods Wil in Genezing," 6.
85. Jamieson, "Divine Healing," 23.

risk. The AFM of SA taught that God gives both forgiveness and healing when the human being believes.

An article in the church's monthly magazine mentions seven natural divine means of healing found in the Bible, including laying on of hands, anointing with oil, touching of Jesus' garment, touching the sweat clothes of holy persons, being touched by the shadow of a holy person, the use of the communion meal, and relationships in marriage. In each case, Scripture references illustrate that, although they refer to the same issue, they do not present evidence for the argument that it represents a "divine means for healing."[86] The same article also refers to seven spiritual divine means of healing: the word of God, faith, prayer, unified prayer, confession of sin, the forgiveness of sin, and deliverance from demonic spirits.[87] The systematization of biblical material clearly demonstrates an arbitrary and artificial way of dealing with the Bible.

The need for ill believers to understand God's will for their lives is critical enough that one finds references at several places in the church's publications. "How can they trust God to heal them, when in their hearts they believe He might want them to remain sick for some mysterious good, which Satan always puts into their imagination to thoroughly deceive them?"[88] God's will is demonstrated in the events in the wilderness when everyone among the Israelites who looked upon the copper snake lived, according to Osterhus.[89] It is still God's will for every sick person who trusts in God's power and believes in the power of Christ's atonement to be healed.

In his sermon to the General Conference in 1918, Moffat also referred to the origins of illness. He emphasized that the discipline and chastisement that Hebrews 12:6–7 refers to is never illness.[90] The reference is related to Christ's experience of being tempted in all respects; the Bible nowhere states that Christ was ill. Moffat argues that Paul's reference to Trophimus's disease in 2 Timothy 4 is due to a lack of support for Paul, including on the part of Trophimus. That is the reason why he became ill; he forsook Paul in Paul's time of crisis! And Paul's thorn in the flesh (2 Cor 12:7) does not refer to illness but a messenger from Satan

---

86. Borrowed, "Gebruik die middel," 3–4.
87. Borrowed, "Gebruik die middel," 4.
88. Osterhus, "Have They Real Faith?," 4.
89. Osterhus, "Have They Real Faith?," 4.
90. Executive Council of the AFM of SA, "Minutes," July 16, 1918.

fulfilling his master's wishes to tempt Paul to forsake his faith in Christ. Moffat's egg dance to read into texts what he needs to support his viewpoint that God always wills that believers get healed shows the lack of explicit biblical support for the perspective.

What about Those Who Are Not Healed?

How did the church take care of believers who remained sick despite trusting God for their healing and visiting various "divine healers" for prayer? And what about those with chronic and permanent sickness, injury, and disability?[91] Shane Clifton refers to people with a disability as being the "elephant in the room" because they form a part of the "obviously unhealed in a social space in which supernatural healing is understood to be connected to the gospel, a reward of faith, and a central part of the life and ministry" of Pentecostals.[92]

In this regard, Johannes Henning writes that Paul's advice to Timothy to use some wine for the sake of his stomach and frequent ailments (1 Tim 5:23) should be viewed in the light of Timothy's weak constitution and the local water found in that region that was detrimental for his body.[93] Believers do not use alcohol at all, and this is clearly an exception, argues the author, showing the damaging effect of the water that Timothy should avoid at all costs. G. D. Morgan argues that theological speculation that believers such as Timothy stayed sick is not valid because the Bible does not provide any evidence that anyone remained ill, implying that God would have healed them very quickly in response to their faith.[94]

The discussion illustrates the church's embarrassment with biblical references that do not support their perspective that all believers would be immediately healed in answer to prayer. Some of the arguments are clearly not convincing. The embarrassment is based on the connection between the healing of diseases and forgiveness of sins to the divine historical intervention of the cross. If God forgives each time a sinner turns to Christ in faith, God should also heal when a believer trusts in Christ's sacrifice for healing. If it does not happen, it cannot be God's fault.

---

91. Clifton, "Dark Side of Prayer for Healing," 209.
92. Clifton, "Dark Side of Prayer for Healing," 206.
93. Henning, "Vragen en Antwoorden," 7.
94. Morgan, "Goddelike Genesing," 17.

Since the 1930s, several voices reminded the church that not all believers are healed. L. Jones, for instance, stated in an article in 1935 that Epaphroditus (Phil 2:25–30) and Trophimus (1 Tim 4:20) remained ill.[95] For that reason, one finds the instruction in James 5:14–15 that sick believers should call for the church elders to pray for them and anoint them with oil in the name of the LORD; the LORD will raise them, heal them, and even forgive the sins they have committed. Jones concludes, however, that although believers do not "refuse to consider present-day exceptions," they refuse to "interpret Scriptures by present-day exceptions. Salvation is for all, yet all are not saved! The Baptism of the Holy Spirit is for all of God's children, yet all God's children have not the baptism in the Holy Ghost. If we accept this, why should we experience difficulty in believing that healing is for all, yet all are not healed?"[96]

Thoughtfully, Eva Stuart remembered the earlier days in the AFM of SA when believers consistently experienced the victory of healing through the prayer of faith.[97] These days, she argues, the elders' prayers for the healing of believers are not answered anymore but only for young Christians and sinners. She finds the reason for her (somewhat bizarre) observation in the lack of knowledge about the "higher things of God" among the older believers who looked at the elders for healing and did not put their trust in God. They did not grow in their study of the word of God and did not progress into a deeper life with God, and did not develop in the faith. They were still attending kindergarten.

The meeting of the General Conference in 1931 attended to the question of why some were not healed. The discussion concluded that "unbelief was to a large extent the sin which prevented people from receiving Divine Healing."[98] They also discussed whether healing might serve as a form of chastisement that God could use to discipline the believer. "Several asserted that the LORD allowed sickness to come upon us as a chastisement to bring us back to him." The meeting accepted the argument of P. L. Le Roux that the word "chastisement" in the Greek language conveys the idea of an earthly father who corrects and educates his children; illness is not a fit manner for a father to reach such a goal.[99]

---

95. Jones, "Is Divine Healing for Everybody?," 7.
96. Jones, "Is Divine Healing for Everybody?," 7–8.
97. Stuart, "Goddelike Genesing," 4.
98. Executive Council of the AFM of SA, "Minutes," April 1, 1931.
99. Executive Council of the AFM of SA, "Minutes," April 1, 1931.

Are there exceptions to the rule that God heals the believer in answer to the prayer of faith? In an article in the church's monthly magazine, R. A. Crane accepts that such exceptions might occur and gives the reasons for it as to test the faith of believers, to test whether the believer will turn from God to call on medical help, to serve God's glory by granting healing, to prove that the prayer of faith saves the ill person, and to teach believers empathy with those who suffer from diseases because they had experienced illness firsthand.[100] P. G. Parker disagrees and argues that cases may occur where healing does not take place. God has reasons for not granting healing, and believers would do well to leave the exceptions to God, trusting the biblical principle that a saved person would be healed in body and soul.[101]

For the first time, one finds the acknowledgment that some believers who were healed then lost their healing.[102] C. R. Robinson adds that it might even be the experience of most believers. The most important reason for this sorry state he ascribes to the believer who was healed but still "persists in his life of careless disobedience."[103] In later years, the church's experience that many believers remain ill despite praying for healing would lead to accepting medical help. However, in the fifties, it would contribute to a schism when some more conservative AFM members left the church and established the Pentecostal Protestant Church, due in part to what they perceived as a lack of faith among AFM pastors to trust God exclusively for healing all illness.

Interpretation and Application of Scripture in the AFM of SA

It was customary among early Pentecostals to provide textual references to their statements about healing. However, as stated above, the desire to ground the doctrine in the Bible did not leave room for discussing each text in terms of its genre, context, or original intention. A good example is found in an article by P. C. Nelson with the subheading, "The Scripture on Divine Healing," which provides fifty-five references to texts in the Old and New Testament without any further discussion of the texts.[104]

---

100. Crane, "Why Believers Experience Sickness," 9–10.
101. Parker, "Sewevoudige Evangelie," 4.
102. Robinson, "Keeping Healing," 3.
103. Robinson, "Keeping Healing," 4.
104. Nelson, "Instruction to Those Seeking Healing," 23.

No attempt was made to systematize and process the biblical data about healings into a systematic theological reflection. Pentecostalism as such was skeptical about theological attempts to formulate propositions and doctrines and preferred to experience encounters with God instead. In an article published in 1946, P. L. Le Roux writes that speaking in tongues serves as an initial sign of Spirit baptism. Still, other signs follow it, such as a hunger to read the word of God, continuous prayer, and unity among believers. He writes about the desire in young Christians to be trained in the word, "The Holy Ghost leads us to the Word, not away from it . . . The enemy tells some people that when they have the Baptism they do not need the Word any more. Those who listen to his voice generally fall into error, into fanaticism, and sometimes into grievous sin."[105]

The church's use of the Bible was characterized by literalist interpretation, based on the conviction that the Bible was verbally inspired and should be accepted word-for-word as God speaking to humankind. In an article entitled "Is the Bible Verbally Inspired?," the author asserts that the Bible is a document "inspired, word for word . . . no word in it save such as God has selected."[106] And C. S. Osterhus maintains the same viewpoint when he writes, "There is no guesswork about God's declarations. They are explicit and emphatic. They make no mistake."[107]

When the Bible is read literally, the pronouncements of Jesus and the apostles seemingly leave no doubt that God wants to heal all people at all times. The practice for believers was to literally stand on God's word, the Bible, binding God to the promises that the Bible provides and reminding God of the commitment to heal them.[108] Such arrogance, however, betrays the presumption that God is bound by what the Bible states, making God a prisoner of what the Bible says. This attitude leaves no room for God's sovereign decision over the lives of individuals and does not acknowledge the unique journey of God with individual believers. God is imprisoned by human interpretation of the Bible, as if that is possible at all. What is needed is "to have the living Word that moves beneath

---

105. Le Roux, "Pentecostal Signs," 3.

106. Godet, "Is the Bible Verbally Inspired?," 25.

107. Osterhus, "Have They Real Faith?," 4.

108. Pentecostals love to sing the song: "Every promise in the book is mine / Every chapter, every verse, and every line / All are blessings of his love divine." One of the verses read: "By his stripes, the book says I'm healed / Until the day of redemption / The book say's I've been sealed / To prosper and be in health is right in line." Hymnary.org, "Every Promise in the Book Is Mine."

the literal words of the Bible erupt to call people into life," in the words of Bishop John Shelby Spong.[109]

Isaiah 53 and Its Use in the New Testament and the AFM of SA

The Bible-reading practices of the AFM are demonstrated by the way they interpreted Isaiah 53.[110] A recurring theme in Pentecostal parlance is the assertion that divine healing is founded on Christ's work on the cross (see discussion above of the grounding of healing in the AFM). It is based on an interpretation of Isaiah 53:5 that states, "by his (the servant's) bruises we are healed," and the references to the text in the New Testament (Matt 8:17; 1 Pet 2:22–25). The interpretation influenced the AFM of SA. In research done among AFM members of all races, its influence in thinking demonstrates the hermeneutical stance found among most members who read the Bible literally.[111]

Isaiah 52:13—53:12

Most contemporary Old Testament scholars accept that Isaiah 40–55 (Deutero-Isaiah) should be distinguished from chapters 1–30 (Isaiah) and chapters 56–66 (Trito-Isaiah). Deutero-Isaiah exists as an essential unity, although it does not imply that only one author wrote it, and a group of passages designated as "servant songs" (42:1–4; 49:1–6; 50:4–9; 52:13[112]–53:12) characterizes it.[113] The distinction of the servant songs is recognized, but scholars differ in their opinion about the referent of the servant.[114]

Isaiah 53 continues the prophetic "narrative" of chapters 40 to 52 which describes divine intervention in the Babylonian exile that ushers

---

109. Spong, *Rescuing the Bible from Fundamentalism*, 184.

110. In a following section, the Bible-reading practices among AFM members are investigated in an empirical research project.

111. See discussion about hermeneutical developments within the AFM of SA that follows.

112. Most scholars view Isa 52:13 as marking a significant turn. The use of *hinnēh* ("there") never serves to mark a wholly new beginning but at most a new section that links with what precedes it (Goldingay and Payne, *Isaiah 40–55*, 273).

113. J. C. Döderlein (1775), J. G. Eichhorn (1778–83), and Duhm's Isaiah commentary of 1892 served to establish such a distinction.

114. Childs, *Isaiah*, 290.

in God's eschatological reign. Traditional psalmic conventions (especially Pss 30, 54) underlie it, although it is unique because it serves as prophetic liturgy, characterized by mourning, thanksgiving, and penance.[115] The irregular meter, simile (vv. 2, 6, 7), sacramental and political/military metaphors, thirteen pairs of parallelism, and word order show that it represents poetry.[116]

As argued above, to understand a book in the Bible, one needs to understand something about its original historical setting and reason for being written. What is the historical referent for this song? Deutero-Isaiah originated during the exilic period when Judah was taken to Babylon. They received permission only after fifty years to return to their country.[117] However, the servant songs are concerned with the plight of the poor people that Babylonia left behind to take care of the land. These Judahites found themselves in a hopeless situation when exile threatened their survival as a distinct nation with its own religion. The Babylonians desecrated their temple in Jerusalem along with the city and annihilated the monarchy and independence. Would Judah lose its identity in exile, as was the case with Israel?

The servant's identity is unknown and without direct or clear meaning to later readers, even though the songs are abundantly rich and theologically suggestive, as Walter Brueggemann emphasizes.[118] However, it seems as if the servant in Isaiah 53 serves as a referent to Jacob-Israel, who YHWH called to present the nations with God's "justice" (*mišpāṭ*). In Isaiah 49, the identity of the servant is connected to an individual, unnamed prophetic figure.

In Isaiah 50, the servant is tortured and humiliated by opponents from within the nation of Israel itself. The following song also deals with his humiliation but ends with reference to his exaltation (see especially 53:11–12). Now the servant is among the great because he bore the sins of many and prayed for his transgressors.

Paul Hanson argues that Isaiah 52:13—53:12 represents Deutero-Isaiah's response to how God can address Israel's ages-long pattern of sin and consequent divine punishment.[119] The new initiative consists of a

---

115. Elliger, *Deuterojesaja in Seinem Verhältnis zu Tritojesaja*, 19 was the first to describe its genre as "prophetic liturgy."
116. Goldingay and Payne, *Isaiah 40–55*, 276.
117. Goldingay, *Isaiah for Everyone*, 142–43.
118. Brueggemann, *Isaiah 40–66*, 141.
119. Hanson, *Isaiah 40–66*, 156.

servant who submits to oppression and affliction when YHWH crushes him with pain (53:10), as a bold choice to participate with God by offering his life as an offering for sin (the Hebrew meaning is uncertain) aimed at breaking the stranglehold of sin in Israel's stead.[120] Although not all scholars agree, it is accepted that the servant's suffering can be interpreted as vicarious.[121] His suffering also holds consequences for Israel's illnesses—the servant's bruises heal Israel because he has borne their infirmities and carried their diseases (vv. 4–5, 10).

Isaiah 53 in the New Testament

Pentecostals interpret Isaiah 53:4–5 by viewing healing as a benefit of the atonement of Christ, along with forgiveness of sins.[122] However, also in these cases, they consider neither the larger textual context nor the rest of the Scriptures. These verses refer to salvation in terms of the forgiveness of sin. For that reason, the text refers to "all" (v. 6) that are "healed," without exception; the referent is the forgiveness of sins. If this is not the case, then all believers should experience healing because Christ died for them.[123]

That the New Testament interprets the text by identifying healing of illness with forgiveness of sins is evident from 1 Peter 2:24, that the servant bore others' sins in his body on the cross, so that they may be freed from sins and live for righteousness. His wounds brought healing. Forgiveness and healing constitute one act, according to this interpretation of the song. Edouard Nsiku reminds us that Peter's explication of

---

120. Hanson, *Isaiah 40–66*, 159–60.

121. Childs, *Isaiah*, 415.

122. Pentecostals followed in the footsteps of the Holiness movement in accepting the construct of "healing in the atonement." Holiness teachers of the late nineteenth century, like A. B. Simpson, R. Kelso Carter, Smith Wigglesworth, Alexander Dowie, and others, had been promulgating this position (Holm, "Healing in Search of Atonement," 55). For instance, Wigglesworth writes, "There is healing through the blood of Christ and deliverance for every captive. God never intended His children to live in misery because of some affliction that comes directly from the devil. A perfect atonement was made at Calvary. I believe that Jesus bore my sins, and I am free from them all. I am justified from all things if I dare to believe. He himself took our infirmities and bore our sicknesses; and if I dare believe, I can be healed" (quoted in Holm, "Healing in Search of Atonement," 55).

123. Mbugua, "Misunderstanding the Bible," 19.

Isaiah 53:7–8 led to the conversion of the first African (Acts 8:26–39) who had visited Jerusalem to worship.[124]

The *Torah* explains that moral guilt due to sin can only be reconciled by an adequate offering to affect forgiveness. Thus, the innocent servant is put to death (Isa 53:7–9) to comply with the guilt offering regulations found in Leviticus 5:15 (Isa 53:10a), requiring a ram without blemish from the flock. Interestingly enough, the beneficiaries of the servant's offering have gone astray like sheep, and the servant is led away to be slaughtered in their stead like a lamb that does not object (see Jer 11:19 for a similar comparison).

Such concepts do not apply to sickness or healing; they cannot be "forgiven." Illness is never connected to sin in a causative manner. In conclusion, one cannot read Isaiah 52:12–53:12 in terms of healing because the context is determined by discussing sin and its forgiveness. The servant is humiliated before being exalted, for the salvation of the nations (52:13–15; see Phil 2:6–11), just like Judah in exile is to be exalted when their land is restored to them. In his analysis of the text as a ring composition, John Goldingay finds that verses 4–6 provide the most significant statement that forms the theme of the song, that the servant suffers for the sins of others.

That the text had "a more colorful afterlife" than most of the Old Testament, in Goldingay and Payne's terms,[125] is demonstrated in references that interpret it in terms of supposed similarities with Christ's death and resurrection (Matt 8:17; Luke 22:37; John 12:38; Acts 3:26; Rom 15:21; 1 Pet 2:22–25).[126] Whether Jesus interpreted his calling in terms of Deutero-Isaiah's suffering servant is unclear, but later Christian interpretation saw him as fulfilling the prophecy.

Pentecostals should be repeatedly reminded that Old Testament prophecies were addressed to their first audience and found their intended "fulfillment" within that situation. Otherwise, the prophets had no message for their own day. Some prophecies might find further fulfillment or be interpreted as such by believers in New Testament times.

---

124. Nsiku, "Isaiah," 845.
125. Goldingay and Payne, *Isaiah 40–55*, 284.
126. Hanson, *Isaiah 40–66*, 163.

Isaiah 53 in Literature in the early AFM of SA

As the empirical work (in the next section) demonstrates, some AFM members believe that forgiveness of sin and healing are equal and equivalent parts and benefits of the work of atonement on the cross. But does that imply that unconditional forgiveness is replicated in unconditional healing?

The early literature of the AFM read Isaiah 53 christologically, ignoring the historical context and connecting salvation and healing to the cross. "He heals as He saves—out of boundless, fetterless, fathomless love."[127] As we accept in faith that God saves us, we should believe that God heals us. Believers should assume they are healed when they pray for healing, notwithstanding the symptoms of the illness they might still experience. And they should cease using any medication to show that they trust God for their healing. C. S. Price encourages readers to claim healing from God as their inheritance; it was locked up in the atonement of Christ and formed an "essential part of the cross."[128] Like salvation, believers need to claim it and take it in possession by way of their faith.

In 1918 the Executive Council of the AFM of SA discussed the "heretical teaching" of a certain brother M. A. Botha that illness came from the LORD. He responded to their query that it was due to his "thoughtlessness." In response to Botha's opinion, at the next Annual Conference of the church on July 16, 1918, Scott Moffatt referred to Romans 5:12 and explained that sickness resulted from the fall and its remedy was the cross. The cross guaranteed that healing would take place if one believed.[129]

Matthew 8:16–17 played a definitive role in AFM publications; J. N. Hoover referred to it as the "inspired and therefore a correct interpretation of Isaiah's prophecy . . . To the rational mind this is final proof that provision was made in the divine atonement for every infirmity and sickness of man."[130] The context is Jesus' healing of Peter's mother-in-law and of many who were possessed with demons and others who were sick by Jesus to fulfill Isaiah's prophecy, "He took our infirmities and bore our diseases" (Isa 53:4). The reference in Matthew 8 is not about Jesus but his ministry of healing (see also Matt 8:1–13). Jesus carried people's illnesses, healing them.

---

127. Editor, "Healing Helps," 15.
128. Price, "Healed by the Lamb," 2.
129. Burger, *Geskiedenis van die Apostoliese Geloof Sending van Suid-Afrika*, 409.
130. Hoover, "Divine Healing," 9.

To the question of why illness still occurs among believers after the crucifixion, the early AFM argued that it followed on a lack of faith, as many nonbelievers also choose not to believe for their salvation.[131] Believers who did not trust God for healing were accused that "they believe He might want them to remain sick for some mysterious good, which Satan always puts into their imagination to thoroughly deceive them."[132]

Not all early Christians interpreted healing as directly linked to the atonement, as 1 Peter 2:24 shows. The context is an encouragement of believing slaves to accept the authority of their masters, even hard masters. Enduring pain in unjust suffering illustrates that God's approval rests on them (v. 20). They should follow Christ's example of suffering unjustly without resistance. Such slaves should instead trust the one who judges justly (vv. 21–23). The text modifies Isaiah 53:4—by adding (italicized here): "He himself bore our sins in his body on the cross, *so that, free from sins, we might live for righteousness,*" followed by "by his wounds you have been healed" (v. 24).

Jan Smith applies the text to believers' suffering, encouraging readers to suffer with "happiness" for Jesus's sake.[133] However, such an interpretation does not fit the context that addresses slaves who were owned by their proprietors in the ancient world, who could punish and execute them at will. Moreover, no references in AFM publications were found that read it within the context of slaves.

Connecting healing to the atonement in a rectilinear way led to the pragmatic challenge that not all believers were healed. In the New Testament, one also finds several such cases. Johannes Henning teaches that Timothy was encouraged to use a little wine and not only water "for the sake of your stomach and your frequent ailments" because he had a weak constitution due to residing in an unhealthy region. He should avoid all harmful water.[134] To the remark in 2 Timothy 4:20 that Paul left Trophimus ill in Miletus, Henning ascribes the illness to Trophimus's living in iniquity.[135] Paul's torment at the hand of a messenger of Satan (2 Cor 12:7) refers to a bodily weakness (perhaps poor eyes) that God allowed. The purpose is to keep Paul humble about his successes in the mission

---

131. Stuart, "Gods Wil in Genezing," 6.
132. Osterhus, "Have They Real Faith?," 4.
133. Smith, "Wonderbare Genesings," 158–59.
134. Henning, "Vragen en Antwoorden," 7.
135. Henning, "Vragen en Antwoorden," 7.

field.¹³⁶ It certainly is not any bodily illness.¹³⁷ It is clear that it presented a challenge to read about unhealed believers in the New Testament, as shown by the far-fetched and imaginative ways to justify it occurring. To find a direct causative link between forgiveness and healing, early authors had to oversimplify the issue.

Empirical Research

Empirical research was utilized to test whether the early AFM's connection of forgiveness and sin as different elements of the atonement is held by contemporary AFM members. The research, completed during February 2019, utilized grounded theory, a form of qualitative research as a process of examining and interpreting data.¹³⁸ The three groups associated with the AFM of SA as members, attending "cell groups" or Bible study groups and representing three of the four former racial divisions of the AFM of SA.¹³⁹ The three groups consisted of African youth using English as their second or third language (Group A); a mixed-race group of older people using Afrikaans, their mother tongue, with one exception, an English lady (Group B); and a group of White adults consisting primarily of professional people (Group C). Group A meets in Promosa, Potchefstroom, in the North-West Province, a township consisting mostly

---

136. Henning, "Vragen en Antwoorden," 7.

137. Also Morgan, "Goddelike Genesing," 17.

138. I made an audio recording that was typed *verbatim*. Sociological data: Group A consisted of seven girls and eleven boys aged between twelve and seventeen. They were all learners at the same secondary school. Group B consisted of ten women and four men of whom five were married and nine were widowers or widows. Four of them were in the age group of fifty-one to sixty-five and ten were older than sixty-five years. They were all pensioners. Thirteen completed secondary school as their highest qualification and one had a university degree. Group C consisted of five women and six men of whom ten were married and one was divorced. Eight of them fell in the age group thirty-six to fifty and three in the age group of fifty-one to sixty-five. Seven were college graduates, while eleven attended secondary school as their highest qualification. Two were medical doctors, three were businessmen and one was a businesswoman (Nel, "Isaiah 53 and its use in the New Testament").

139. The AFM of SA was unified in 1996, two years after the establishment of a democratic South Africa. However, in reality it still mostly exists in terms of racially divided assemblies. The area involved, in the North-West and Free State provinces, does not have many Indian inhabitants and neither Potchefstroom nor Parys have a sizable Indian community. Under apartheid laws, Indians were not allowed to reside in the Free State.

of mixed-race people, at their church on Wednesday evenings. Group B meets at their church in Parys, Free State, on Wednesday mornings, and Group C meets at different participants' homes on Thursday evenings in Parys. The distinct group leaders read through Isaiah 53:4–6 and invited the listeners to share their interpretation and understanding of its meaning. The purpose was to build a theory based on the acquired data and the generation of concepts.[140] The Bible study leader used two questions in an unstructured study: What do you think Isaiah 53:4–6 is all about? And is there anything in the text that grabs your attention? I attended in all three cases, but I was relatively unknown to the participants and did not participate in any way in the discussion. In the case of groups B and C, I at times preached at the two churches that their members attended. I did not participate in the discussion but left it to their study leader, a trusted leader in each case. In all cases, the leaders deliberately involved each member in the debate, as agreed between us.

The data reveal varieties in how members described their interpretation of the relevant text. From these discussions, I formulated a sensitizing concept, in addition to the main research question. Some emerging categories became apparent, and I sought to illuminate and define the boundaries and relevance of these categories.

In all groups, the enthusiasm with which participants participated in the discussion was remarkable. Among members of Group A, the young adults at first were hesitant to speak their minds until one young man took the lead, explained what he thought, and then encouraged the other members to follow suit. Each group leader limited the discussion to twenty minutes; it was clear that the debate would have continued for much longer if they were allowed to do so. The research was done in two weeks in February 2019.

Isaiah 53 in Practice

Grounded theory, a form of qualitative research as a process of examining and interpreting data, was used to survey the responses of three groups, all of them associated with the AFM. As explained, participants were given the opportunity to read through Isaiah 53:4–6 in order to elicit meaning,

---

140. Bryant and Charmaz, "Grounded Theory Research," 1, and for application, Verweij, *Positioning Jesus' Suffering*, 64.

gain understanding, and develop empirical knowledge. The purpose was theory building based on data and the generation of concepts.

The groups were unanimous in responding to the first question, reflecting the view found in the early literature of the AFM of SA that forgiveness of sin and healing represented two aspects of the atonement that were equal in scope. The suffering servant was interpreted as Christ without any reference to the author's historical context or the audience's situation. They clearly used the lens of the New Testament to read the prophetic text in the Hebrew Bible. Their immediacy in reading the text implied that they ignored the hermeneutical distance between the reader and the text; it resulted in confusion between the sixth-century BCE context, the interpretation that the New Testament provides for the text, and their own present-day context. Jacqueline Grey found this shortcoming occurring widely in Pentecostal Bible-reading practices.[141] By reading the text literally, they sacrificed the uniqueness and immanence of God's message to the original audience.[142]

The groups emphasized that Jesus' sacrifice demonstrated God's grace. One participant in group B said, "God saw in Jesus our sins; God saw our face when God looked at the Son, and God punished the Son for these people's sins. That shows how great God's grace for us is." However, passersby did not interpret Jesus' death as sacrificing his life as a sacrifice for their sins. They probably thought that the Roman authorities punished Jesus and God rejected him. The lady continued her explanation by stating that many people still did not understand what the cross was about in today's world, demonstrating God's grace. A female in Group C responded that Isaiah states that Jesus was to be crucified because God rejected and punished him; only faith could enlighten anybody to understand that his crucifixion demonstrated the mystery of how God saved people.

In discussing the words, "by his wounds we are healed," the young people of Group A did not reply at all. They live mainly in a squatter camp characterized by poverty and misery; perhaps their economic circumstances required them to concentrate on more mundane issues. Their attention was not primarily on healing but on God's provision for their urgent daily needs. Participants in Group B were convinced that Isaiah states explicitly that "Christ died on the cross so that believers are already healed, all of them." The crucifixion is a historical fact. "And if

---

141. Grey, *Three's a Crowd*, 143.
142. West, *Stolen Bible*, 348.

you are sick as a Christian, it is because you did not stand on the fact that you are already healed and base your life on Jesus' death for your illness on the cross." A medical doctor in group C verbalized it as "it happened in history, and nobody can contest the fact that Jesus died on the cross. What we now need is faith, that he had died for our sicknesses. As we need faith to accept that he died for our sins, we also need to accept in faith that he had already died for our illnesses. When we realize that, healing becomes a reality in our lives." The argument is clear: that Jesus died to affect our salvation and heal our illnesses are on the same level; the cross guarantees both.

Is there anything in the text that jumps out? To the second question, a female in group C responded, "For me, this text is nearly a summary of the whole New Testament in three verses. If you look at what these three verses teach, you will find that it summarizes what happened in the whole of the New Testament." A female medical doctor in group C responded in tears, "Jesus did it for us. This is the most poignant element of the passage for me." Again, the passage reminded them of God's grace. "Jesus was crucified and died without God intervening to save him because God's grace is so great that he was willing to pay any price to save sinners like us." A female in group C said, "What Jesus went through he did not deserve; I have deserved to die in that manner because of my sins." A female in group A said that the passage was about human beings' sinfulness and the hopelessness of their situation but that God "is full of love for human beings and he is gracious enough to forgive us our sins, even though it cost him everything, even his Son." A young female in group A stated that she heard in the text that Jesus died for her sins. Members in this group repeatedly appropriated Christ's atonement for themselves.

Some respondents also brought the text in relation to healing. For example, an older female in group B heard an invitation for the ill to trust God for their recovery. "Like at the bath of Bethesda, we can get into the water and experience the healing power of God," ignoring the fact that only one person was healed there, leaving the others still sick (John 5:2–9).

Conclusion

The theme of the song in Isaiah 52:13–53:12 is that the servant gives his life as expiation for others. Healing of infirmities functions in the context of the servant's crushing "for our transgressions" (v. 5). "Infirmities" are connected to the effect of moral guilt, a result of sin. By forgiving their iniquities, the servant, the righteous one, heals the many unrighteous ones (v. 11).

As already stated, the New Testament presents more than one voice when it brings the servant song in relation to Jesus. It never mentions the atonement at all in its interpretations of the song. Matthew interprets the servant's suffering in relation to Jesus's healing ministry. The author of 1 Peter 2:24–25, on the other hand, refers to the unjust suffering of slaves and encourages them to defer to their masters, following Christ's example. Nowhere do the New Testament's references to Isaiah 53:4–6 bring divine healing directly and causative to the atonement. Thus, early and contemporary AFM members oversimplify the relationship between healing and salvation when they view both as equal benefits of the atonement.

Pentecostals who read the Bible literally in a biblicist sense dissolve all genres into one category that they refer to as "the word of God," making the mistake of thinking that the Bible is addressed primarily to their situation and ignoring the Bible's original context and intention.[143] The case study discussed above illustrated that the movement could benefit from a more intellectually sophisticated hermeneutics. In the last two chapters, an attempt is made to read the Bible from another angle, of a new Pentecostal hermeneutics that has been developing since the 1980s. The theme of the following discussion is the hermeneutics of Bible-reading practices and should be read in conjunction with the first chapter's discussion of Pentecostal hermeneutics.

Hermeneutics of Bible-Reading Practices in the AFM of SA

In research done at the request of the AFM of SA's Education and Training Department in 2019, the author used a questionnaire sent to all AFM congregations by the denomination's general secretary. Pastors and members participated, and 77 percent of congregations responded with an average of eighteen completed questionnaires that were returned.[144] The response of the data collection reflected South Africa's demographic

---

143. Grey, *Three's a Crowd*, 145.

144. Nel, "Bible-Reading Practices in the AFM." The positive response of congregations to the request to complete the questionnaire can be ascribed to the involvement of the office of the general secretary, making the questionnaire an official document of the church.

realities. The questionnaire analysis clearly reveals the hermeneutical model that AFM members use to read the Bible if one accepts that it represents a representative sample of the church in all its diverse forms.

Most AFM members regularly read the Bible (74 percent indicated that they do so daily).[145] Forty-one percent indicated that they read more than one chapter daily, while 30 percent read one chapter every day. Thirty-five percent of members read the Bible as a family daily together, implying that the practice occurs among a third of church members. The implication is that most participants spend time with the Bible regularly and use their Bibles well.

No less than 96 percent indicated that they do have access to a Bible. Seventy-two percent indicated that they read the Bible in its printed form, while 24 percent read it on an electronic device. That the Bible is available on iPad, tablets, and smartphones is an exciting development because it implies that people carry the Bible with them everywhere they go. The conclusion is that the Bible informs the daily practice of at least some AFM members.

Forty-seven percent of participants indicate that they only read the Bible, while 33 percent use the Bible and a commentary, and 23 percent use the Bible and a daily devotional.[146] The quality and paradigm of some material used to interpret the Biblical message may confuse believers. For that reason, it is encouraging that many members also focus on the Bible.

Interestingly, 30 percent indicated that they attend a Bible study weekly while the same percentage never attend such a study. Forty-two percent of participants had read most of the Old and New Testament, 33 percent think they had read all the New Testament, and 35 percent have read all of the Old Testament.[147]

Of participants, 75 percent indicated that they had experienced a distinct Spirit baptism and the same percentage indicated that they pray more than once during the day.

---

145. Even if one accepts that some participants responded to the questions in the way they thought the church would like (as is probable), such high percentages indicate that at least a majority of AFM members read the Bible regularly, if not on a daily basis.

146. It should be kept in mind that many pastors also completed the questionnaire; it might explain why many indicated that they use commentaries while interpreting the biblical text.

147. That Christian believers read the Old Testament seemingly more than the New may seem improbable, but it may have to do with the length and narrative structure of the Old Testament, with its many beloved "bedtime stories."

When asked about the quality of sermons in their worship services, a worrying trend was revealed. Only 49 percent state that reference was made to the Bible during sermons that they had listened to, 52 percent of participants thought that their minister's sermons were based on the Bible, and 58 percent thought that the Bible was taught well at their church, indicating that preachers may be using other-than-biblical material in preaching.

The section concerned with such relevant questions is of specific relevance for this study based on Pentecostal hermeneutics. Two-thirds of participants (67 percent) believed that the entire Bible is the inspired word of God and that everything the Bible says is true (66 percent). Less than a third (30 percent) indicated that they believed that the Bible has to be interpreted in the context and culture of its time. That the context should determine the interpretation of an ancient text, even in the case of poetry, is an integral element of healthy hermeneutical practice. The case study's conclusions support the contention that most Pentecostal believers interpret the Bible in a fundamentalist, biblicist, and literalist way.

Theodicies of Divine Healing

Courtney Campbell discusses four theodicies of faith healing, a term preferred by many Pentecostals. The first is that divine healing fails because of human sinfulness.[148] This assertion is based on the supposition that sickness and death are the results of the "fall" of Adam and Eve in the garden of Eden, implying that disease is the result of a spiritual rather than biological pathology. Many Christians understand the fall metaphorically or symbolically. Still, Pentecostals look for the literal meaning of Genesis 3 and find the reason and explanation for disease in the present in a biblical story that is part of the Bible's protohistory. They view the essence in all diseases in terms of the human propensity to sin. Certain choices made by humans also lead to disease and death, such as those made by a faith community or parents when explaining why a baby is sick or dies. The implication is that different choices would have warded off the disease. Thus, Pentecostals believe that a baby could not be responsible for wrong decisions in the way others might be, placing spiritual responsibility for the illness on someone else's shoulders. This way of reasoning is at the heart of the free will defense or theodicy. The purpose is

---

148. Campbell, "What More in the Name of God?," 18.

to protect the theological affirmation of the ultimate sovereignty of God while at the same time accepting that God's power can and wants to heal all diseases because disease *per se* cannot exist outside the realm of the divine, including God's total control of the universe.[149]

The second theodicy of divine healing considers insufficient faith the reason why healing does not occur after prayer. All diseases represent a "test of faith." When the prayer of faith does not affect a cure, the reason consists of a lack of faith, whether of the patient, family, or faith community members. "The implicit assumption is that had sufficient faith or trust in the divine healing power been exercised, a healing would have transpired."[150] For instance, if death results from the disease, it serves as a wake-up call to the family and faith community that they should reconsider the quality and integrity of their relationship with God.

Third, theodicy is explained in terms of human limits and finitude in knowing why an illness occurred. It is part of inscrutability. The divine design for the disease is beyond human capacities. The situation requires the believer to be submissive in the face of divine incomprehensibility. In the case of Job, the divine voice affirms that Job in his questions lacked the necessary knowledge and what it requires from him is humble submission to the divine mystery revealed in the theophany. The emphasis is on divine sovereignty and omniscience; the price is that human beings can never know everything about God.

The last theodicy described by Campbell is based on the eschatological consolation that although believers' prayers of faith are not answered with divine healing, they may find consolation and comfort in the hope that they will one day understand why such suffering occurred when they see God face-to-face.[151] Thus, the expectation of a joyous afterlife encourages believers to persist in faith, even in the face of unanswered prayer.

In the following two chapters, a theodicy is developed that contains some of the positive elements of these theodicies by responding to the

---

149. Quayesi-Amakye ("Coping with Evil in Ghanaian Pentecostalism") describes how many Ghanaian Pentecostals interpret evil, a practice probably shadowed by many others in Africa. Common believers approach evil through "witch-demonology," ascribing all evil and suffering to the work of evil powers exemplified in the witch. This view fails to understand the role of evil and suffering in human existence. In contrast, their leadership considers this as inadequate; they tend to promote the devil far above the Almighty God, and the presence of evil may not necessarily contradict God's goodness and purpose.

150. Campbell, "What More in the Name of God?," 19.

151. Campbell, "What More in the Name of God?," 21.

tendency found among Pentecostals to blame unanswered prayers for God to intervene in suffering on the shoulders of believers who did not pray hard enough or did not have the "right" amount of faith.

Pentecostals and Prosperity Theology

That Neo-Pentecostals' prosperity theology influences some Pentecostals is due to their hermeneutics. However, the impact of prosperity theology is much broader than the Pentecostal movement and led to the development of an alternative movement of independent churches. In twenty-first-century Africa, it seems that prosperity churches as an integral element of Neo-Pentecostalism grow exponentially more and faster than any of the other Christian traditions, including Roman Catholicism.[152] Its influence is discussed and limited here to the "Word of Faith" or "Faith Confession" movement, probably the foremost exponents of prosperity theology. Its most prominent proponents are Kenneth Hagin Sr. and Kenneth Hagin Jr., Kenneth and Gloria Copeland, Jerry Savelle, Creflo A. Dollar Jr., Benny Hinn, Jesse Duplantis, F. K. C. Price, Jim Bakker, Buddy Harrison, and Reinhard Bonnke. Bonnke ministered in Africa for the more significant part of his life.[153]

The Word of Faith movement finds its roots in the Pentecostal movement, demonstrated in its practice and theology. Kenneth Hagin Sr. was an ordained minister of the Assemblies of God from 1938 to 1962. In turn, the movement influenced many Pentecostal leaders and other believers, both in the prosperous West and, ironically, the mainly impoverished Global South of the Majority World. Many Western Pentecostals ascribe their prosperity to God's blessing in response to their faithfulness. In contrast, many African Pentecostals dream of the blessings and benefits of prosperity that wealth and health would bring. Yet, at the same time, they languish under challenging circumstances while donating money to the advancement of the prophet's ministry.[154]

It is submitted that the theodicean answer that prosperity theology gives to the challenges that suffering in the face of a good and almighty

---

152. Asamoah-Gyadu, "'From Every Nation under Heaven,'" xxx.

153. See a summary of this theology and its theodicy in Nel, *Prosperity Gospel in Africa*; Torr, *Dramatic Pentecostal/Charismatic Anti-Theodicy*.

154. For further discussion, see Hollinger, "Enjoying God Forever," 19–23; Perriman, *Faith, Health and Prosperity*, 58–77; Warrington, *Pentecostal Theology*, 275–76.

God presents accords with those of Pentecostals because they read the Bible in the same literalist way. For instance, prosperity theology leans heavily on the Deuteronomist Historian's perspective on the formula that the blessings of God are guaranteed for faithful believers. At the same time, suffering and hardship are preserved for the godless.

Prosperity theology provides the answer to the question of where evil and suffering in the world come from and asserts that its origin lies in the first humans' acts shortly after their creation. Adam, a replication of God (*imago Dei*), as representative of all human beings, was given rule over the world for six thousand years, when God would return and establish God's kingdom on earth.[155] However, by the disobedience of the first human couple in the garden of Eden, human beings lost their god-like being; they gave the world into Satan's hands, as it were. Now they had a "satanic nature," and God's hands were "chopped off."[156] Kenneth Copeland argues that because Adam committed high treason, the authority and dominion that God had handed over to him passed into the hands of Satan, without God being able to do anything about it. Instead, human beings had been given the freedom and authority to make such choices.[157] Kenneth Hagin Jr. asks who causes all this world's evil, such as sickness and wars, and answers that the devil is the sole cause.[158]

God responded to human disobedience by making a covenant with Abraham, as the representative of Israel, finding a way back to address the problematic situation in which humans found themselves.[159] God's side of the Abrahamic covenant was to care for Abraham and his descendants in spiritual, physical, financial, and social terms.[160] Israel's side was to keep the commandments that characterized the old covenant.

The difficult situation that human beings found themselves in due to Adam and Eve's disobedience in the Garden and Eve consisted of two

---

155. Perriman, *Faith, Health and Prosperity*, 20. It is crucial to note that the argument is not that Eve serves alongside Adam as representative of all human beings, betraying the notion among Neo-Pentecostals about the gender of the prophet that is mostly exclusively limited to males. The length of human occupation of the world also results from a literal way of reading the protohistory found in Gen 1–11 and rejects evolution as a means of creation as well.

156. The theology prefers a legal framework for its arguments about rights and privileges, making God a prisoner of the way they interpret such arguments.

157. Copeland, *Our Covenant with God*, 8.

158. Hagin, *Executing the Basics of Healing*, 16.

159. Copeland, *Our Covenant with God*, 9–12.

160. Copeland, *Our Covenant with God*, 13.

curses: work and the devil.¹⁶¹ The first curse affects all of creation and includes that human beings would have to earn their livelihood by working hard and that women would experience pain during childbirth. The second curse is found in breaking the laws of God and with sickness, a part of the penalty for doing so. The only way Abraham and his descendants could prevent the fruit of the curse was by obeying God to the letter of the law. In conclusion, evil enters due to the choice the first human beings made, which resulted in handing over the world into the hands of Satan. Still, evil continues in the world due to disobedience, as far as Israel is concerned.

There is in the Bible not one one singular notion of evil. The Bible uses various ways to refer to evil, related to the variety of contexts in which it is discussed. The Bible also does not define evil with philosophical precision.¹⁶² Mark Scott notes that there are at least four prominent themes in biblical discussions of evil, with evil viewed as chaos, sin, satanism, and suffering. First, evil as chaos and destruction threatens or impairs creation. God creates the world, in the first place, by subduing chaos, and this primeval chaos seemingly recurs again and again to threaten God's creation. Second, evil is defined as sin or disobedience against God's law, variously construed and conceived. Third, especially the New Testament takes the reality of hostile spiritual forces for granted in a dualist framework of good and evil forces and ascribes evil to the work of these powers, although some of the prophets already intuited the notion (e.g., Isa 14; Ezek 28). Lastly, the Bible sometimes portrays evil as suffering or misfortune. Clearly, the Bible does not present a singular perspective of evil.

The biblical portrayals of evil tend to avoid ontology.¹⁶³ Evil is described in moral rather than metaphysical terms in the Bible and tends to be spiritual, not syllogistic. As a result, it requires moral and spiritual remedies, not rational or logical solutions. It should be kept in mind that the Bible operates "within a cosmic, moral, and spiritual landscape rather than within a rational, abstract, ontological landscape. Its complex of symbols, then, has more in common with mythology and theology than philosophy *per se*."¹⁶⁴

---

161. Hagin, *Executing the Basics of Healing*, 9.
162. Scott, *Pathways in Theodicy*, 14.
163. Scott, *Pathways in Theodicy*, 27.
164. Scott, *Pathways in Theodicy*, 27.

What does prosperity theology understand by the term "evil"? Because evil causes human beings to lose their being like God as they were initially created, evil can be defined as that which causes or perpetuates the experience of beings who have become less like God.[165] Satan is currently the god of this world, and for that reason, evil reigns in this world. Thus, prosperity theology interprets the world in terms of the dualism of God-Satan and goodness-evil.

The following substantial question is, What can believers do about the evil and suffering that face them in the world? Due to sin, the world legally belongs to Satan, but God re-entered it through the covenant with Israel. Therefore, if Israel would put their entire trust in God and obey all of God's laws and institutes, the result would be that they would experience all God's blessings, including that they would experience no sicknesses.

When Christ died, and God resurrected him from the dead, God untied Satan's legal bind on the world. Now God provided all human beings, not only Israel, the opportunity to turn back to the nature they originally possessed. God gave them access to Abraham's and Israel's blessings.[166] By identifying themselves with Christ, believers experience the full benefits of a restored image of God in their lives; they recover the divine nature that God had given to Adam and Eve at their creation.[167] The fruit of the atonement of Christ consists of being saved from sin and its devastation, the indwelling of the Spirit of God, as well as the recovery of Adam's nature, including being delivered from the curse of the law of Moses.[168] The believer receives several rights, including health and healing in a holistic sense; body, mind, spirit, and soul.[169] Healing is an essential element in the atonement; Christ did not die only for people's sins but also to do away with the effects of sin, of which disease is a significant part. Evil is restrained in the life of the believer through what Christ had realized in the cross.

Prosperity teaching claims that being saved from the effects of evil is the right of every believer; believers should learn to claim these promises for themselves, including that God would remove the effects of sin, such

---

165. Torr, *Dramatic Pentecostal/Charismatic Anti-Theodicy*, 92.
166. Copeland, *Our Covenant with God*, 14–15.
167. Perriman, *Faith, Health and Prosperity*, 27.
168. Hagin, *Executing the Basics of Healing*, 24.
169. Copeland, *You Are Healed*, 19.

as sickness.[170] If a believer for whom Jesus has provided healing is sick, it implies that the person is living far below the promises of God.[171]

To claim the promise and make it true in believers' lives, Kenneth Hagin Sr. formalized a formula. Find the promise in the Bible, believe that what has been asked for has been received, verbally confess one's belief, and act as if it has been received, regardless of the circumstances and feelings.[172] If a believer stays sick, it is because of failure to comply with one of the steps of the faith formula. Either the believer is ignorant about the biblical promises, rights, and privileges that belong to believers or experiences a lack of faith. The prayers of believers who beg and cry but do not believe cannot be heard by God "because I (God) cannot violate my Word."[173]

What can believers do about evil and suffering? The emphasis is on their responsibility; the obliteration of evil rests on their shoulders. They need to hold God to the promises God had made by identifying these promises found in the Bible, verbally naming what they are and what the implication for their situation is, and claiming it as their own.

The presupposition is that promises found in the Bible apply to contemporary times and that each promise is always appropriate to all believers. God does not have a personal will for each believer, but God's will in terms of obliterating evil on earth, in general, includes all believers. Another presupposition is that faith is merely a human choice. Faith is something that believers can and must generate themselves. God has told them in the Bible how to obtain more faith in Romans 10:17, that faith comes from what is heard, and what is heard comes through the word of or about Christ. "If we don't have faith, it is not God's fault. To blame God for our lack of faith is nothing but ignorance. God had provided the way whereby everyone can have faith."[174]

---

170. Songwriter Russell Kelso Carter wrote a song that Pentecostals love to sing that states, *inter alia*, "Standing on the promises I cannot fall / Listening every moment to the Spirit's call / Resting in my Savior as my all in all / Standing on the promises of God. [Chorus:] Standing, standing / Standing on the promises of God my Savior / Standing, standing / I'm standing on the promises of God." Hymnary.org, "Standing on the Promises."

171. Copeland, *You are Healed*, 9.

172. Hagin, *I Believe in Visions*.

173. Hagin, *I Believe in Visions*, 84.

174. Hagin, *Exceedingly Growing Faith*, 9–10.

Seldom does one find an acknowledgment among these teachers that God reigns sovereignly over individuals' lives. At most, one reads the admission that the Spirit can reveal the divine self to the individual: "Where the Holy Spirit is in manifestation, anything can happen. I cannot make it happen, however, just because I want it to happen."[175] In contrast, the teachers emphasize that God's word always works for all people in the same way. One does not need the manifestation of the spiritual gifts (*charismata*) to operate before one is healed; one is healed through simple faith in God's word.[176] Divine mystery or divine will do not play any role in theological endeavors that use the Bible as a manual and keeps God to the Bible as though every verse in Scripture is directly from God's mouth and addressed to the contemporary believer who quotes it.[177]

Concluding Remarks

In this chapter, the focus was on Pentecostal thinking about theodicy, intending to derive a Pentecostal theodicy, given that Pentecostal theology disqualifies Pentecostals to leave room for allowing any unanswered prayers in believers' lives. As indicated initially, the theme was limited by referencing one Pentecostal denomination in South Africa and one article in Pentecostal thinking. Divine healing always played a significant role among Pentecostals. Although only one church's review is discussed, it is submitted that, to a large extent, it represents the opinion of a much wider group of Pentecostals. The developments in the doctrine during the forties and fifties had to do with hermeneutical changes within the AFM of SA. The influence of prosperity theology among Neo-Pentecostals on the worldwide Pentecostal movement is also discussed regarding the relevant Pentecostal hermeneutical models applied in the movement.

The evangelistic impact of the healing ministry of John G. Lake and others did not allow for differentiation in God's will for individuals but absolutized available biblical evidence of the ministry of Jesus and his apostles, making it applicable to all people and all kinds of diseases. The question of believers who were not healed after praying for healing was deferred, and in time it was answered that the problem lies with the

---

175. Hagin, *I Believe in Visions*, 102.
176. Hagin, *Executing the Basics of Healing*, 48.
177. Torr, *Dramatic Pentecostal/Charismatic Anti-Theodicy*, 97.

quality of the believers' faith or knowledge of God's will.[178] Preachers used formulas to teach believers to "keep God to his Word," a blasphemous statement when one considers the sovereign power of God in creating and maintaining everything in the universe. It is argued that Pentecostals need to state it categorically that God is beyond formulas and cannot be made a prisoner of the book God primarily has chosen to communicate with human beings.

The Pentecostal approach to theodicy is pragmatic, and its focus is on what can be done about evil and suffering. Satan is a significant role-player in their dualistic worldview as the leader of demonic forces opposing God and goodness. The responsibility for removing evil and suffering due to satanic influence is placed on the shoulders of human beings. They must choose between Satan and evil, or belief in God and goodness.

Satan's influence is connected to the narrative in Genesis 3 about the first human couple's disobedience to God in response to the convincing argument of the snake. The connection between the snake and Satan is taken for granted in a literal way, an issue that needs to be discussed in more detail (see chapter 6). The role that Genesis 3 plays in Pentecostal thinking will be subjected to a discussion of what the Old Testament teaches about Satan and its relation to the New Testament.

Donald Gee (1891–1961) was a Pentecostal teacher and pastor from England who visited South Africa at the invitation of the AFM of SA. L. D. Hart calls Gee the apostle of balance, especially concerning the practice of divine healing, although he did not enjoy everybody's favor.[179] He visited South Africa three times, from January to April 1934, January to April 1950, and July to September 1956. His views on medical help concerning divine healing, the relationship between the Pentecostal movement and medical science, and those who are not healed after being

---

178. Onyinah ("God's Grace, Healing and Suffering") concurs and argues that the tendency among many contemporary African practitioners of healing is to teach that healing is a sign of living right with God. They ascribe the lack of healing, or suffering of any kind, as a curse, the result of disobedience by the affected person or their progenitors. In contrast, Jesus and the apostles were selective in their healing ministry; not all people were healed. He states that Christians are exposed to all types of suffering, like other people. Prayer for healing is one of the means of dealing with a variety of manifestations of evil and suffering but then always within the context of pastoral ministry to all people, including those that do not get healed in answer to prayer.

179. Hart, "Critique of American Pentecostal Theology."

prayed for influenced the AFM of SA as well as other Pentecostal groups in southern Africa.[180]

Gee writes, "If no apparent reasons for failure to receive supernatural healing are made clear to the conscience or mind of the sufferer we have no recourse but to leave the case in the hands of our heavenly Father—without condemnation of ourselves or others."[181] Although the term "sovereignty of God" is to be problematized in the next section, it is submitted that Pentecostals should reconsider God's will for individuals as unique.

Their high view of Scripture determines the Pentecostal movement's views on divine healing and theodicy. It claims that the Bible is the authoritative foundation for its worldview and practice, but, in reality, the Bible is used only as a source for proof texts used without considering the genre or context. The Bible is used to support the proponent's view in service of the practice of divine healing.[182] In the case of proof texts, the text is not interpreted with seriousness primarily to understand the original author's intention or the situation of the first listeners. Still, it is applied to the contemporary situation. The result is a crooked and distorted use and view of the Bible in thinking about evil and suffering. For instance, the influence and contribution of Satan are sometimes overemphasized when compared to biblical evidence.

The Pentecostal movement should account for the fact that supernatural healing is rare; it does occur, but not to the extent that some Pentecostal leaders might claim.[183] Joni Tada acknowledges that God does heal today; she does not doubt it. But she asks, what about a quadriplegia patient with spinal cord injury with an ongoing battle with pain that is not healed, as she is.[184] She concludes correctly, "Much of why God does what He does and heals when He heals remains cloaked in divine mystery."[185]

In this regard, Shane Clifton's assertion that supernatural healing is rare among Pentecostals cannot be proven conclusively.[186] However, it is difficult, if not impossible, to find substantive evidence that many

---

180. Nel, "Leerstelling van Goddelike Genesing," 197–209.
181. Quoted in Torr, *Dramatic Pentecostal/Charismatic Anti-Theodicy*, 139.
182. See discussion in Torr, *Dramatic Pentecostal/Charismatic Anti-Theodicy*, 140.
183. Clifton, "Dark Side of Prayer for Healing," 213.
184. Tada, *Place of Healing*, 17.
185. Tada, *Place of Healing*, 19.
186. However, see his convincing statistics from the 2011 NCLS Attender Sample Surveys; Clifton, "Dark Side of Prayer for Healing," 214.

people with severe and permanent injuries, disabilities, and illnesses are supernaturally healed. People who suffer from disabilities and permanent, terminal illnesses or those who are severely physically or mentally challenged form an essential part of the life of any congregation.[187]

Clifton's observation is also accurate as anyone with experience in the Pentecostal ministry would confirm that it is much easier for the visiting evangelist to excite the audience with testimonies of people with faith who were healed than for the pastor who daily lives among and with chronically ill and depressed patients as church members. Pentecostals must acknowledge that healing prayers are not customarily answered; supernatural healing is rare.

The problem is that when Pentecostals assert in their preaching that God heals all who believe and trust in God, it negatively impacts people who have not recovered.[188] Believers who are ill or challenged experience doubt and confusion when they pray and get prayed for but still do not receive healing. Doubt and belief are opposite sides of the same coin; unbelief is the opposite of belief. If doubt is not countered, it may eventually become disappointment with God, anger, guilt, frustration, and unbelief. "Anger as a legitimate, even positive way of processing pain is consistent with the enormous value placed on a human life by God."[189]

What Pentecostals need is the realization that the way they read the Bible affects their people. They need to cultivate a historical consciousness that realizes in sensitivity for different contexts, including the context that determined the text in terms of an author's intention and a specific group of listeners, the context of the early church that determined how they read and interpreted the Hebrew Scriptures, and the current context which differs in many respects from the others.[190] It is imperative to keep contemporary readers from reading into the text what was not even conceived in the original context. When one understands the text in its sociohistorical

---

187. Amos Yong is one of the few Pentecostal scholars to engage with disability studies. He writes that the Pentecostal movement's emphasis on healing is counterproductive and even offensive to scholars with disabilities. Such people do not consider their disabilities as problems to be resolved, healed, or cured but as an integral part of their identity (Yong, "Many Tongues, Many Senses," 169). See also the significant contribution to the debate by Clifton, "Theodicy, Disability, and Fragility."

188. Clifton, "Dark Side of Prayer for Healing," 213.

189. Orr-Ewing, *Where Is God in All the Suffering?*, 28.

190. Snyman, *Om die Bybel Anders te Lees*, 16.

context, then one may find a structural resonance between one's own context and the different contexts implied in the Bible.[191]

If the Pentecostal healing message alienates those who remain sick, Pentecostals need to revisit their theology of divine healing. It is probably true to state that the Pentecostals have not attempted to publish a systematic theology of healing, as Gunther Brown argues, making the exercise essential.[192] In revisiting their theology of healing, Pentecostals should reframe it in terms of the fact that illness, injuries, and disability are a part of all people's lives, as are the illnesses that accompany old age. At the same time, no less than one billion people, or 15 percent of the world's population, are disabled to some extent, as the World Bank's statistics show.[193] One-fifth of the estimated global total, or between 110 million and 190 million people, experience significant disabilities. The World Health Organisation reported in 2018 that "one in four people in the world will be affected by mental or neurological disorders at some point in their lives. Around 450 million people currently suffer from such conditions."[194] The incidence of disability is higher for developing countries.

Steven Fettke writes that in many Pentecostal churches, a triumphalist attitude prevails that suggests that a charismatic ministry requires able-bodied and able-minded persons, not disabled ones, to support those considered sick, disabled, weak, and poor.[195] Disabled, chronically ill, or challenged persons are deemed to be unqualified for ministry and/or as not charismatic enough because their illnesses and disabilities do not demonstrate their faith. That these churches lose a lot by not considering such persons as fit for ministry has been shown by Stanley Hauerwas's remark in his "critique of modernity." He writes that once he had been drawn into the world of the mentally disabled, "it did not take me long to realize they were the crack I desperately needed to give concreteness to my critique of modernity."[196] His problem with "modernity" is the basic assumption that humans are meant to be autonomous. It might be that many in the Pentecostal movement embraced this sense

---

191. Snyman, *Om die Bybel Anders te Lees*, 12.
192. Brown, "Introduction," 4.
193. World Bank, "Disability Inclusion."
194. World Health Organizaion, "World Health Report."
195. Fettke, "Spirit of God Hovered Over the Waters," 178. See also the important article of Kgatle, "Triumphalist Theology in the Context of Prophetic Pentecostalism in South Africa," in this regard.
196. Hauerwas, "Timeful Friends," 14.

of autonomy, found in the selfish desire to get what one can from God and attend church as long as it satisfies the individual without considering other people. Fettke calls this "a pretty self-absorbed view of the life of faith."[197] The implication about the disabled is that they constitute a burden and that it would be better if they did not exist.[198]

Pentecostals need the wisdom to view the disabled, weak, and chronically ill as people on whose lives the anointing of the Spirit may rest as in the case of any other Spirit-filled believer, empowering them to participate fruitfully in ministry. The disabled are people like any other. When Pentecostals consider and accept them as such, that they are disabled and weak will not be any hindrance. They are not part of the "others," as some Pentecostals stereotypically judged people with different sexual orientations or races in the past.

Fettke refers to an interview published in *Christianity Today* with deceased Henri Nouwen of L'Arche, the French ministry to the severely disabled. Nouwen said about the philosophy of ministry at L'Arche (in Toronto): "L'Arche exists not to help the mentally handicapped get 'normal,' but to help them share their spiritual gifts with the world."[199] The disabled need to be recognized for what they are, fellow Spirit-filled servants of Christ who have been empowered to provide in the need of others through their *charismata*.

Amos Yong asks the question of where disability can be categorized with regard to the problem of evil.[200] He classifies the sufferings related to disability under "natural evil" because it forms part of the "workings of nature." However, there is also a social character to disability that classifies its suffering under the category of "moral evil," for instance, in the case of congenital disabilities including genetically or chromosomally related syndromes like trisomy 21 (Down syndrome). Such diseases do not represent natural or moral evils in terms of their etiologies. It seems that a third classification may be needed in disability directly related to human responsibility, for instance, in the case of fetal alcohol syndrome.

The question remains how a good and almighty God can allow such evils in the world. The standard reply is a pragmatic and eschatological one. God will heal all individuals, presumably also those with genetic

---

197. Fettke, "Spirit of God Hovered Over the Waters," 178.
198. Hauerwas, "Timeful Friends," 14.
199. Fettke, "Spirit of God Hovered Over the Waters," 179.
200. Yong, "Disability and the Love of Wisdom," 166.

variation, when the new world of God's peaceful reign dawns over the earth. However, Yong complicates the response by asking how someone with, for example, trisomy 21 can be the same person without that specific chromosomal configuration.[201] If that person gets "healed" (whatever that means), then God would in effect not allow what is precisely that person to continue to exist. The eradication of the disability will lead to the elimination of the person.

Pentecostals should also acknowledge that divine healing is God's work and decision and that no human being can claim anything from God. In the words of Joni Tada, "God reserves the right to heal or not . . . as He sees fit."[202] Furthermore, no human being can comprehend God's ways, as the author of Romans 11 asserts in a song of praise: "O the depth of the riches and wisdom and knowledge of God! How unsearchable are his judgments and how inscrutable his ways! For who has known the mind of the LORD? Or who has been his counselor? Or who has given a gift to him, to receive a gift in return? For from him and through him and to him are all things. To him be the glory forever. Amen" (vv. 33–36).

Amos Yong proposes that the new theology of healing should contain the pneumatological imagination that characterizes Pentecostal spirituality and does not consist of a fixed orthodoxy but shifting foundations, because it bases its orientation on the experience of the Spirit.[203] The movement's history shows that early Pentecostals concentrated their evangelistic outreach on those marginalized and rejected by society, such as drunkards, whores, fornicators, criminals, etc. The movement should regain such an inclusive approach, including those who are chronically ill, mentally and physically challenged, and marginalized in other ways. It should deliberately confront exclusion by gender, culture, class, sexual orientation, disability, and permanent illness.[204]

A positive emphasis in the Pentecostal theology of healing is that healing should be viewed holistically, including the human being in its entirety. God does not care only about human beings' souls but also their daily lives; it implies that what people experience is vital to God and, by extension, the church. It includes unanswered prayers and the

---

201. Yong, "Disability and the Love of Wisdom," 166.
202. Tada, *Place of Healing*, 19.
203. Yong, "Many Tongues, Many Senses," 177.
204. Yong, "Many Tongues, Many Senses," 177.

disappointed expectations that it might hold for believers. The movement should honestly address such questions.

According to Luke 14, Jesus tells a parable to illustrate that when his disciples give a luncheon or a dinner, they should not invite their friends, relatives, and rich neighbors. Instead, they should ask the poor, the crippled, the lame, and the blind (vv. 12–13). In the same way, the church should be the home where these people are made to feel welcome, regardless of whether they get healed in the ministry of healing. Of course, that does not imply that the church should not pray for and with the sick for healing. Still, suppose Pentecostals suggest that God's compassionate love is manifest only when a person is healed. In that case, the movement cannot offer any hope for most ill and disabled persons.[205]

---

205. Clifton, "Dark Side of Prayer for Healing," 224–25.

5

Reflecting on God in Theodicy from a Pentecostal Hermeneutical Perspective

Introduction

IN THE PREVIOUS CHAPTER, a possible Pentecostal theodicy was described in terms of Pentecostals' teaching of divine healing. It seems that Pentecostals ignore the urgent challenges that theodicy poses to suffering people, including believers, by concentrating on God's salvation and deliverance from all hardships and ills without leaving room for any exceptions or unanswered prayers for deliverance. When the theology is not realized in practice, Pentecostals argue that it is because of a lack of faith, placing the blame on the believer's shoulders. Before that, an overview was presented of theological and biblical proposals to respond to the challenges theodicy poses to faith to form an idea of the complexity implied by theodicy as a theological challenge.

Next, a reflection is done about the most significant aspects of theodicy, including its view of God, the use of language in speaking about God, eschatology, and evil, but now from the perspective of the new Pentecostal hermeneutics that has been developing during the last two or three decades as an alternative to traditional biblicist views. It critiques the traditional Pentecostal theodicy with its easy formulas that coincide with the Deuteronomist Historian's retribution and reward theory. Instead of developing a specific theodicy, it is proposed that theodicy from a Pentecostal hermeneutical perspective should limit its discussion to victims' subjective experience and perception of suffering and their attempts at explaining it that answers questions that the post-World War II and post-COVID-19 world pose. In some cases, suffering is without any meaning or sense. In such cases, the only possible outcome is for the believer to trust God, whose ways in many cases remain incomprehensible. In Psalm 92, the author contrasts the righteous and foolish person's perceptions and refers in verse 5 to God, translated literally: "How great are your deeds, O Yahweh; how very deep are your thoughts."[1] Theodicy leaves room for divine decisions that cannot be accounted for in human thought.

Thinking about God

Every theodicean question is premised on an understanding of "God." In many instances, philosophical reflections are based on the god of deism or philosophical theism.[2] The concept of *Theos* has transitioned and changed in time, as the first chapter argued, and for that reason, each contribution to theodicy should state exactly to which *god* it refers.

The "god" of modern theodicy, a deistic god, is "good," "sovereign," and "all-powerful" (or "almighty"). The terms used to describe the characteristics are, however, determined by the user's own perceptions. God's power is displayed through the acts of creating and maintaining everything, as Christians accept. What is the difference between the god/God of the deist and the theist? Deism is based on the Enlightenment requirements for faith to be made explicable in terms of the demands of reason. The implication is that anything Christians believe (including everything in the Bible) must be compatible with reason. The result is that the biblical account of creation, miracles, prophecies, and much of theological dogma became suspicious to leave room for a respectable and viable god.[3] This led to the perspective of cessationism, that miracles and wonders ceased at the end of the first century CE with the death of the last apostle and the closing of the missionary era. Daniel Castelo explains that one feature of Christian identity was especially singled out as unacceptable. That was the scandalous particularity of a God who revealed the divine self to a particular people, and through Jesus Christ, to all people.[4] Natural religion's god does not have any history and does not

---

1. Harris, *Lexham English Bible*.
2. Surin, *Theology and the Problem of Evil*, 4.
3. Castelo, *Theological Theodicy*, 30.
4. Within the South African context, with its sad history of apartheid laws that

communicate with anyone; the god's involvement in the world is reserved to the creative act. Its existence is attributed to some intuitive sense of transcendence that (many or some) people share. This god also does not own any characteristics, like goodness or love. The god is an object of reasonable devotion, engaging with people's thinking minds rather than the rest of their existence as bodies with experiences and the accompanying affections, such as passions, joys, and heartache. To "serve" the god, one does not need a temple or liturgy, dedication or devotion, or personal piety; worshipers bow before the supremacy of reason.

Deism does not disbelieve in evil but does not accept the idea of evil as an opposing and equal force to goodness, related to God. For the most part, monotheistic believers such as Jews did not accept a strict dualism of evil and goodness because they viewed God as the source of all that is, including evil (and evil forces). It would have been convenient for religious believers to have accepted such a strict dualism that evil originated and existed apart from God because it would have kept God from any blame in the occurrence of evil in the present world. As a result, most Christians believe that although evil existed apart from God, it originated with God. They hope that evil will be finally conquered and destroyed by God, whose power includes everything in the world. Otherwise, the potential might have existed that evil powers might conquer the Christian God.

Christians accept neither deism nor deism's god nor dualism. They believe in a God, the primordial reality, who created everything. God's existence is accepted in faith; nowhere is it explained or justified. God is different from and distinguished from creation in a real sense because God represents primordial creation; everything that is created depends on God. God is essentially relational as a triune God and stands in a relationship with human beings. The fact that the Bible portrays God in terms of the Father, Son, and Spirit explains that relationality is a significant part of the existence of God. That God consists of three persons shows how God is but also who God is. It is consistent with God's nature and is the essence of "love" when the Bible states that "God is love" (1 John 4:8), love that includes friendship, loyalty, and other-directed compassion, in

---

destroyed the dignity of large groups of people for the way they look, Gerrie Snyman opines that reformational theology with its literalist reading of the Bible and identification with Israel as the elected people, reflecting the Calvinistic election theory, is prone to discrimination. The Afrikaans-speaking churches did not only support apartheid but justified it theologically by using the doctrine of election (Snyman, *Om die Bybel Anders te Lees*, 11).

contrast to human perceptions of love that may include elements of passing away after a period, spontaneity, fickleness, inconsistency, etc.

Creation is a sign that God wanted to extend the divine self.[5] This God has a history with human beings because God created the universe to participate in relationships with human beings. In some way or another, the fact that God created human beings in God's image presupposes that human beings would have the free will to choose or reject this God's advances. It also assumes that human beings become rulers or have dominion over the rest of creation (Gen 1:26). This is another sign of God's emptying of the divine self to stand in a relationship with human beings.

This God is "good" and created a "very good" creation (Gen 1:31). That creation is good reflects the goodness of the Creator. It affirms that God created human beings in God's likeness, something that was not annulled by the human choice for anti-God or evil because human beings are still a part of God's creation and purpose with creation, despite their (nearly) universal choices for evil. For that reason, human beings retained the capacity to do good, as God originally intended for them. Thus, even though God's image in them was corrupted to a certain degree, human beings are still the objects of God's revelation in the history of salvation.

Did evil only enter the world when human beings exercised their capacity to choose between good (and God), or did it negatively reflect on God's goodness?

Adam and Eve's choice to disobey God's clear command not to eat of the tree in the garden of Eden was birthed from their desire to be like God, a desire awoken in them by the serpent's opinion that God's motive for the command was to keep their eyes from being opened, which would have resulted in their becoming like God (Gen 3:5).[6] It is possible to explain the narrative in Gen 3 as a symbolic explanation of the origins and existence of evil in the world, as the result of (all or most) human beings using their God-given capacity to choose for or against God in a negative way, rather than the story about two people whose choice determined the history of everyone else who lived in their wake. The serpent then represents the human inclination to choose for evil in selfishness and pride. Instead of realizing the purpose of their creation, to stand in a

---

5. Castelo, *Theological Theodicy*, 35.

6. The serpent said, "You will not die; for God knows that when you eat of it your eyes will be opened, and you will be like God, knowing good and evil." See discussion about Gen 3 and theodicy in the next chapter.

relationship with God, sin leads to human beings setting themselves up as rivals of God.

In this work, God is defined in terms of theology, and specifically from a Pentecostal angle. In developing a doctrine of God, the purpose is to distill in conceptual form what we know about God through revelation. The warning of Clark Pinnock is timely: that we should always clearly distinguish between the Bible and our attempts to interpret it, while we also remember that humility is essential because we are trying to say something about God, while we know "only in part"; some things are just too high for us.[7]

In this discussion, two models of God are described, referring to the traditional doctrine accepted by most Christian traditions and a doctrine with affinities with an open view of God. It is crucial to note the pervasive influence of one's concept of God that one uses to think of God. Traditionally, God was viewed primarily as an aloof monarch who occupies a heavenly throne high above the world of human beings, far removed from the world's contingencies. God is characterized by God's immutability and omnipotent power that no power can resist. God has determined everything that will ever happen. The traditional view was defined by Augustine, who was deeply influenced by the Neo-Platonist philosophy he learned from Plotinus.[8] His idea of God conformed to the Neo-Platonic notions of God as a creative force or metaphysical principle. He speaks of God in terms of the traditional list of divine attributes, that God is self-sufficient, impassable, immutable, omniscient, omnipotent, timeless, ineffable, and simple. That God is unchangeable implies that neither divine knowledge nor divine will ever change.[9] God knows everything, including all future events, in one eternal moment of "spiritual vision."[10] Since Augustine, traditional theism has accepted God's immunity to time, change, and responsiveness to God's creatures.

Augustine did not see any incompatibility between his idea of divine foreknowledge and human freedom. In his perspective, God knows exactly what will happen in the future. That God knows is, however, not the cause of those future events.[11] While the early church fathers had

---

7. Pinnock, "Systematic Theology," 93–94.
8. Augustine, *Confessions* 7.9.
9. Augustine, *Confessions* 7.11; 11.18; 12.15; 13.16.
10. Sanders, "Historical Considerations," 70.
11. Augustine, *Confessions* 11.18.

taught that God knows who will have faith and then elects them, leaving the decision in the hands of the individual, Augustine argues that human beings lost the freedom necessary to respond positively to God in the garden of Eden's fall. It is up to God to decide who will become believers, earning God's approval, and who will reject the offer of salvation, earning eternal punishment. God can never be dependent upon what human beings decide because God is immutable and incapable of suffering or feeling pain. "The will of the omnipotent is always undefeated."[12]

What about texts stating that God desires that all people be saved (e.g., 1 Tim 2:4)? Augustine replies that it means either that no person is saved unless God wills their salvation or that "all people" refers to some individuals from all classes and ranks of people, but it does not include every individual.[13] What about people who live as Christians for a time but then leave the faith behind? Augustine responds that such people have never been and cannot be genuine Christians because God did not grant them the persevering faith necessary for salvation. That a Christian will persevere until the end depends on it being the decision God made in eternity about the individual. Those that did not persevere were never indeed predestined for salvation. What about infants who suffer or die before the age when they can make a conscious decision for or against Christ? From Augustine's perspective, God knows what child God will save, as God also knows why such things happen. "Perhaps God is doing some good in correcting parents when their beloved children suffer pain and even death."[14] Believers can trust God in such cases because God always acts justly. Therefore, it is imperative never to question God's judgment.

What about texts that state that God changed the divine mind (literally, "repented")? These texts, Augustine argues, were written for "babes in the faith" and did not properly refer to God.[15] To find a true description of God, other texts should be consulted, specifically those that state that God never changes. Clearly, Augustine decides what applies to God and uses this understanding to filter the biblical message.[16] In his perspective, God can never repent and choose not to fulfill the divine will because God knows all that will happen; after all, God had decided what

---

12. Augustine, "Enchiridion" 26.
13. Augustine, "Enchiridion" 26.
14. Augustine, "Enchiridion" 24.
15. Augustine, "De Trinitate" 1.1.2.
16. Sanders, "Historical Considerations," 72.

will happen from eternity.[17] God can never change the divine mind (e.g., by removing the kingship from Saul and giving it to David); God only changed the divine work and not the divine will.

Augustine sees the essence or being of God as being alone in the trinity. Because God's external relations with the temporal creation are accidental, it does not affect the essence of God. The implication is clear that God does not have a "real relationship" with human beings. If such relationships were essential to God, they would have hindered God's immutability, because love always holds the risk of disappointment for one of the parties. The divine essence consists of "absoluteness and impassibility rather than based on the active involvement of God in creation and redemption."[18] God is a remote deity, perilously close to being impersonal.[19]

Augustine views the essence of human beings in the same light. The essence, that is, the image of God within human beings, refers to their inherent faculties, such as memory, understanding, and will. External relations with others, including other human beings and God, do not determine humanity's essence.[20] These ideas have been formative in the development of Western individualism. As in the case of God, the essence of the human being is to be alone. To get to know God, humans should turn inward to find the essence of God in their aloneness. God exists in the higher intellect, not in history or human relations. Augustine realized that relationships always hold risks for human beings, and he disqualified interpersonal models from explaining the being of the Godhead or humanity.

An alternative view of God is that God is a husband or parent who cares with self-sacrificing love in response to a wife or children with generosity and sensitivity. This implies that God is vulnerable in the relationship with those God loves. As a person and not a principle, God responds to what happens in the created order in a dynamic and active give-and-take relationship with humans.[21] "God is more like a dynamic event than

---

17. Augustine, *City of God* 11.18, 21; 14.9, 11.
18. Pelikan, *Christian Tradition*, 2:296.
19. Sanders, "Historical Considerations," 75.
20. Augustine, "De Trinitate" 12.5–7.
21. Sanders ("Historical Considerations," 52) describes the Greek philosophical concept of God as the ultimate metaphysical principle called the "unlimited" that is indescribable in human language (ineffable) because God is beyond all reality that humans can know.

a simple substance and is essentially relational, ecstatic, and alive."[22] In the first model, God has affinities with the god of Greek philosophy, although some references in the Bible support this view.[23] Greek thinking located God as the ultimate and perfect in the realm of the immutable. God is the absolutely transcendent one.

It is submitted that an open view of God, consisting of the emphasis of God in relationship with human beings, is more consistent with the picture found in the Bible. In the first view of God, the emphasis is on God's transcendence; in the second, God's immanence is highlighted without denying God's transcendence. God's immanence refers to God's presence and involvement in the universe, and specifically in the lives of human beings, a world characterized as being changeable and contingent. God is active in the whole long process of its development and the risks it holds for God.

God is the creator of the world who maintains all of creation, who revealed the divine self to Israel, and then in the incarnation of Jesus. God is the triune God, as a self-revealed mystery. Indeed, God did not need human beings in any sense; God is self-sufficient without creating any world. However, God chose to create human beings to interact with them. It is imperative to realize that God created humanity to be able to respond to God. God created them for their God-instilled ability to grow in a relationship with God. It is argued that this ability is what is meant by the expression that God created human beings in God's image or likeness (Gen 1:26–27; 9:6). The word for "image," ṣelem, refers to something that is a likeness or representation resembling something or someone else. It describes humanity created in the "image of God," in the same way that Adam passed on his "likeness" to his son Seth (Gen 5:3).[24]

God exists in "eternity" as the "holy" one, two terms that require a theological definition since it does not (in theological terms) refer to any concepts that agree with ideas or characteristics that human beings can fashion. What does the word "eternity" imply? The Hebrew term ('ad) refers to time as a continuum of experience, without beginning in the past or end in the future. It is found alongside another word for "a very

---

22. Pinnock, "Systematic Theology," 98.

23. See discussion of Sanders, "Historical Considerations," 49–90, about the god of Greek philosophy, especially Middle Platonism.

24. The term also refers to idols (Num 33:52; Amos 5:26; Ezek 7:20) and animal figurines (1 Sam 6:5, 11; Ezek 16:17; 23:14) (see Mangum, "Idolatry.")

long time" ('*ôlām*, in, e.g., Isa 30:8; Mic 4:5; Ps 9:5).[25] Does it imply that God is temporally everlasting or timelessly eternal? Traditional theism saw God as timeless; God exists outside creation characterized by time, sequence, and space limitations. God's transcendence as an immutable and impassable being implies God's lack of involvement in creation.

The traditional view of God as the timelessly eternal implies that God does not experience the flow of temporal passage or experience anything like a surprise. God knows everything before it happens. However, the Bible depicts God as being intimately involved in the life of people, urging them to stay loyal to God, praising them when they succeeded and punishing them when their disloyalty damaged God's reputation among the nations. For the timeless God, the future is ultimately settled. However, the God of the Bible reveals the divine self in the redemption of human beings in time. The eternal God is temporally everlasting because God is related to the temporal world and faithful over time. God cannot be threatened or become undone by time. For God, the past is actual, the present is evolving, and the future is possible. God's eternity means that there has never been and never will be a time when God does not exist. However, saying that God is in time does not mean that God is exhaustively in time. Even human beings partially transcend time through memory, imagination, and reason; God transcends time much more perfectly.

The term "mystery" also needs to be qualified theologically to be helpful in the discussion. In many theodicean discussions, "mystery" is used as the "trump card" when one does not know the answers to challenging questions. Still, here its meaning is somewhat limited to the "essence" of God, as far as it is possible to say anything about it, since God exists in a frame of reference that human beings cannot comprehend (as the term "holy" refers to; see discussion beneath).

When one opens a standard book on the introduction to systematic theology, the first chapters discuss God's general and specific revelation, creating the impression that human beings can know and understand God. However, in similar books in the Eastern Orthodox tradition, one finds that its first discussion is concerned with "God as mystery," the unknowable and incomprehensible being that is the source of all life. In Western theology, "mystery" does not function in the same way as in Orthodox theology. It is submitted that Pentecostal theological endeavors

---

25. McGuire-Moushon and Klippenstein, "Eternity."

connect more closely to Orthodox spirituality and theology than Western ones, as far as God's (un)knowability is concerned.[26]

God is the radically transcendent entity, the *Ganz Andere*, who exists in a dimension and state that differs from anything human beings can devise. God is beyond human words and concepts. What human beings can say about God is what God said about the divine self and how God revealed the divine self to human beings in the history of salvation. Human beings cannot access the essence of God; they can at most refer to God's energies in creation and self-revelation. They know that God is the source of love, goodness, beauty, and truth, but they understand that the human definition of these terms does not do justice to the divine clothing of the concepts.

The heading of a section of Karl Barth's *Church Dogmatics* is "The Being of God as the One Who Loves." Barth argues that divine revelation is the essence of God. Wolfhart Pannenberg agrees with Barth when he states, "Only in the love of God does the concrete form of his essence come to expression."[27] The view presented here disagrees with Barth; God's revelation defines God's relationship with human beings in only partial essential terms. Although divine self-revelation gives a picture of God's essence, it does not exhaust God's essence. The vastness and beauty of the universe, for example, present another picture. God's revelation is always more than "self-revelation," but the other aspects of the divine essence fall outside the human frame of reference or understanding. However, Barth is correct when he states that the divine self-revelation to human beings shows "the Godhead of God . . . consists in the fact that He loves";[28] the divine act of love is God's being, essence, and nature. "Love is what it means to be God."[29]

God as the completely other stands in contrast to humanity. However, this does not imply that God is inaccessible to human beings. On the contrary, God revealed the divine self, first through the voice of angels and prophets and then through Jesus Christ. Klaas Runia is correct when he refers to the one-sidedness of the early Karl Barth in his exclusive emphasis on God as the completely other or completely different at the expense of humanity, in Barth's reaction to establish a self-conscious contrast with

---

26. See fuller discussion in Nel, "Pentecostal Spirituality in Dialogue with Early Fathers."

27. Pannenberg, *Systematic Theology*, 1:396.

28. Barth, *Church Dogmatics* II.1, 275.

29. Rice, "Biblical Support for a New Perspective," 11.

Schleiermacher and his followers with their depiction of a god of philosophers.[30] Barth employed *diastasis* to explain divine knowability, ignoring the complementary concept of analogy. However, by emphasizing God's transcendence, the other aspect must be kept in perspective: God revealed the divine self to human beings by taking the form of a human being in the incarnation of the Christ, signifying God's togetherness with them (immanence). In the later Barth, one finds the confirmation that "God shows and reveals who He is and what He is in His Godness not in the vacuum of a divine self-sufficiency, but genuinely just in this fact, that He exists, speaks, and acts as a partner."[31] In Christ, human beings find God as God is, and the God in sovereign freedom decides to be human beings' partner. Only in Christ, one finds human beings as they are, the being for whom Christ was born, suffered, died, and rose again. The change from the early to the later Barth consisted of increasing all his theological endeavors upon Christology.[32] Barth even asserted that the whole of creation from its very beginning to all eternity stands in the light of God's grace in Jesus Christ. The purpose and meaning of creation are "to make possible the history of God's covenant with man, which has its beginning, its center and its culmination in Jesus Christ."[33]

Although Christians believe they can state something true of God, they understand that they can never speak exhaustively of God or God's work. They recognize the importance of keeping the limitations in mind when they talk to and about God to prevent self-deception and self-projection in religious dialogue.[34] They can worship and praise God and pray to God, but they have to keep in mind that God is a mystery that far transcends the revelation of God that they know something about. Among Pentecostals, theological endeavors are not high on the agenda. They believe it is more important to experience God's present revelation in encounters than to talk about historical encounters related to the Bible. Perhaps they understand the danger that "easy talk" about God can easily lead to self-delusion and even arrogance.[35]

---

30. Runia, *Karl Barth's Doctrine of Holy Scripture*, 209.
31. Barth, *Church Dogmatics I.2*, 37.
32. Runia, *Karl Barth's Doctrine of Holy Scripture*, 209.
33. Barth, *Church Dogmatics III.1*, 42.
34. Castelo, *Theological Theodicy*, 19.
35. Compare arguments in Nel, "Pentecostal Talk about God."

The best way to talk about (and with) God is by worship and silence born from the realization of own ignorance about God. Whatever believers say about God should always be seen as provisional, even when referring to God's goodness and power. Because they use human language with its limitations, they can only stutter when speaking about the one who exists outside the human frame of reference. This is also true in terms of theodicy. What John Shelby Spong emphasizes should be kept in mind: "Words are always but a human vehicle through which ultimate meaning seeks to find expression. The words cannot be identified with the ultimate meaning."[36]

The Bible's language to refer to God is metaphorical, with the word "God" the exception.[37] A metaphor can be defined in terms of its power to bring "two separate domains into cognitive and emotional relation by using language directly appropriate to the one as a lens for seeing the other."[38] Metaphors are central to a richness of association in the human experience. Metaphors work not simply at cognitive levels but at the levels of emotion and will as well. Terence Fretheim remarks that the biblical metaphors are proper to human life, replete with meaning. They capture, organize, and communicate human experience, demonstrated by their use by believers through centuries. Significantly, they also represent "a two-way traffic in ideas" where human beings can learn from and imitate some aspects the metaphors ascribe to God, such as references to the fatherhood and motherhood of God.[39] In the incarnation, God acted anthropomorphically, implying that human beings can talk about Christ and his life and ministry on earth.

Christians also realize that they can only speak about evil in reference to God's goodness. Evil is the absence of goodness; it is the deprivation and corruption of goodness, the opposite of God and goodness. Evil is not only a problem that needs to be solved; it is also an entity that exists in direct opposition to God. God is the infinite mystery who, by love and grace, reveals the divine self to human beings while evil is not infinite or eternal, nor necessary in any way. For that reason, Christians believe and expect that evil will end in the foreseeable future. Evil is not a mystery in the sense that God is. Instead, it is a disorder, sickness, or corruption that

---

36. Spong, *Rescuing the Bible from Fundamentalism*, 242.
37. Fretheim, *Suffering of God*, 162–63.
38. Fretheim, *Suffering of God*, 157–58.
39. Fretheim, *Suffering of God*, 227–30.

coincides with the state of being anti-God, of opposing God's purposes for creation and God's character. It does not exist as long-term viability.[40]

God as the Almighty?

As the complication of the relationship between God and human suffering, theodicy arises from two assumptions: that God is almighty, and that God is good.[41] That God is almighty implies that everything happens as God wills it to happen. Everything that people experience comes from God's hand. For many Christians, it is encouraging to remind themselves that "God is in control" and that nothing happens outside of God's will. They feel safe because they "know that all things work together for good for those who love God, who are called according to his purpose" (Rom 8:28). They find comfort in the thought when they face difficulties and mishaps: God is in control, and God will protect them. However, if God is in control, why does evil occur? If God is good, on the other hand, why do people experience suffering? What are God's purposes when people suffer innocently? What purpose can justify a baby born with severe challenges, suffers for many excruciating months of suffering for the baby and parents, and eventually dies? Why does God allow such a harrowing experience in the lives of believing parents? Where is the good God then?

The problem originates when the assumption is that the good God is also all-powerful or almighty. If God were good but cannot do anything because God is not omnipotent, the argument would have been that God does not want bad events to occur in people's lives. Therefore, God is powerless to do something about it even though God would have stopped the events from happening if it were in God's power. But if God is all-powerful, the question is why God does nothing about suffering that characterizes all biological life forms that exist on the planet. Everything animate and inanimate is subject to the law of entropy, associated with a state of disorder, randomness, or uncertainty.

In traditional theology, both omnipotence and goodness are ascribed to God's character. Jürgen Moltmann explains that these two characteristics form the basis for atheism's arguments about God.[42] Tra-

---

40. Castelo, *Theological Theodicy*, 20.
41. Van de Beek, *Why? On Suffering, Guilt, and God*, 5.
42. Moltmann (*Crucified God*, 221) writes that "there is something that the atheist fears over and above all torments. That is the indifference of God and his final retreat

ditional theology describes God's sovereignty as the victory of God's will in creation, implying that nothing happens without conforming to God's will. The purpose and goal of divine creation is divine glory; God created the world to display divine glory by fulfilling God's purposes. God's will is irresistible to human beings, implying that everything happens as God dictates and fits into the divine grand design. No human beings or power can thwart God or hinder the accomplishment of divine purposes. God rules and controls creation. Righteous people's obedience and sinners' disobedience, the resultant redemption of the first group, and the destruction of the wicked serve God's purposes. Nothing can catch God off guard because nothing can happen that God's will has not ordained. God's will cannot fail to reach fulfillment in each case, and God cannot change the divine mind.

In traditional theism that emphasizes God as the eternal God, God sees past, present, and future together, and at the same time, God exists in timelessness. God remains essentially unaffected by anything in creation because God knows the past, present, and future as well as what human beings intend.[43] This view preserves God's radical transcendence and affirms that God reigns sovereignly; God has complete control over the universe.[44] Unfortunately, the price the traditional idea of God paid for their view of God was that it thought of God's relation to the world in static terms.

However, a more dynamic view is preferred, based on the biblical observation that God interacts with God's creatures in an intimate relationship characterized by divine love and grace. In the relationship, God influences human beings; however, they also exert an influence on God. That is why the course of salvation history is not about divine action alone but shows that God responds to humanity's propensity to sin in many cases, saving them from some of the destruction caused by their sins. God's will is not the ultimate explanation for everything that happens; human decisions and actions significantly contribute to it. "The will

---

from the world of men."

43. Rice, "Biblical Support for a New Perspective," 2.

44. It is possible to support this view with biblical quotations such as Gen 17:1; 18:14; Exod 15:11; 20:3; Num 23:19; 1 Sam 15:29; 2 Chron 20:6; Job 37:23; Pss 18:31; 139:4, 16; Isa 37:16; 46:10; Mal 3:6; Matt 19:26; Eph 3:20; Heb 4:13; Jas 1:17; and Rev 4:8.

of God . . . is not an irresistible, all-determining force."[45] Thus history is the combined result of what God and God's creatures decide to do.

What does "omnipotence" mean, a word adopted in the creed by the First Ecumenical Council in Nicaea in present-day Turkey in 325 CE (and amended in 381 CE at the Second Ecumenical Council, at Constantinople), and used in the Apostles' Creed that originated in the fifth century CE, probably in Gaul? Besides the predicates that God is "Father" and "Creator," God is also almighty. Although the term is not used in the New Testament, the idea occurs there, leading the early church to coin it to describe God's power. The Heidelberg Catechism (Lord's Day 10), written in 1563, answers the question as to the providence of God by stating that it refers to the "almighty and ever-present power of God by which he upholds, as with his hand, heaven and earth and all creatures, and so rules them that leaf and blade, rain and drought, fruitful and lean years, food and drink, health and sickness, prosperity and poverty—all things, in fact, come to us not by chance but from his fatherly hand."[46] Thus, for centuries, Christians experienced security in the belief that God reigns in their lives and that they are safe. In the words of Romans 8:35, "Who will separate us from the love of Christ? Will hardship, or distress, or persecution, or famine, or nakedness, or peril, or sword?" The author responds, "In all these things we are more than conquerors through him who loved us. For I am convinced that neither death, nor life, nor angels, nor rulers, nor things present, nor things to come, nor powers, nor height, nor depth, nor anything else in all creation, will be able to separate us from the love of God in Christ Jesus our Lord" (vv. 35–39). However, if God is almighty and good, why is prayer necessary at all? What good can prayer do when everything has been determined to happen in eternity? Would human beings then not be in the position to trust God to serve their interests without asking God to change their circumstances? Prayers of request typically are concerned with needs and challenges that reflect the imperfect world in which human beings live.

Today, many believers experience the confession of God as the almighty as challenging to accept in the face of the post-Second World War and post-9/11 world. With many people exposed to pictures and videos of the suffering implied in catastrophes, wars, famines, and genocide daily thanks to modern means of communication, few people

---

45. Rice, "Biblical Support for a New Perspective," 28.
46. Bierma, "Heidelberg Catechism."

accept the worldview of a well-ordered system with a supreme being in control of everything. The prevailing sentiment finds little room for the supernatural as a power or influence of direct causality that is empirically verifiable.[47] In the contemporary world, science explains why things happen and how they can be improved. Human beings have to complete what can be achieved globally, and nothing is achievable beyond that. And thanks to the prosperity that characterizes many Westerners' lives, life on earth has become valuable, and earlier longing for heavenly bliss in a paradise has been exchanged for investment in life here and now.

To state that God is almighty implies that God can manage everything, and God can do anything. Thus, it refers to the power of God as it accords with God's will. The statement that God can do anything is the crux of the problem because it asks why evil and suffering continue to exist globally. If God can manage everything, why does God not manage human suffering, especially innocent suffering, sin, and injustice? Why did God not stop human beings from sin, preventing the suffering and destruction that followed their evil acts?

The Middle Ages responded to the logical problems presented by this challenge by stating that God is not omnipotent in some respects. For instance, God cannot create a stone that the divine self cannot lift, implying that absolute omnipotence is not possible. However, it is foolish to argue such a hypothetical case.

The question evoked by the debate is: Is the traditional notion of the omnipotence of God correct? Can God make a world that the divine self cannot manage? Can the Creator create a world that is not subject to the divine self? The answer is clear. Yes, the present world cannot be subject to God's will if we hold to the statement that God is good. But, if the present world is not obedient to God's will, can God still be omnipotent? Is God really able to manage the world, given the current state in which the earth and human beings find themselves? Or has the world slipped out of God's hand?

Can one presume, given the fact of the existence of the present world, that God could not have created a better-functioning world? Why did a good God not create a perfect world of peace and justice? If God's power was absolute, God could have done it. The fact is, God did not create an ideal world. Why did God not make things differently?[48]

---

47. Van de Beek, *Why? On Suffering, Guilt, and God*, 9.
48. Van de Beek, *Why? On Suffering, Guilt, and God*, 13.

To describe God as the almighty is at odds with itself. It seems absurd to confess that God is the almighty. Jewish rabbi Harold Kushner argued for a God who hurts with hurting people because this God is not actually omnipotent. Things are happening in people's lives and on earth that God cannot do.[49]

How does one reconcile the statements that God is almighty and that God is good? It is submitted that the description of God's essence and character always leads to these kinds of contradictions, as demonstrated in other statements about God, such as that God is the triune existing as one. Such contradictions warn us that to speak of God requires the utmost care, because we are talking about what we do not know and cannot even understand, at least not while we are limited to the dimensions in which our lives occur. "For that reason, it is vital to emphasize that God did not reveal the divine self for us to know and comprehend God but to have communion with the one who created us for such communion. Trust in God, not explanations from God, is the pathway through suffering."[50]

The most human beings can say about God is that God limited the divine self by creating free human beings and with Jesus' incarnation. God's *kenosis* (first implied in the self-emptying of Jesus to do the divine will completely, indicated in Phil 2:7) led to God limiting the divine power invested in God. To what extent these limitations apply falls outside human capability to know. If God is almighty, God deliberately limited the divine self to stand in a relationship with human beings characterized by human freedom. It also implies that the deliberate *kenosis* of the mighty God determines and limits God's sovereign rule.

God created human beings with independent status alongside the divine self, accepting limitations God imposed on the divine self. For that reason, instead of God responding with holy anger to humankind's disobedience in the garden of Eden and humanity's continued sin, Genesis describes God's reaction as simple grief, so deep that God contemplates removing the most favored of the creation, humankind, which God created in the divine image, from it.[51] Divine restraint is illustrated by Genesis 6, which explains that when YHWH saw how great humankind's wickedness was and that all their thoughts were only evil continually, YHWH was sorry for creating humanity. It grieved the divine heart, and

---

49. Kushner, *When Bad Things Happen to Good People.*
50. Ortlund, "Book of Job."
51. Potgieter, "Divine Exultation and Agony in the Face of Evil," 210.

YHWH decided to blot out from the earth the human beings that God created (vv. 5–7). The only reason God did not continue with their destruction is described in verse 8, that Noah found favor in YHWH's sight.

God voluntarily relinquished absolute rule over the world of human beings by granting them dominion over it. God chose to not be all-determining. That does not imply that God cannot realize God's goals; instead, God achieves these goals through other agents and means. "Sometimes he accomplishes things through the cooperation of human agents, sometimes he overcomes creaturely opposition to accomplish things, sometimes he providentially uses opposition to accomplish something, and sometimes his intentions to do something are thwarted by human opposition."[52] Clark Pinnock argues that this does not mean that God is weak; actually, it requires more power to rule over a world not determined by God than it would over a determined one.[53] Only an omnipotent God might have the requisite degree and quality of power to create free creatures that cooperate with God and granting them the right to reject God working with them. God is an *"ad hoc"* God who sets goals for creation and redemption and realizes them *ad hoc* in history. God responds and adapts to surprises that result from human beings' free will.[54]

In line with this argument is the solution proposed by Clark Pinnock, that to talk sensibly about God in the context of theodicy, the definition of "omnipotence" should be redefined. He explains that "omnipotence does not mean that nothing can go contrary to God's will (our sins go against it) but that God can deal with any circumstance that may arise."[55] Because God is the most intelligent, wise, resourceful, and adaptable being, God can achieve God's goals in various ways. God is like a master chess player who can counter any moves that the human opponent may make.[56] That does not imply that God knows about everything that is going to happen in the future. "The future is determined by God not alone but in partnership with human agents. God gives us a role in shaping what the future will be."[57] God does not need foreknowledge to achieve God's purposes and fulfill divine promises. Pinnock adds that

---

52. Rice, "Biblical Support for a New Perspective," 27.
53. Pinnock, "Systematic Theology," 103.
54. See full discussion in Boer, *Ember Still Glowing*, chapter 8.
55. Pinnock, "Systematic Theology," 114.
56. Pinnock, *Most Moved Mover*, 52.
57. Pinnock, "Systematic Theology," 107.

Reflecting on God in Theodicy from a Pentecostal Hermeneutical Perspective   161

God knows everything that has ever existed, now actually exists, could possibly exist in the future, and what God has decided to do.[58] Pinnock is critical of traditional predestinarians' conclusion that God is the author of evil. "The logic of consistent Calvinism makes God the author of evil and casts serious doubt on his goodness. One is compelled to think of God's planning such horrors as Auschwitz, even though none but the most rigorous Calvinists can bring themselves to admit it."[59] Calvinism's emphasis on God's sovereignty extended to evil. Despite trying to blame creaturely agents, God's powerfulness as the almighty is so decisive that evil is included, making it difficult to think of God as good.[60] Calvinistic explanations of God's relationship to evil either make God the author of evil or are contradictory or nonsensical.[61]

As mentioned above, if God does not know what the future holds, it has implications for prayer. Pinnock agrees that God may provide guidance about what a believer should do in a given situation in response to the believer's prayer, but what is more important for God is that believers should be people who love and obey God, making responsible decisions that serve the interests of others and the planet.[62] If God has predestined everything that happens, it can be argued that it would be what God had wanted them to do, making prayer a meaningless venture no matter what people do. Pinnock suggests that even if God does not know what the future holds, God's exhaustive present knowledge allows God to predict the future much better than any human being can, implying that believers' reliance on God to guide them is always better than trusting their own judgment. It also suggests humans can proactively avoid evil without thwarting God's "plan" for the future, since God never causes evil.[63] And we are not doomed to a particular fate because God foreknows it.

God's love for them determines God's relation with human beings, and God manifests divine omnipotence paradoxically by suffering for and in Christ. God limited the divine self in the relationship with human beings by this love because it includes servanthood and self-sacrifice.[64]

58. Pinnock, *Most Moved Mover*, 138.
59. Pinnock, "From Augustine to Arminius," 21.
60. Zeeb, "Open Theism and the Problem of Theodicy," 305.
61. Pinnock, "Systematic Theology," 104.
62. Pinnock, *Most Moved Mover*, 175.
63. Zeeb, "Open Theism and the Problem of Theodicy," 310.
64. Plato was correct in observing that a god who loves always lacks because love in a relationship always holds the risk of disappointment and rejection. Plato's

For God to redeem humankind and restore their relationship with God cost the highest price imaginable. In the words of Philippians 2, Christ Jesus was in the form of God but did not regard equality with God as something to be exploited; Jesus emptied himself and took the form of a slave. He humbled himself even further and became obedient to the death on a cross (vv. 5–8).

God's creation of human beings, along with the rest of the universe, displays God's power; God's relationship with humanity displays God's love. God's love led to divine powerlessness because God did not force human beings to serve God by creating them without freedom and free will. God did not subject their wills to the divine will; instead, God transforms human hearts to display divine love towards each other and God. The future is determined by God in partnership with human agents, implying that God provides people with the opportunity to participate in shaping what the future and end will be.

That does not mean that God's omnipotence ceased to function when God created human beings; it does imply that omnipotence should instead be redefined not as the power to do anything but rather as the power to deal with creation in which God is not all in all. The author of 1 Corinthians 15 reasons that all things in creation are subjected to death, but when the eschatological future dawns, all things, including death, will be subjected to God "so that God may be all in all" (vv. 26–28). For the moment, God is not a puppeteer but a loving partner, requiring the human images of a mother and father, a brother and husband to portray the potential of the intimacy of God's relationship with humanity.[65] These metaphors serve as "controlling metaphors" because "they are able to bring coherence to a range of biblical thinking about God; they provide a hermeneutical key for interpreting the whole."[66]

God does not exercise total control over the lives of human beings, not even believers' lives. Complete control does not leave room for the destruction that results from the human propensity to sin. Full control

---

philosophical god or demiurge does not love; his god lacks nothing. His god is a self-sufficient being without any need, that also has no need of love (Sanders, "Historical Considerations," 53).

65. The image of God as a jealous husband of a wayward wife led to some of the most remarkable texts in the Old Testament, like Hos 2:2, 4, 9–10, 14, 19–20; Jer 3:1–3, 20, 22; cf. 2:20; 13:26–27; and Ezek 23. Hosea also compares God's feelings for Israel with a parent's tender longing for a wayward child (11:1–8).

66. Charnock, *Discourses upon the Existence and Attributes of God*, 1:434.

would have made God's creation of free human beings impossible, and that God could change the divine mind unthinkable. Else human beings could not have decided to sin in the garden of Eden, and God would not have been sorry that God had made humankind on earth (Gen 6:6), as God was also sorry and sad that God made Saul the king over Israel (1 Sam 15:35). God can relent from sending calamity (Jonah 4:2) or the disaster God had threatened (Exod 32:14). God also has powerful rivals in this world that God struggles with, showing the limitation to omnipotence that resulted from God's decision to create human beings in the divine image. God limited divine power by delegating some of this power to human beings. That people are created in this image implies that they received the ability and potential to stand in a reciprocal relationship with God. The risk was that they also received the ability to become disloyal to God by their disobedience in choosing other gods. The creation of free human beings demonstrates God's paradox of strength and vulnerability, requiring dialectical language to speak sensibly about God.

Some references in the Bible connect God directly to evil, as in Ecclesiastes 7:14, Isaiah 45:7, and Amos 3:6. God sent the evil spirits to plague Saul (1 Sam 16:14–23), the leaders of Shechem (Judg 9:23), and Ahab's prophets (1 Kgs 22:19–22). God destroyed Sodom and Gomorrah, sent plagues to Egypt, poisonous snakes to the Israelites in the wilderness, and a pestilence that killed many Israelites (2 Sam 24:15). These texts represent traditions that support a view of God as violent and patriarchal, without regard for the dignity and worth of men, women, children, and slaves, prompting Phyllis Trible to refer to these traditions as "texts of terror." "It depicts the horrors of male power, brutality and triumphalism, of female helplessness, abuse, and annihilation. To hear this story is to inhabit a world of unrelenting terror that refuses to let us pass by on the other side."[67]

How do we account for the reality of evil that permeates the world? Pinnock argues that at present, what God wills is resisted fiercely by powers of darkness; believers should participate in combating them through spiritual warfare.[68] Jesus referred to deformity, blindness, leprosy, and fever as signs that darkness reigns over the human world. They do not represent God's providence (see, e.g., Matt 17:14–20; Luke 13:11; John 12:31; 14:30; 16:11; also 2 Cor 4:4; Eph 2:2; 1 John 5:19). The Old Testament, as

67. Trible, *Texts of Terror*, 65.

68. Pinnock, *Most Moved Mover*, 148; Smith, "Spiritual Warfare in African Pentecostalism."

noted, refers sparsely to demonic powers. However, a new note appeared when in the book of Daniel, the angel explains the temporary delay of a response to Daniel's prayer as due to an evil power (Dan 10:13–14).[69] Humans suffer under the rule of the power of this world and not because of God's will.[70]

However, believers expect that the day will come when nothing and no one can resist God's will, with the introduction of God's reign of peace. At present, evil is still mounting a challenge to God's rule, and human beings are, *inter alia*, the victims of this battle. Pinnock writes that the powers of darkness put up stiff resistance and do their utmost to thwart God's will, even restricting God's ability to respond to a given crisis.[71] Until then, the Spirit suffers and groans with creation and human beings. That God's reign suffers temporary setbacks are "unfortunate by-products of the freedom which is necessary to achieve God's ultimate purpose: people who freely love him."[72]

This perspective justifies God as the good God because it ascribes evil to the misuse and abuse of humans' God-given free will instead of being God's will. Humans are morally responsible for their choices and decisions, including the evil ones with destructive effects. It encourages believers to combat evil actively because it never represents God's will. God's omnipotence implies that God can realize good out of evil, but God is not predestining it.

Michael Welker agrees that the theodicy requires that the false notion of divine omnipotence of God as the all-causing reality, the ground of being, the *causa prima*, ultimate reference point, and highest and final cause should be left behind.[73] "Divine omnipotence consists not in God's intervention into every possible situation in time and space like some instantaneous fire extinguisher but rather *in God's power to create something new and good even from suffering and distress*. It is this power which in the Bible is closely connected to discourse on the recreative work of the Holy Spirit."[74]

---

69. Pinnock, *Most Moved Mover*, 148.

70. Zeeb, "Open Theism and the Problem of Theodicy," 314.

71. Pinnock, "Systematic Theology," 115.

72. Pinnock, "Systematic Theology," 115.

73. Welker, "Theodicy, Creation, and Suffering," 282. "Ground of all being" was Paul Tillich's favorite name for God (Spong, *Rescuing the Bible from Fundamentalism*, 241).

74. Welker, "Theodicy, Creation, and Suffering," 285; author's use of italics.

Welker emphasizes that God created human beings and endowed them with some power; at the same time, however, they are also transient, finite, and mortal beings that live at the cost of other living beings. God does not spare them the experiences of suffering and death that all other creatures share. On the contrary, it demonstrates their powerlessness and helplessness in the face of the challenges that life poses. At the same time, they encounter God in God's power and goodness in their daily provision as well as the Spirit's immanence. In a world characterized by racism, genderism, injustice, heartless exploitation, and falseness, they share in the power of the Spirit that steadily transforms and restores the world to justice, mercy, love, and truth as an introduction to the eschatological future.[75]

God as the Immutable

Traditional theology viewed God as changeless, unchangeable, or immutable, based on several biblical passages (like Exod 3:14; Mal 3:6; Jas 1:17; Num 23:19; 1 Sam 15:29). God does not change in several respects: God cannot fail to exist and cannot die, like God's biological creatures (Pss 9:7; 90:2; 1 Tim 1:17; 6:16). God is also completely reliable in divine behavior (Mal 3:6). God is not fickle or capricious, and God's love (also called *hesed*, apart from other Hebrew terms) implies steadfastness, loyalty, and faithfulness. God's love never changes. God also cannot repent or change the divine mind (Num 23:19; 1 Sam 15:29). God also cannot lie but always tells the truth. Everything about God is changeless.

However, this view is one-sided because it does not account for the change that occurs in different aspects of the divine being. Indeed, God's existence, God's nature, and God's character are changeless. In God's concrete relation to the world, however, God is dynamic because, in the divine response to what happens in the world, divine decisions about what to do in the world and divine actions within the world changes can and do occur. These changes are because what happens to God's creatures and how they respond to it deeply affect God.[76] While God's love never changes, God's experience must change to do justice to divine love. Therefore, it is imperative to distinguish between God's unchanging nature and his dynamic experience.

75. Welker, "Theodicy, Creation, and Suffering," 291–92.
76. Rice, "Biblical Support for a New Perspective," 37.

Divine immutability is defended by referring to the name God used to identify with in Exodus 3:14, "I AM WHO I AM," commonly interpreted as "I am the self-existent one." YHWH was a word that derived its meaning and its power from the verb "to be."[77] However, Wolfhart Pannenberg correctly asserts that the name rather expresses God's freedom to act; it relates divine identity to divine action. The revelation of this name occurs at a crucial moment in salvation history, introducing God's deliverance of the elected people, Israel, from Egypt. The name asserts that God "will show himself in his historical acts."[78] What God is saying with this name is that God will be there for Israel.[79] Or, as Richard Rice puts it, "I am the one you can always count on."[80] God's name emphasizes the dynamic quality of divine activity rather than its static quality, leading Adrio König to argue that to describe God's being in terms of disengagement, remoteness, self-sufficiency, and the ground or origin of all that is does not do justice to the biblical message.[81]

Traditionally, predestination and divine foreknowledge are interpreted in terms of divine changelessness. It accepts that the future is entirely foreseeable to God, and "foreknowledge" and "predestination" indicate that God determines the entire course of history (or at least substantial portions of it). God chooses, wills, or ordains certain things to occur, sometimes as long ago as when the world originated. God's people are the object of divine calling, foreknowledge, and predestination (Gen 12:1–2; 15:18–19; 25:23; Jer 1:5; Eph 1:4–5; Rom 8:28–30; 9:10–13; 1 Pet 1:2). Even those who oppose God also serve divine purposes without knowing it (Exod 4:21; 8:23; 9:16; John 13:18; 17:12; Acts 1:16). One of the most influential exponents of the doctrine of predestination was John Calvin. He asserted that God's election of individuals to salvation is based solely on God's will and decision in eternity. He did not accept that God could see what individuals would choose for faith in Christ and then elects them.

In his view, God foresees all future events for the simple reason that God decreed that they should take place.[82] That implies that God also

---

77. Spong, *Rescuing the Bible from Fundamentalism*, 241.
78. Pannenberg, *Systematic Theology*, 1:205.
79. Murray, *Problem of God Yesterday and Today*, 8–15.
80. Rice, "Biblical Support for a New Perspective," 39.
81. König, *Here Am I*, 43.
82. Calvin, *Institutes* 3.23.6; 3.23.7; 3.21.5.

decreed that the first human couple would choose to be disobedient to God's command not to eat of the tree's fruits. With the resultant effect, all their descendants are born totally depraved and unable to do good. Is God then responsible for sin, as seems the logical conclusion to these assertions? Calvin replied by defining human freedom to sin in compatibilist terms that God works through secondary causes. Compatibilism states that two propositions are accurate at the same time, that God is absolutely sovereign, but that God's sovereignty never functions in such a way that human responsibility is minimized or mitigated. They have the freedom to rebel against God and disobey God's commandments or to obey and honor God. However, they choose evil because they are morally responsible beings. They are also held accountable and responsible for their own decisions. However, that does not imply that God is absolutely contingent and dependent on humans to act.[83] The implication is that God does not directly determine the events where the first couple sinned or the decisions people make, but God only establishes the causes by which they come about. In this way, Calvin tried to absolve God from blame and responsibility for the existence of sin and evil.[84] He warned that Christians should not question God's will for their lives. He referred to Romans 9:20–21, which discourages readers from arguing with God about these matters: Like a potter, God has the right to decide what God wants to make with an individual, either an object for special or ordinary use. God always has good reasons for whatever God wills and chooses about humans' lives. In the personal relations between God and an individual, God is the cause, and faith is the effect.[85] If God had predestined a human being to salvation, faith would follow. The individual is never an active agent in the process of regeneration.[86]

The result of such argumentation is that God can never change the divine mind. God can never repent of any decision God had taken because it would contradict God's immutable and impassible will and foreknowledge, determined by God's predestination.

However, there is other biblical evidence that God's will does not guarantee that the divine desire is always served. For instance, God is "not wanting any to perish, but all to come to repentance" (2 Pet 3:9;

---

83. Carson, *How Long, O Lord?*, 177.
84. Calvin, *Institutes* 1.16.3.
85. Calvin, *Institutes* 1.17.1.
86. Sanders, "Historical Considerations," 80.

see 1 Tim 2:4; Titus 2:11). However, not all are or will be saved. Some human beings set themselves against God for eternity (Matt 21:41–46; Rev 20:14–15; cf. Matt 7:13–14). In other words, that God foreknows or predestines something is no guarantee that it will happen. That God elected and called a specific people, Israel, does not imply that all Israelites responded correspondingly, as the eighth-century Assyrian exile of the northern kingdom that led to the extinction of Israel as a nation suggests.[87] The Old Testament depicts God's disappointment and frustration with Israel in the many prophecies that preceded their destruction as a separate people.

At times God acts by fiat, directly causing something to happen, like the parting of the Red Sea when delivering Israel from Egyptian oppression. That does not imply that God determined all events in Israel's life. God's will for them was to serve God; their forty-year stay in the wilderness before conquering the promised land as punishment for their disobedience shows that God can be frustrated in the execution of the divine will. God cannot achieve divine objectives unilaterally when the human decision is presupposed; God requires human cooperation. Free creatures can decide what to do and, to a great extent, what occurs in their lives. History is not something that runs the course that God decides; both God and human beings contribute. That God calls human beings to live in the right relationship with God through Christ similarly does not imply that God directs how individuals decide about it.

It is crucial to see that divine election is concerned with a corporate call to service to understand the biblical notion of election. God called prophets, kings, and prophets to specific tasks, but these were the exception. This leads William Klein to conclude that because plural language dominates texts related to the election, it shows that "God has chosen the church as a body rather than the specific individuals who populate that body,"[88] to serve, perform tasks, functions, and ministries in divine service. Klein's conclusion is, "Election is not God's choice of a restricted number of individuals whom he wills to save, but the description of that corporate body which, in Christ, he is saving."[89]

---

87. Albertz, *Israel in Exile*, 2, suggests that the largest group of inhabitants of the northern kingdom were assimilated while a small group probably linked up with the Judean exiles.

88. Klein, *New Chosen People*, 258–59.

89. Klein, *New Chosen People*, 266.

Limitations of Language: Theological Concepts and the Essence of God

Theodicy requires that one thinks about and reflects on the Bible in such a way that one brings it to bear on this aspect of human life, of suffering. Because our hermeneutics determines our interpretation of the Bible, as argued above, one must also reflect on one's hermeneutics as an introduction to defining one's theodicean theories. All human language by its nature uses words that serve as symbols to convey meaning and requires hermeneutics that determines the rules for reading and understanding. In the case of biblical writings that represent the words and thoughts of people using languages that are not in use anymore and representing cultures that we do not understand fully, sound exegesis is irreplaceable. There is a vast distance of time and culture between contemporary readers and the ancient authors; to try to understand the meaning of their thoughts requires that we wrestle with words, syntax, and literary forms which express their ideas. Understanding these ideas requires that we hear them within the author's and the hearers'/readers' cultural contexts and presuppositions (these may even differ between authors and listeners). It is no easy task to understand in every case what they intended by their words.[90]

That is not the end of believers' problems in interpreting the language of the Bible. To speak about God is *per se* a difficulty because we talk about one who is living in a dimension that falls outside our frame of reference. We cannot see God because God's essence does not accord with the dimension we live in and the state we find ourselves in.

The limitations of language are discussed in this subsection in terms of several aspects that demonstrate these limitations, such as God's *kenosis*, holiness, existence in eternity, God's unpronounceable name (YHWH), existence as a triune God, the gift of glossolalia, and the scandal of the cross.

To talk about how God revealed the divine self to human beings in the history of salvation is less complicated because we repeat what biblical authors said about their perceptions and how they understood God's word (or revelation). However, then the hermeneutical issues mentioned in the previous paragraphs find themselves on our agenda.

Pentecostals emphasize that the Bible should be interpreted as a book of testimonies about people's encounters with God. In the Pentecostal

---

90. See discussion in Fee, *Gospel and Spirit*, 25–27.

world, testimonies have always played a crucial role because their religion is based on their charismatic experiences rather than their theological reflection about the Bible and the charismatic encounters it describes. The Bible serves for them as a kind of menu, explaining what God wants to do for humans, the way God works, and what contemporary readers or listeners may expect when they encounter God. For that reason, they reinterpret and redeploy biblical language when they testify in their worship services and prayer meetings about their encounters with God and leave ample room that God may act in different ways than the Bible describes. They use biblical language because everyday speech does not provide the jargon necessary to talk about their charismatic experiences. The biblical events served as precedents for their expectation in seeking the face of God and defining what they experience during those moments. They turn to the biblical world to make sense of their encounters.

However, when it comes to speaking about the essence of God, we can say no more than what God's character consists of. God is love, and good, and faithful, and just, and powerful, etc. Here as well, it is vitally important to realize that the terms that we employ to describe God's characteristics bring down and lower God to the level where we understand these terms. What we understand by these terms is necessarily determined by our experiences and perceptions. If we are not careful, we may be degrading and even debasing God's character by using references that do not do full justice to the character and nature of God, even depicting an idol instead of the transcendent God presented in the Bible.

We must understand that for God to communicate with creatures of God's creation, *kenosis* was required from God. *Kenosis* refers to the relinquishment of some of God's transcendence, glory, and attributes to enable human beings to perceive something about God by bringing God into the sphere of human reflection. Jesus' incarnation was a form of *kenosis* (from Greek "emptying") and his suffering and death on the cross as well, to such an extent that God abandoned the divine self on the cross, found in Jesus' words, "*Eli, Eli, lema sabachthani?*," that is, "My God, my God, why have you forsaken me?" (Matt 27:46). The context was the darkness over the whole earth for three hours that accompanied Jesus' death, indicating the God-forsakenness of the world during Jesus' crucifixion, and the tearing of the curtain of the temple just after his death, indicating the opening of God's presence to people in the world (Matt 27:45, 51). It was followed by the resurrection of (some of) "the saints" and their appearance to many in Jerusalem (Matt 27:52–53).

The other side of the *kenosis* is that all language about God is also subjected to the *accommodatio Dei*. To reveal the divine self to human beings, God had to accommodate God's divinity and essence in order to become comprehensible to human beings. God does not and cannot speak according to God's nature; if God did, no human being would have been able to understand it, writes John Calvin.[91] God had to stoop down to reach human beings and communicate in human words. The whole incarnation of Jesus is *accommodatio Dei*. The Father is boundless but becomes bounded in the Son to accommodate human capacity. If this did not happen, human beings would have been swallowed up by the immensity of God's glory and holiness.[92] God, as it were, transfigured to partake in the incarnation.[93] Calvin emphasizes that it belongs to the essence of God's revelation that it is given in the form of accommodation because it comes to human beings.

To understand God's *kenosis*, it is imperative to know what God's holiness consists of. The Hebrew word for "to be holy" (*qadash*) is derived from the root *qad*, which means "to cut or to separate."[94] The term is applied mainly to God but also to the persons or things dedicated to God's service. Their holiness is derived from their association with God. Holiness is not primarily a moral or religious quality, such as love, grace, and mercy, but a term that refers to God's essence that also applies to a position or relationship existing between God and some person or thing.

A. A. Hodge says that the holiness of God is not one attribute among others in God but rather a general term representing the "conception of God's consummate perfection and total glory." It refers to God's infinite moral perfection (Lev 11:44; Ps 145:17) that crowns infinite intelligence and power (Isa 6:3; Ps 22:3; Rev 4:8).[95] It denotes that God is absolutely distinct or totally different from all God's creatures. God cannot be compared to anything that God created; human beings can, to a certain extent, be compared to God, as far as they have been made in God's image or likeness. Holiness refers to one of God's transcendental attributes, to God's supreme perfection and goodness. God's holiness is co-extensive with and applicable to everything that can be predicated of God (Exod

---

91. Calvin, *Opera Quae Supersunt Omnia*, 26.387, 478.
92. Calvin, *Institutes* 2.6.4.
93. Calvin, "Sermon on Job 1:6–8," 3.
94. Berkhof, *Systematic Theology*, 73.
95. Quoted in Cairns, *Dictionary of Theological Terms*, 211–12.

15:11; 1 Sam 2:2; Isa 57:15; Hos 11:9). Rudolf Otto, in *Das Heilige*, asserts that holiness is most essential in the numinous God. God cannot be thought of conceptually but can be understood only as the one defined by "absolute unapproachability," "absolute overpoweringness," or "awful majesty" that reminds human beings of their absolute nothingness, a "creature-consciousness," or "creature-feeling," leading to absolute self-abasement.[96] In arguing about the limitations that language sets to humans speaking about God, the concept of God's holiness should be kept in mind. It implies that God exists in a dimension that human beings cannot access or comprehend, that the Totally Different exists as an essence in a state that falls outside the human frame of reference. When speaking about God's involvement with human beings, creation, and the occurrence of evil, it should be considered.

As discussed above, the Tetragrammaton (YHWH) with which God revealed the divine self to Moses also refers to God's essence. The name is unpronounceable; today, no one knows how it should be pronounced, and Jews never use the word but instead refers to God by name as "the Name" (*Hashem*). To obey Exodus 20:7, a part of the Ten Commandments, they never use the word itself: "You shall not make wrongful use of the name of the LORD your God, for the LORD will not acquit anyone who misuses his name." According to Exodus 3, Moses responded to God's call to free Israel from Egyptian slavery by asking, "If I come to the Israelites and say to them, 'The God of your ancestors has sent me to you,' and they ask me, 'What is his name?' what shall I say to them?" God said to Moses, "I AM WHO I AM." He said further, "Thus you shall say to the Israelites, 'I Am has sent me to you'" (vv. 13–14). YHWH is the God of Abraham, Isaac, and Jacob, the ancestors of Israel. God adds, "This is my name forever, and this my title for all generations." God is the one who has been from all time, is, and will be, from a human perspective. As the one who is, God exists for an indeterminate period of time.

The same is implied by referring to God's state in terms of eternity. J. A. McGuire-Moushon and Rachel Klippenstein define "eternity" as the concept of endless time, or more fully, of being beyond time; only God is intrinsically eternal.[97] The Hebrew word ' *ôlām* translates as a "long time." The singular word can indicate the remainder of a person's lifetime, i.e., as long as someone lives (e.g., Exod 21:6; Deut 15:17; 1 Sam 1:22; 27:12).

---

96. Berkhof, *Systematic Theology*, 73.

97. See also discussion above. McGuire-Moushon and Klippenstein, "Eternity."

In some contexts, it can mean "unending," and it is often used to describe the attributes of God. It can also mean "forever;" humans were banished from Eden in Genesis 3 so that they would not take fruit from the tree of life and live "forever." The term for "a long time" is frequently used with a word meaning "lasting time" (*'ad*) in constructions such as "to *'ôlām* and *'ad*" (e.g., Exod 15:18; Ps 9:5), "a long time ago" (e.g., Josh 24:2; Isa 46:9), or "for a long time, since long ago" (e.g., Isa 42:14; 57:11; 64:4). The Greek term translates as "age" or "eternal, long-lasting" (plural) and refers to "the ancient past, the distant future, or a long time."

"Eternity" is generally understood as endless time, but instead, it is essential to realize that it refers to eternity's infinite nature that transcends time. God is eternal (e.g., Gen 21:33; Ps 93:2; Isa 40:28) and, as the creator of all things, must transcend all God has created, including time. God can give this substance to people in the divine ability to transcend time; the New Testament refers to it as "eternal life," promised to those who believe in Jesus (e.g., Mark 10:30; John 3:15–16; 17:2–3; Rom 6:23). What is eternal derives its quality ultimately from God, who is eternal. This remark explains Jesus' definition of "eternal life" in his prayer in John 17, that "this is eternal life, that they may know you, the only true God, and Jesus Christ whom you have sent" (v. 3). "Eternal life" then refers to a quality of life that the one receives who believes in Jesus, a life that does not end with death but continues within the divine dimension where space and time cease to exist.

God's holiness also has an ethical aspect that consists of separation, a separation from moral evil or sin. God can have no communion with sin (Job 34:10; Hab 1:13). However, ethical holiness is not merely negative, as separation from sin, but its positive element is moral excellence or ethical perfection. Human beings can respond to God's presence only by feeling utter insignificance and awe before the holy God, resulting in the consciousness of their sin (Isa 6:5) and repentance.

God's nature or essence is also demonstrated by the concept and doctrine of the Trinity developed in the Christian church. Although the term does not appear in the Bible, the concept is based on several emphatic assertions that are found throughout the biblical writings, that there is only one God (Deut 6:4; Isa 43:10; 46:9; Rom 3:30; 1 Cor 8:4; Jas 2:19); that Jesus is God's incarnate Son (Matt 1:23; John 1:1; Rom 9:5; Col 2:9; Titus 2:13–14; Heb 1:1–3); and that the Holy Spirit acts in the world (Acts 5:3–4; 28:25–27; 2 Cor 3:7–18). The Father, Son, and Spirit possess all the attributes of God.[98] From 325 to 787 CE, the church deliberated about the doctrine at seven ecumenical councils. In writing about the Trinity, Augustine admits that humanity must ultimately regard any exploration of the doctrine as being handicapped by insufficient language and, when necessary, be content to rest in what God has revealed of divine mystery.[99] The term serves to cover the church's embarrassment in attempting to speak about an incomprehensibly great and awesome God.

According to Pentecostal theology, human beings find it difficult to speak about or to God, leading to the observation that the spiritual gift of speaking in tongues (glossolalia) is helpful in worshiping God. For the worshiper, it is difficult to find the right and suitable words and concepts to worship and praise God in a manner that does justice to God. For instance, Wolfgang Vondey explains that because Pentecostals operate at the limits of speech because of their practice of emphasizing testimonies and stories of their encounters with God, worship, and praise, they are not comfortable with the definitions, concepts, propositions, theses, systems, philosophies, and methodologies that characterize and dominate the world of Western theology.[100] In their worship services and spirituality, the "heavenly language" serves as a means to express the most profound awe of finding themselves in the presence of God in words and expressions that they ascribe to the Holy Spirit. In this regard, Pentecostal speaking in tongues serves as a prayer and worship "metalanguage" that allows the worshipper to enter God's presence and worship God intuitively and affectively, bypassing the intellectual for the moment. Speaking and singing in tongues provides for an encounter with God that involves the entire human being.[101] This is how they interpret Paul's teaching about a negative assessment of the gift of speaking in tongues in the worship service. In 1 Corinthians 14:18–19, the apostle writes, "I thank God that I speak in tongues more than all of you; nevertheless, in church I would rather speak five words with my mind, in order to instruct others also, than ten thousand words in a tongue." Paul confines the practice of glossolalia mainly to the individual's private worship practices.

The most effective way to speak about and to the incomprehensible God who inhabits another dimension than ours and as a substance and

---

98. Meeks, "Trinity."
99. Augustine, "De Trinitate" 15.
100. Vondey, *Pentecostalism*, 121.
101. McGee, "Brought into the Sphere of the Supernatural," 10.

essence that fall outside the human frame of reference is by means of stuttering. In fact, if we do not stutter when we attempt to speak about God, we may be sure that we refer to our own image and idea of God. This is because human language fails to define the One who defines our lives and reality.

The scandal of the cross also illustrates the limitation of language. The author of 1 Corinthians 1 argues that he proclaims the gospel, instead of eloquent wisdom, to prevent the cross of Christ being emptied of its power. He then explains that the message about the cross is "foolishness to those who are perishing, but to us who are being saved it is the power of God" (vv. 17–18). In discussing the theodicy of the New Testament in chapter 3, reference was made to how Roman citizens viewed the crucifixion of habitual criminals as their deserved fate, probably the most repulsive way to die. To consider the cross of Jesus not as scandalous but as a redemptive act as the Christians did seemed to them as impossible, ridiculous, and superstitious.

In considering the cross in legal terms, one may use the philosophical argument: Why would an omnipotent divine being require human beings to atone for their sin by sacrificing their lives? Why did God need Jesus to die in their stead to save them from the just judgment for their sins? Why did God not just forgive them, as Jesus taught his followers to pray: "Forgive us our debts, as we also have forgiven our debtors" (Matt 6:12)? For example, Bishop Spong discusses the issue and concludes by stating his view: "I do not believe in a God whose inner need for justice is satisfied when his son is nailed to a cross. I regard the substitutionary version of the atonement as a barbaric attack on both the truth of God and the meaning of human life."[102] That Jesus should suffer such a shameful, scandalous, and horrible death might seem unconvincing to someone who argues that it seems unnecessary for God to take such an action to save people if God could have redeemed them as God did in the case of liberating Israel from Egypt. To respond to the argument is to speak about God's essence or substance and motivations. It seems that human language and logic are just too limited to argue the case convincingly.

---

102. Spong, *Rescuing the Bible from Fundamentalism*, 69.

God and Suffering

How do Pentecostals respond to the question of God's role and contribution to a world characterized by evil, disease and suffering, and tragedies? Where is God when a young child dies after suffering horrendously from cancer or is being raped and beaten to death in ethnic conflict? Many observations of suffering clash with human sensibilities of what is right and good. While Christians believe that God is working actively in the world, cares for them, answers their prayers, and that God is the source of goodness and justice, how do they explain the absurdity of suffering and death? Pentecostals have traditionally responded by praying and seeking God's intervention, not accepting that God's providence would not include an answer to their prayers. As Harold Kushner notes, leaving the room that God would not answer necessarily leads to the unacceptable perception that God is too weak to deal with some afflictions and hardships.[103] To live with suffering as an unexplained mystery in the power of the Holy Spirit, to accept that believers might have to go through a dark night of the soul, or might suffer from depression fall outside the Pentecostal frame of reference.[104] "Pentecostals have no place in their schema for the dark night."[105]

Christians believe that the most significant event of the history of salvation is the incarnation of Jesus Christ, his ministry to love, heal, and forgive, and his crucifixion and death that was a ransom for sin. The answer to the question of where God is while people suffer is found in Christ. God is healing and repairing the world, and people, in Jesus. While he was living on earth, people in need found help in Jesus' presence and touch. When he died, his agonized cry was directed to God, "My God, my God, why have you forsaken me?" These words come from the psalm of lament, Psalm 22, which continues with the complaint, "I cry by day, but you do not answer; and by night, but find no rest" (v. 2).[106]

---

103. Kushner, *When Bad Things Happen to Good People*.

104. Fettke and Dusing, "Practical Pentecostal Theodicy?," 170. See also Allan, "Sertraline, Suffering, and the Spirit."

105. Chan, *Pentecostal Theology*, 75–76.

106. While the ancestors trusted God and God delivered them, the psalmist thinks that perhaps he is not worth God's attention: "I am a worm, and not human; scorned by others, and despised by the people" (v. 6). Still, the psalmist trusts God because God cared for the psalmist since birth (vv. 9–10).

God in Christ identified with human pain and suffering, and in Jesus' crucifixion achieves victory over it.

As the Word of God, Jesus reveals God. The best way to learn to know somebody is by listening to and observing the person. For example, Jesus' proclamation and behavior towards marginalized people revealed God's will and character. He became the bridge between God and human beings, and his brutal death of atonement demonstrated God's heart for them. He died to bring salvation for all human beings who became separated from God due to their sin and rebellion.

In facing death, Jesus used a lament to verbalize his deep emotions, identifying with all people who experience suffering and death in its diverse forms. Later in the chapter, it is submitted that the lament serves well to relate to innocent and incomprehensible suffering. Jesus faced death, the challenge to all existence, and experienced the God-forsakenness felt by the many others who share suffering and death. As God-with-us, he became one or united with every human who is challenged by the adversities that characterize the reality of brokenness. In identifying with human beings, he also identified with their state of being anti-God due to their choice to disobey God, demonstrating the grace that Adam and Eve, Noah and his family, Abraham, and Israel had experienced in Old Testament times. God did not write off human beings who had rejected God for the whole of history; divine mercy leaves room for restoration and healing, culminating in the promise of a new heaven and earth (Rev 21).[107]

There is not anything that human beings experience that Jesus did not identify with in his life of betrayal, humiliation, rejection, crucifixion, burial, and ascension. As God with Us, Jesus' life demonstrates God's involvement in the lives of human beings, that God has not abandoned the creation. In Jesus, God became like human beings so that human beings can become like God, regaining the image of God.

The restoration of the earth has not occurred yet, but Jesus became the establishment of the reign of God; his resurrection demonstrated how God would finally conquer death and sin. The answer to theodicy is in the God who revealed the divine self to human beings, showing an incarnate God who suffers alongside and with people and creation. God's suffering does not bring an immediate end to suffering but guarantees creation's restoration, redemption, and healing. The final answer to

---

107. See the discussion of eschatology later in this chapter.

theodicy is for that reason found in Christians' eschatological hope of a new creation where God reigns.

The answer to the question of where God is when people suffer is clear. God is closer to people who suffer than the people are to themselves; the broken body of Jesus on the cross demonstrates God's solidarity with people. The resurrected body that is not subject to the limitations of time and space shows that suffering will not have the final say.

A theology that emphasizes the significance of the cross does not invite those who are suffering from pondering the hidden things of God, writes Tullian Tchividjian. Instead of asking "Why me?" it brings the sufferer face-to-face with the suffering Servant, in contrast to a "theology of glory" that emphasizes the Christian as a conqueror.[108]

What Pentecostals need is a new view of God to discount for the suffering of believers despite their faith in God's promises, a view of God that does not confine God to what only some parts of the Bible state about God, and trying to manipulate and domesticate God into doing what Pentecostals "demand" God should do for them.[109] In 2 Corinthians 1, the author begins the letter with a song of thanksgiving after his current afflictions and shows that there are different ways that sufferers may look at their suffering. Next, he testifies to God's consolation in his time of affliction (vv. 3–4). Paul does not qualify the affliction but writes that what he experienced in Asia nearly crushed him to death. He despaired of life itself, and it felt as if he had received the death sentence (vv. 8–9). However, he learned not to rely on himself in the affliction but on God, who raises the dead. Now he knows how to encourage his fellow believers in their affliction: he is able "to console those who are in any affliction with the consolation with which we ourselves are consoled by God" (v. 4). "If we are being afflicted, it is for your consolation and salvation; if we are being consoled, it is for your consolation, which you experience when you patiently endure the same sufferings that we are also suffering" (v. 6). God provides suffering people comfort so that the comfort they receive from God can bless other suffering people.

Pentecostals' claim that all people should always be healed in reply to faith and prayer denies that God works in humans as individual people in ways that may, in some cases, be incomprehensible. Reference was made to Paul's experience that his profound spiritual experiences were followed

---

108. Tchividjian, *Glorious Ruin*, 159.
109. Fettke and Dusing, "Practical Pentecostal Theodicy?," 171.

by afflictions that threatened his life. Even though he prayed three times that God should remove them, he did not receive a positive answer. In the same vein, Paul refers to Epaphroditus, who was sick unto death, but God had mercy on him (Phil 2:27), and Trophimus, whom Paul left ill in Miletus (2 Tim 4:20). Paul did not blame them for remaining sick or refer to some unconfessed sin that might have caused the illness. The discussion about Romans 8 also showed how Christians share in Christ's suffering when they experience weakness and hardship (v. 17), while the Spirit prays for them in such a time (vv. 26–27). What Pentecostals need is a more nuanced view that leaves God the room to work uniquely in everyone's life. For instance, in the case of Joseph's hardships as a slave in Egypt brought on by his brothers, he explains that when his brothers intended to do him harm and sold him to slave traders, and he ended up in Egypt, God intended it for good (Gen 50:20). Joseph did suffer at the hands of his evil brothers but not because of them; God was unfolding a much larger plan that changed the course of Israel's life and fate.

It is not only arrogant to claim that God has to do what some parts of the Bible seemingly promise, but it denies the reality that God works in a myriad of mysterious ways. For some, God's intervention includes deliverance from their hardship and affliction. For others, it introduces a period of testing and disciplining.[110] That evil continues to exist in the world no Pentecostal would deny. Rather than denying that its influence on believers is limited unconditionally by believers' faith, they should consider addressing evil's presence in the world. The cross of Christ is still the response to the problem of evil. The urgency of their participation in the *missio Dei* should encourage Pentecostals to continue with the task of reaching all people with the good news of Jesus Christ. At the same time, Pentecostals can address causes of evil and suffering as far as possible by becoming imaginatively involved in job creation, healthcare, education, care of the poor and elderly, etc.

Why did God not prevent the suffering of Jews in pogroms through the ages or the *Shoah* during the Second World War? The inability of Job's friends to justify God in the distress that Job experienced warns contemporary believers to state that the best answer to the question is the admittance that the answer is not known to human beings. We cannot comprehend the essence of God. In discussing Jewish reaction to Jesus and the good news his life and death brought, the author of Romans 11

---

110. Fettke and Dusing, "Practical Pentecostal Theodicy?," 172.

argues that God's gifts and calling are irrevocable, implying that all Israel will eventually be saved (vv. 25–29). The impression that such mercy made on the author leads him to sing about God's goodness, including the words, "O the depth of the riches and wisdom and knowledge of God! How unsearchable are his judgments and how inscrutable his ways!" (v. 33). Because God's ways and decisions are inscrutable, mysterious, and incomprehensible, except insofar as the revelations in the history of salvation are concerned, believers should limit themselves to the language of restraint, recognizing their powerlessness and inability in speaking about God. Our silence is restless, but it is also holy, since we acknowledge faith in the God in whom we entrust our future. When we suffer, we verbalize our emotions in psalms of lament, confirming the existence of the God of goodness and justice. Daniel Castelo states that Pentecostals need to cultivate an appreciation for the role of apophaticism, the view that God is both indescribable and inconceivable, or negative theology as a form of thinking and practice that attempts to approach the divine by negation, can play in their theological endeavors. They need theological initiatives that attempt to speak about God through negation, stating what cannot be said about God rather than self-assuredly speaking about the inexplicable One. The best way to reply to questions about God and suffering that we do not know the answers to is to keep silent.[111] Castelo argues that Pentecostals should resist their urge to exercise power by controlling and narrating their experiences to solve and figure out why they suffer. Jesus' life serves as a faithful performance before the forces of suffering, pain, and evil, empowering Christians to bear their own pain and suffering by engaging in longsuffering so as to witness to the Spirit's steadfast presence in the many dimensions of life, including suffering.[112] When the Spirit empowers them to endure suffering and pain, they believe that these do not determine their lives' meaning and significance. While many people find pain and suffering as reasons to question or reject God, Christians exhibit their love for God by their longsuffering.[113]

Is the restoration and healing of creation postponed to the time after the second coming of Christ? Do Christians have to wait for the new earth, or may they pray for healing and redemption in their present situation? Some Pentecostals separated themselves from the world, living with

---

111. Castelo, "What If Miracles Don't Happen?," 243.
112. Castelo, "What If Miracles Don't Happen?," 244.
113. Castelo, "What If Miracles Don't Happen?," 245.

an other-worldly orientation.[114] However, before Jesus left the earth, he promised, according to the testimony of John, that he would not leave his disciples orphaned but would be returning to them in the person of another advocate or *paraclete*, the Spirit of truth that would remain in them (John 14:18, 17). As Jesus' life and ministry entailed the confrontation with evil and suffering and its defeat, God continues with the restoration and healing of creation (integral to God's *missio Dei*, or mission of God). God uses the agency of the church for this work in the world (described in Mark 16:14–18; Matt 28:19–20; Luke 24:36–49; John 20:10–23; Acts 1:6–8). As the representative of the church that is the body of Christ on earth, the local faith community retells the Jesus stories to keep the memory of Jesus alive. Its ministry is the embodiment of God's love.[115] Anointed with the Spirit of Jesus, they continue Jesus' ministry in their preaching and teaching, healing, and deliverance. It displays the first fruits of the reign of God in a new world, depicting the hope for the world.

At least, the church is supposed to love the world in God's stead. That did not always happen, as many events in the church's history demonstrate. Instead of revealing the face of God in the world, its history is linked to human history in general, characterized by sin and rebellion against God. However, the *missio Dei* continues despite human failure. God works without and outside the church and through faith communities that remain faithful to their calling as representatives of God in the world (Gen 1:26–27). Daniel Castelo emphasizes that the restored image of God in human beings cannot be limited to faithful believers but to all people who contribute by doing good, listening to, and caring for others, including the marginalized and needy, and respecting the dignity of all people without exception. Christians confess that Christ is the only way to God; whether God will reject Buddhists or Muslims who lived a good life because they did not go through Christ to God is an issue that they leave to God to decide. No human being ever ceases to be a creature of God, created in God's image and equipped with the capacity to restore that image in part (contra Calvinist teaching).

The discussion challenges the faith community to concern itself with its primary purpose and business, consisting of the world's restoration and healing. It includes the proclamation of the good news that sins are forgiven through Christ's atonement but also through the feeding of

---

114. See discussion in Nel, "Pentecostalism and the Early Church."
115. Castelo, *Theological Theodicy*, 66.

hungry people, involvement in creating jobs, caring for the sick and elderly, and caring for a world threatened by climate change, partly due to human abuse of the environment.

The Example of Job

All theodicean questions from a Christian perspective at one point or another refer to the book of Job, which is dedicated to the subject of the suffering of a believer and his family. The book addresses the loss of loved ones, wealth, health, and various persons' desire to make sense of why it happened. However, to find in the book a modern theodicy is anachronistic, as David Castelo explains.[116] What the book of Job does is rather the opposite, by deconstructing theodicy rather than supporting it.[117] David Burrell interprets the three rounds of exchanges between Job and his friends to demonstrate the observation that Job's friends explain what happened to Job in order to justify God. At the same time, Job rejects their explanations out of hand. In this way, Job calls into question the logic that the covenant implies a formula or simple set of transactions that consists of the set rule and formula: Do good and blessings will follow, or do evil and difficulties, diseases, and mental illness will follow.[118]

By the time Job's friends arrive and showe their empathetic support of Job, readers have been informed that Job is blameless and upright, a man who fears God, keeps God's commandments, and does not do evil (Job 1:1). The friends' arguments that Job's difficulties result from his sins because they represent God's punishment or God's discipline, in line with the thinking represented by the Deuteronomist Historian, do not hold water. Burrell concludes that the primary function of the book of Job in the Hebrew canon is to correct "mechanical readings" of the Deuteronomist Historian that "remain heedless of the graceful divine initiative the covenant embodies."[119] The difference between the work of the Deuteronomist Historian and the character of Job is that the Deuteronomist refers to Israel, as applied by the prophets who warned Israel of impending doom and exile for their disobedience and disloyalty to God, while Job is an individual. While God gave the people of Israel what they deserved,

---

116. Castelo, *Theological Theodicy*, 22.
117. As Burrell (*Deconstructing Theodicy*, 16) explains.
118. Burrell, *Deconstructing Theodicy*, 16–17.
119. Burrell, *Deconstructing Theodicy*, 125.

God treats every individual in a unique manner related to the individual's choices. God permits what has happened to Job in a real sense, but God does not will it.[120]

What is important to realize is that the deliberations of the friends, as well as Job, illustrate the limits of all human theodicean reflection. Job's friends represent the alternative biblical theodicean explanations that serve as justifications for God. In the process, they certainly do not console and comfort Job as they intended to (Job 2:11).

In Burrell's opinion, Eliphaz the Temanite is the "dogmatist" because he talks about God and God's ways so that he comes to Job from an "above" vantage point. Eliphaz acts in the assurance that he views Job's situation from God's angle, and that is why he knows exactly the reason for Job's suffering: Job is facing God's reprobation. "Job, God is disciplining you" (Job 5:17).

In Burrell's categorization, Bildad the Shuhite is the "jurist," raising the question of the justice of Job's response to the suffering. For him, God is the ultimate guarantor of justice: God cannot pervert justice or pervert the right in any way (Job 8:3). Hence, his advice to Job is, "For that reason, Job, the only way back is to seek and make supplication to God and be pure and upright. Only then will God restore you to your rightful place" (Job 8:5–6).

In Burrell's eyes, Zophar the Naamathite is the "philosopher" because he is concerned with the epistemological question about human knowledge of the divine. No one can find out the deep things or find the limit of God (Job 11:7). "Job, you deserve the pain and suffering because God is punishing you fittingly and justly. God's justice is always perfect, and God's ways are not humankind's ways, and your insistence on being innocent is nothing else than a denial of God."

The three friends' explanations can be found in many contemporary believers' logic when discussing suffering, whether their own or that of other people. Many Christians use a text to explain it, such as Romans 8:28, which states that all things work together for those who love God and are called according to God's purpose. The text seems to suggest a kind of determinism in line with the calculus that the Deuteronomist Historian supports, that God works all things in believers' lives according to their just deserts; the book of Job subverts this logic. Daniel Castelo argues that the parable of the vineyard laborers in Matthew 20:1–16 and

---

120. Castelo, *Theological Theodicy*, 22.

Luke 13:1–5 subverts Romans 8:28 in its turn, while Jesus' suffering represents the most significant subversion of this logic.[121] Job's subversion is supported by the unraveling of the book when the "voice from the whirlwind" repudiates the four friends and seemingly hails Job. YHWH tells Eliphaz that God's wrath is kindled against the three friends because they have not spoken what is right, as Job has. For that reason, they need to bring seven bulls and seven rams to Job and offer for themselves a burnt offering while Job prays for them that God would not deal with them according to their folly (Job 42:7–8). Job's insistence that he is innocent and that his suffering cannot be related to God's punishment and discipline is clearly correct.[122]

It is significant to note that the explicit purpose of the friends' explanations was to preserve God's character by justifying Job's plight due to his sins. The friends provided answers to Job's situation to reach their goal by declaring what God's purposes were. The divine wrath is directed against their justifications for suffering. Hence, the book of Job does not justify theodicy; it serves as a biblical witness to confound all theological endeavors to provide a theodicy. In the words of Gustavo Gutiérrez, the book of Job intends readers to "learn how to speak of God in the midst of suffering."[123]

In the last five chapters of the book, containing YHWH's voice from the whirlwind, God does not provide any explanation for Job's suffering. Instead, God only explains God's works in order to emphasize the greatness of God. At the same time, God shows the relative position of a human being, as an insignificant creature. "Where were you when I laid the foundation of the earth? Tell me, if you have understanding" (Job 38:4).

The principle is essential for discussing an alternative Pentecostal theodicy, since it emphasizes the human inability to comprehend God and God's ways entirely because of God's holiness and great power. The resolution to Job's questions about his distress is found in God's revelation and the human encounter with God. Job does not find answers to his questions, but he finds more. For that reason, he responds to the encounter by saying, "I know that you can do all things, and that no purpose of yours can be thwarted . . . Therefore I have uttered what I did not understand, things too wonderful for me, which I did not know . . . I had

---

121. Castelo, *Theological Theodicy*, 22.

122. See also scholarly work in Carter, "The Book of Job through Central African Eyes."

123. In Gutiérrez, *On Evil*.

heard of you by the hearing of the ear, but now my eye sees you; therefore I despise myself, and repent in dust and ashes" (Job 42:1–6). Encountering God is the condition for living with suffering.

Theodicy and Eschatology

A meaningful way to impact theodicy's discussion of evil and suffering is in eschatology that contains the ultimate resolution to the problem of evil. Thus, eschatology plays an essential role in the historical life of Pentecostalism. Most Pentecostals would present an eschatological resolution for the unresolved challenges for theodicy when confronted with the mystery that most suffering entails.

Early Pentecostals viewed the second coming of Christ as imminent, and it motivated them to reach the ends of the earth with the proclamation of the gospel before the end occurred. Their missiological urge was strengthened by a restorationist and primitivist urge to imitate the early church.[124] The experience of Spirit baptism with the sign of glossolalia convinced Pentecostals that God is restoring the early church in preparation for the final age that would introduce the eschatological end.[125]

Reference has been made to the work of Marilyn M. Adams, who emphasizes the importance of eschatology in theodicy. She writes about the beatific vision: believers' expected face-to-face encounter with God (1 Cor 13:12; 1 John 3:2). She opines that evil would be defeated in seeing God.[126] Encountering God in the new world (Rev 21:5) will alter believers' personal experience of suffering, and their perspective will shift. They will recognize its worth in terms that earthly life cannot explain. "Retrospectively, I believe, from the vantage point of heavenly beatitude, human victims of horrors will recognize those experiences as points of identification with the crucified God, and not wish them away from their life histories."[127] In the words of Romans 8:18, "I consider that the sufferings of this present time are not worth comparing with the glory about to be revealed to us." Evil is incomprehensible to human beings living in this world, but it will become comprehensible in a new world where evil

---

124. Archer and Hamilton, "Anabaptism-Pietism and Pentecostalism," 189.
125. Nel, *African Pentecostalism and Eschatological Expectations*.
126. Adams, "Horrendous Evils and the Goodness of God," 155.
127. Adams, "Horrendous Evils and the Goodness of God," 167.

will not occur at all. Eschatology does not solve the problem of evil; it dissolves it and renders it obsolete.[128]

A popular song among Pentecostals refers to eschatology as the means to find answers to the challenges that suffering on earth posed. "We'll talk it over in the bye and bye . . . I'll ask the reason, he'll [God will] tell me why."[129] This rather crude belief may be comforting; however, there is no biblical precedent for this belief. Eschatology will instead render the need to understand obsolete.

Pentecostals use the concept of hell to explain the urgency that sinners should repent. It forms an essential element of their missiological drive. However, it is also one of the most unpalatable doctrines of the New Testament for contemporary people.[130] Divine justice requires that "good" people be rewarded while "bad" people receive their due, implying the need for formulating a theological view about the afterlife for nonbelievers. It is a good question whether child rapists, serial killers, and perpetrators of genocide should share the fate of those people who tried their best to act in a good way in imitating Jesus, as universalism asserts.

It is submitted that "hell" serves as a symbol to explain the need for divine justice in the light of those who misused their freedom for evil in differentiation from those who did good.[131] God created human beings with free will; it was argued that it forms a vital element of God's creation of humankind in God's image. Freedom to act and decide establishes the

---

128. Scott, *Pathways in Theodicy*, 198.

129. "Tho' shadows deepen, and my heart bleeds, I will not question the way he leads; This side of heaven we know in part, I will not question a broken heart. / We'll talk it over in the bye and bye. We'll talk it over, my Lord and I. I'll ask the reasons—he'll tell me why, When we talk it over in the bye and bye. / I'll hide my heartache behind a smile, and wait for reasons 'til after a while. And tho' he try me, I know I'll find that all my burdens are silver lined." eHymnbook.org, "Though Shadows Deepen and My Heart."

130. Nel, "Rethinking Hell from a Classical Pentecostal Perspectives."

131. "Hell" translates the Hebrew term *sheol*, which refers to the place where the departed is kept, and the Greek *gehenna*, the divinely ordained place of punishment for the wicked after death. The name *sheol* seems to derive from *sha'al*, "to ask, inquire" and to reflect the practice of necromancy (Crenshaw, *Defending God*, 240). Rev 2:11; 20:14; etc. refers to it as the "second death," and it is symbolized in those who are cast into a lake burning with fire and brimstone (Rev 21:8; 19:20; 20:10). These texts are read in an over-literal way by Pentecostals and other conservative and fundamentalist groups, resulting in the popular ideas of hell. In modern times, most theologians emphasize that hell is rather the logical consequence of one's own decisions that necessarily separate the soul from God (Cross and Livingstone, "Hell," 753).

room to reject the divine grace that is offered in the sacrifice of Christ on the cross. C. S. Lewis captures the essence of hell with the words: "I willingly believe that the damned are, in one sense, successful, rebels to the end; that the doors of hell are locked on the inside."

With its promises of heaven and hell, reward and punishment, and the eradication of evil, eschatology demonstrates the heart of the problem in religion. Biblical evidence of these concepts must be accepted in faith and cannot be proven as true and accurate, at least not until the eschatological future dawns. A problem with which biblical eschatology confronts New Testament believers is the lack of evidence of an afterlife that includes reward and punishment in the Old Testament. From ancient Near Eastern literature, it seems that there are two rival views of the destiny of the dead, traced back to the Paleolithic and Neolithic periods, that also function in the Old Testament. One thought, held by the wandering semi-nomads, is that the dead rested in their graves as "living corpses," articulated in Genesis 3:19's view of death, that dust returns to dust, and its corollary is the conviction that the animating breath was reclaimed at death by the one who had bestowed it (Eccl 12:7). The rival conception, which functioned mainly among the city-dwellers in ancient Mesopotamia, was that the dead descended to a watery underworld, the equivalent of what the Old Testament refers to as *Sheol*. There they wandered as restless "shades." Whatever view ancient people held, one thing they believed in common was that nobody ever returned from the realms of the dead. There was no expectation of a resurrection that would occur somewhere in an eschatological future. The narrative in 1 Samuel 28 records how the medium of Endor called up the prophet Samuel at the behest of King Saul. The prophet did not take kindly to having his sleep disturbed, asking irritated, "Why have you disturbed me by bringing me up?" (v. 15). That a netherworld is a place of rest that brings an end to all suffering in the present world is poetically envisioned in Isaiah 57:1–2. However, death might also imply that the dead are brought to the king of terrors. Job 18:17–18 states that their memory perishes from the earth. They have no name in the street but are thrust from light into darkness and driven out of the world.

Ancient people did not see any link between the present world and the place where the dead were kept. The dead who were inhabitants in *Sheol* did not give any thought to their beloved ones that stayed behind. They also did not have any communion with YHWH. God had nothing to do with the world of the dead. The underworld is characterized by tempestuous and turbulent waters that could even threaten the citizens of the present world. The solid wall between the present world and the domain of the dead might be breached, resulting in the waters underneath the earth ascending in flood, threatening human survival on earth. Usually, these waters fed fountains, but the waters might rise, risking life and order in the world inhabited by living human beings. These waters, also found above and surrounding the flat earth, were associated with the primeval chaos that formed the substance from which God created the existing world. Primeval chaos was also identified with evil. Deliverance from *Sheol* could come only from God's hand. People who perceived themselves to be caught up in these dreaded waters petitioned God in the belief that the deity was mighty enough to rescue them from the dangers of physical threat and sickness that end in death.[132]

In developing a theology of evil in the next chapter, the place of disability in the perspective of suffering and evil will be discussed in more detail. At this point, it is necessary to state that eschatological perspectives on theodicy have to be aware of the challenge that the "eschatological healing" of disability to realize the promises of a new world might lead to the elimination of the disabled person because of the unbreakable bond between the person and the disability.[133] The issue is made even more significant with the question of how personal identity can be retained in the afterlife in terms of intellectual and physical disabilities, not only in terms of congenital conditions. Will the afterlife require retaining or obliterating how human lives have been shaped over time by capacities, environments, and relationships?[134] Will it not lead to the obliteration of the person's identity?

The expectation of an afterlife as promised in the New Testament leads to the question: Is there an afterlife? If there is an afterlife, what are the relations between what has traditionally been labeled the human soul and the body? And what is the nature of the body in the afterlife? From the perspective of the disabled person, these questions lead to various responses. Some disabled persons may think that any thought of "more of the same kind of (physical and mental) suffering" in terms of "living eternally" with their disability conditions is unacceptable and does not represent any encouragement or consolation. Others may hope for and

---

132. Crenshaw, *Defending God*, 149–50.
133. Yong, "Disability and the Love of Wisdom," 167.
134. Yong, "Disability and the Love of Wisdom," 167.

believe in an afterlife that represents divine justice because it implies that they will, at last, be free from their disabilities. The injustices they have experienced in this life, resulting from what they may perceive as bad luck (chance mutations producing congenital disabilities) or moral irresponsibility that made them its victim, will, at last, be vindicated. For those who desire to live eternally free from their disabilities, the questions pertaining to the relationship between the human soul and the body and the nature of the body in the afterlife become pertinent. For some physically disabled persons, the belief in the resurrection may imply a competent and whole body. For those with various types of sensory and physical disabilities, like blindness, deafness, or prostheses, the question remains whether they will be resurrected without what has become an integral aspect of their identity.[135] That Jesus' resurrected body retained the wounds in his hands, side, and feet may suggest that the resurrected bodies of people with disabilities may also retain signs of their impairments in the world to come.

The same questions pertain to people with intellectual disabilities. With what bodies and what kind of personal identities will they be resurrected? Will those with chromosomal variations which are identity-constitutive, such as trisomy 21 (Down syndrome), be resurrected as "healed" persons, implying that they lose their true self?

Practice of Lament

Human suffering introduces death, which is the denial of life. Despite Christians' belief that death introduces them to the rest in God and eternal life, death is not good because it ends life. God created everything good, and for that reason, it is accepted that death could not have been a part of the original creation. Death always includes farewell, sorrow, and heartache for human beings and is not good. How do believers respond to death and the suffering and disease that introduce it? How do they react to the reality that characterizes human life?

It is suggested that sufferers consider the biblical practice of lament, found in several places in the Bible but also in indigenous practices among Africans and other groups, as a means of responding more efficiently to suffering. Lament provides a minor-key language for those who suffer,

---

135. Yong, "Disability and the Love of Wisdom," 173.

helping them navigate the wilderness of their grief.[136] For the Western world, the expression of sorrow has become inhibited, frowning on the unrestrained, uninhibited, and spontaneous expression of heartache (and other emotions). As a result, grief has become, in many instances, privatized and internalized. This is not how people in the West traditionally responded to sorrow; in earlier times, the expression of sorrow was much more public, with, for example, mourners wearing black clothes for years and refraining from attending social functions.[137] Lament deliberately creates ample room for public and corporate sharing of sorrow that acknowledges the pain and grief caused by suffering and death. Instead of explaining the purpose of pain, mostly with senseless and insensitive remarks such as "God takes away the best of God's children to be with God" or "maybe other people will come to God because of the death of your child," lament permits a person to wrestle with sorrow instead of rushing to end it. The reason is clear: "Walking through sorrow without understanding and embracing the God-given song of lament can stunt the grieving process."[138]

Israel established a liturgical practice that incorporated the expression of grief and sorrow in their spirituality, illustrated in the lament that played an essential role in the book of Psalms, necessitating the need to create a category consisting of laments.[139] Walter Brueggemann analyzes lament into psalms of disorientation, psalms of orientation, and psalms of new orientation. The psalms of disorientation accommodate the honest evocation of emotions in the form of prayer, addressed to God. The psalmists voice their complaints, grief, anger, bitterness, and rebellion about their difficult circumstances in the psalms. They expose their emotions in their stark reality without being afraid of being rejected by others or God.

---

136. Vroegop, *Dark Clouds, Deep Mercy*, 16.

137. See further detail in Duff, "Recovering Lamentation," 6.

138. Vroegop, *Dark Clouds, Deep Mercy*, 18.

139. Personal psalms of lament of an individual that vocalize pain, grief, fear, or some other emotion: 3, 4, 5, 7, 10, 13, 17, 22, 25, 26, 28, 31, 39, 42, 43, 54, 55, 56, 57, 59, 61, 64, 70, 71, 77, 86, 120, 141, 142; corporate lament psalms of a group or nation that vocalize strong emotions: 12, 44, 58, 60, 74, 79, 80, 83, 85, 90, 94, 123, 126; psalms of repentance of an individual or group that express regret or sorrow for sin: 6, 32, 38, 51, 94, 102, 123, 126; psalms of imprecation, where an individual or group express outrage and a strong desire for justice: 36, 69, 83, 88, 109, 137, 140; partial sections of lament within other psalms: 9:13–20; 27:7–14; 40:11–17; psalms that might be a lament in total or in part: 14, 36, 41, 52, 53, 63, 78, 81, 89, 106, 125, 129, 139 (Vroegop, *Dark Clouds, Deep Mercy*, 188; Thompson, "Where Is the God of Justice?," 31).

Even when they accuse God of being guilty of their suffering, as Job also does, their prayers are not unfaithful, and they do not fear that God will take offense. In the case of Job, his complaint that God had cast him into the mire, causing him to become like dust and ashes, led to the prayer, "I cry to you and you do not answer me; I stand, and you merely look at me. You have turned cruel to me; with the might of your hand you persecute me . . . I know that you will bring me to death, and to the house appointed for all living" (Job 30:19–23). However, in the end, God vindicates him when God tells Eliphaz the Temanite that what he and his two friends said was not correct, unlike God's servant Job (Job 42:7). God did not blame Job for the honest lament that portrayed his deepest emotions. Experiences of disorder are a proper subject of discourse with God, with nothing considered out of bounds and nothing excluded or inappropriate.[140]

In my estimation, some or many Pentecostals read lament psalms with a feeling of embarrassment, wondering where they fit into the Bible as God's word.[141] Pentecostals probably argue that belief in God changes the believer's situation in relation to that of unbelievers and the unrighteous, taking away the need for lament. The theological problem is that they do not recognize the significance of the Easter event and its explanation of the suffering of God in the recovery of lament.[142] Pentecostals argue that some christological claim supersedes the lament. While it is true that how one interprets the Old Testament should be affected by the incarnation and crucifixion of Christ, it should also be acknowledged that the suffering of people at all times amounts to the same experience.

Their theology does not allow them to express their honest reflection about their suffering because of the teaching that one should confess that you are healed, blessed, and delivered from mishaps the moment you end the prayer of faith for its removal.

They must consider incorporating lament as an essential element of their liturgy, not only at funeral services but other services of the faith community that celebrate the lives of saints who died.[143] Especially in times of pandemics, as during COVID-19, consisting of a microbial virus that cost the lives of millions and halted the economy of half the planet

---

140. Brueggemann, *Message of the Psalms*, 52.

141. Lament received some attention within Pentecostal scholarship during the past decade of two, testified to in the thinking of Michael K. Adams, David Molzahn, Larry R. McQueen, Scott A. Ellington, and Leonard Maré.

142 Torr, *Dramatic Pentecostal/Charismatic Anti-Theodicy*, 16.

143. Duff, "Recovering Lamentation," 8–9.

and that struck the world in 2020, corporate expression of mourning and grief is necessary for believers to find healing. In many cases, family and friends were denied access to those suffering from COVID-19-related symptoms while they were hospitalized.

Stephen Torr explains that the suffering victim's vocalization of pain and suffering in the form of lament is an essential biblical practice.[144] It enables the sufferer to maintain an honest relationship with God while not understanding the reasons for their distress. Unfortunately, the essence of what they need to vocalize can often fracture the limits of language, implying that the sufferer cannot find words to express themselves. The gift and practice of glossolalia address the shortcoming and bridge the gap with "sighs too deep for words" (Rom 8:26). Lamenting in tongues could pave the way to healing.

Believers' laments do not end with complaining but flow into a call for change in the context of humans' awareness of their dependency on God. It can express faith that facilitates an authentic life.[145] As Stanley Hauerwas explains, lament can express and shape individuals and communities that support them during times of pain and despair.[146] Lament accommodates the hermeneutical grid for establishing memories that initially defied meaning until they were brought into contact with the living God in fellowship. And lament stands in the gap between pain and promise because it is prayer loaded with theology.

Lament is the loud cry, howl, and passionate expression of grief, including verbalizing rage and anger at life and God and wrestling with questions, doubts, pain, and sorrow. It asks two questions: Where is God in what happened to me, and why does this happen if God loves me? It is a prayer in pain, and because it is a conversation in the presence of and, at times, with God, it leads to trust. Lament is the direct opposite of praise, but in many cases, it eventually becomes a path to eventual praise, transitioning the space between brokenness and pain and God's mercy through disappointment and doubt to promise and hope. It consists of an address to God, a complaint, a request, and, in time, an expression of trust and praise.[147] In other words, lament implies that suffering people

---

144. Torr, "Lamenting in Tongues," 40.
145. Castelo, *Theological Theodicy*, 57.
146. Hauerwas, *God, Medicine, and Suffering*, 82.
147. Vroegop, *Dark Clouds, Deep Mercy*, 28.

turn to God, complain, ask, and regain hope and confidence. Therefore, it takes faith to lament.

Lament provides the language for verbalizing loss as a solution to silence. As a category for complaints, it becomes a framework for expressing feelings as a part of the process for dealing with pain, which eventually becomes a way to worship and trust God.[148]

Another element of lament provides the means to unite people when hurt and misunderstanding are in the air.[149] To become fully present to serve others who are suffering requires empathy that can be enhanced by interceding for them in prayer, defined by Fettke and Dusing as standing before Christ and sharing in his mercy for the suffering, in solidarity with the victims of suffering.[150] It means that the praying person may be drawn into the lives of those for whom they are praying. Lamenting is included in intercession for others by verbalizing the pain, sharing the sufferer's hurts and disappointments. It strengthens the concern for the hurting person.[151] People who are suffering or have suffered are probably the best pastors to minister to other hurting people, as the author of 2 Corinthians 1 explains.[152] Catastrophes and disasters can provide the impetus for reflection, deep prayer, and a call to carefully process one's own or another's hurt and trauma.

In an informative article, Raymond Potgieter discusses the example of the healing of emotions within the extreme situation of the Holocaust.[153] Etty Hillesum, known as "the adult Anne Frank," threw a postcard from the train en route to Auschwitz from Westerbork transit camp. At first, her diarizing aided her therapeutically in analyzing her personal feelings rationally, but eventually it turned into a highly private inner conversation. Although she initially addressed herself, in time, she recognized that she was conversing with God. As a result, her life changed as she took on a New Testament servant mentality and attitude of forgiveness towards her Nazi enemies, compelling her to serve the younger women of Westerbork transit camp and tell them of God's power in forgiveness and hope for the future.

---

148. Vroegop, *Dark Clouds, Deep Mercy*, 158.
149. Vroegop, *Dark Clouds, Deep Mercy*, 183.
150. Fettke and Dusing, "Practical Pentecostal Theodicy?," 174.
151. Cartledge, *Testimony in the Spirit*, 15–20.
152. Yong, *Bible, Disability, and the Church*, 38–40.
153. Potgieter, "Etty Hillesum."

Mark Vroegop discusses the practice of lament in the context of racial issues. He explains that lament can provide the language needed to weep with those who weep when the lamenting person has not experienced the pain and humiliation of unfair treatment because of their ethnicity.[154] It provides the opportunity for believers to mourn the racial tensions that mark and scar many societies, separating people and even faith communities.[155] Lament becomes the God-given means for vocalizing complicated and loaded pain that prays with and for other people, resulting in constructive empathy that partakes in integrating separated people and groups.

---

154. Vroegop, *Dark Clouds, Deep Mercy*, 185.

155. I discussed the use of an indigenous language spoken by some White South Africans and developed in Africa from Dutch (Afrikaans) to define worship services for some of those communities and separate them from and exclude people of other languages, in some instances intentionally. Afrikaans became a hated language when the apartheid regime forced Africans to attend primary and secondary education in Afrikaans, even though their home language differed. It eventually led to the Soweto uprisings in June 1976, in which twenty thousand schoolchildren participated. Their resistance was met with fierce police brutality, and many were shot and killed. See Nel, "Moedertaal in die Kerk."

6

Reflecting on Evil in Theodicy from a Pentecostal Hermeneutical Perspective

Introduction

THE DISCUSSION IN THE second and third chapters shows that there is no consensus in the philosophy of religion or biblical studies about the viability of any one theodicy proposal. It is probably more accurate to state that the agreement is that there is a plurality of theodicies.[1] Most theodicies have strengths and sufficiently glaring weaknesses that one can be inclined to give up on the project of formulating theodicy merely as an academic and theoretical enterprise. In practice, it seems true that while some people subjectively perceive a reason for their suffering, in many other cases, their suffering seems senseless to victims of suffering. For that reason, one should rather speak of several theodicean views of suffering that are true and applicable to various situations while leaving room for the mystery that suffering is in some other cases. The biblical evidence provides the motivation to think in terms of several responses to different situations, requiring a diversified theodicy.

To do justice to Pentecostal sentiments, it is necessary to limit theological endeavors to reflections based on encounters with God's Spirit to keep the enterprise from devolving into theorizing and ending with "eternally valid propositions." The same is true of theodicy; Pentecostals should develop theodicies that view each suffering victim uniquely, making their theodicean explanations existential and individual. No single

---

1. Yong, "Disability and the Love of Wisdom," 161.

answer fits every case, and to value pastoral sentiments, each particular case should be reviewed on its own.

It is important to emphasize that theodicy should not be practiced only at a theoretical level, because the Bible does not contain a "one-size-fits-all" answer but hints that every individual case should be reviewed independently and on its own. A person may experience suffering as a catalyst for changing their ways and ascribing the suffering to God's grace, while another may experience suffering as senseless and meaningless. The perception of the individual is essential. The pastoral task of the church is to assist people, especially believers, to use the perspective of faith in God as far as possible as a significant factor in considering the meaning of their individual suffering. It underlines the importance that the church considers its view of God critically to ensure that faith in God does and can explain suffering without the contradictions caused by, e.g., the view of God as almighty and omnipotent.

There are no ready-made answers to the complex phenomenon of suffering because of the diversity of its range and individual perceptions. When natural catastrophes are considered, it becomes even more complicated. Now the church should apply its eschatological perspectives to explain what to expect in the expected coming world. The problem is that the New Testament is vague about the detail of such a world, providing no hard and fast facts. For example, it seems that the earth will be renewed as the place where God will establish the divine kingdom. Will the renewal include that natural weather cycles and movements in the center of the planet are "interrupted" and "repaired" to exclude phenomena such as droughts, floods, earthquakes with the accompanying danger of tsunamis, hurricanes, typhoons, etc.? The Bible does not provide any indications, and for that reason the church cannot clarify the future state of things and the possible occurrence of suffering in such a world.

Amos Yong refers to several theodicies that qualify to explain suffering from a perspective of faith. In the first place, there are ontological and/or theological models, consisting of responses that understand evil as either intrinsically (ontologically) woven into the fabric of the universe or as being the result of God's (at least permissive) will for the world.[2] A second type is freewill theodicy, which views the problem of evil either as the result of creaturely freedom unleashed by the fall of humankind (Gen 3) or the primordial fall of angels. God is not *per se* responsible for evil;

---

2. Yong, "Disability and the Love of Wisdom," 162.

instead, God created a world of free creatures. Free creatures can choose to commit good or evil acts, which can bring about evil consequences for themselves, other people, and the environment.[3] A third type is the so-called "soul-making theodicy" that believes that evil is allowed by God because of its formative capacities to develop moral virtues, especially in terms of but not exclusive to believers. Evil becomes beneficial because of its soul-shaping outcomes.[4] The last type that Yong refers to is developed in cruciform theology that states that God enters the world's suffering in the cross of Jesus Christ and the current suffering of the individual. It does not (and cannot) explain the origins of evil. Still, it admits to the intractability of the problem of evil, insisting at the same time that God is not removed from human suffering but has entered into and embraced it in God's own life.[5]

In the last chapter, the challenge of evil is discussed and brought into relation to the several theodicies that Yong describes. While the previous chapter concentrated on God as the prime mover and master of the universe, this chapter is concerned with God's opponent and adversary, the antigod power of evil, and the evil one(s).

The Bible's View(s) of Evil

Romans 12 opens the third part of Romans with its famous discussion of the church having "many members in one body" and "one body in Christ" (vv. 4–5). The description of the church as the body through which Christ lives is then followed by the injunction about love for fellow Christians and fellow human beings. Paul encourages believers to "hate what is evil; cling to what is good. Be devoted to one another in brotherly love" (v. 10). Furthermore, the author encourages believers not to "repay anyone evil for evil. Be careful to do what is right in the eyes of everybody" (v. 17). Instead of taking revenge (12:19–20), doing good to enemies can bring about their repentance. Therefore, "be not overcome by evil but overcome evil with good" (v. 21)

This does not by any means imply that Christians should passively put up with evil, argues E. W. Davies.[6] It is how evil is overcome that is at

3. Yong, "Disability and the Love of Wisdom," 163.
4. Yong, "Disability and the Love of Wisdom," 165.
5. Yong, "Disability and the Love of Wisdom," 165–66.
6. Davies, *Immoral Bible*, 210.

issue. Here one can find the reason for extending kindness to enemies, the difficult demand that Jesus made of his disciples (Matt 5:43–44). If believers retaliated in kind for all acts of hostility against themselves, they would shortly find themselves engaging in all kinds of equally wicked conduct. To prevent such a development, they must launch a counterattack, returning good for evil and deploying good actions against the evil actions of the enemy. In other words, while on the one hand, they find themselves living and operating in a world where one bad apple can spoil the whole bunch, on the other, they can proceed on the premise that one good apple might make a barrel of rotten apples good.[7] If avoiding being overcome by evil in the world is difficult enough, then overcoming and even crushing it with good is extremely difficult. Christians do not see God face-to-face, but at best through a glass darkly, in a multi-layered and fractured sociopolitical and relational world. The alternative is to accept that God does not exist, which reminds one of Ivan Karamazov's remark in *The Brothers Karamazov* by Fyodor Dostoevsky. In a moment of self-tormenting doubt, when Ivan evaluates the moral chaos when one denies God, he says, "If God does not exist, then everything is permitted."[8] Human beings need the notion of God to be able to survive in their relationships. Dostoevsky recognizes that if there is no limit on human freedom, then indeed, everything is permitted, and human beings can act in any way, whether cruel or criminal. Chaos is the inevitable result.

The Greek word for "evil" (*kakos*, "bad, wicked, evil") corresponds to the Hebrew stem *ra*, which brings out the one-sidedness and impressiveness of the moral and religious judgment which Judaism pronounces on evil and wickedness. The term refers in the sense of "evil" or "disaster" to two ideas, of which the first is that evils are God's punishment for sin when God withdraws the divine hand (e.g., Deut 31:17). Evil is a divine act of discipline and punishment, and the reason for punishment is to be sought in idolatry and apostasy (Wis 14:27). The second idea is that God is the Redeemer from evil. Thus the prophet in Jeremiah 16:19 calls on God and prays to God concerning the results of ungodliness. The question of evil is projected into the national and political life of the people. God and the people are involved in the question. The political woes come from God as the LORD of history, and they are a punishment for sin, which consists of apostasy and relapse into idolatry. Human guilt

---

7. Davies, *Immoral Bible*, 215.
8. Dostoevsky, *Brothers Karamazov*, 72.

and divine action are in this way combined in the question of the origin of evil, which is viewed in the Bible as mysterious. The question of the root of evil finds its answer not in a metaphysical dualism, but in ethical monotheism, in the knowledge of the God to whom the evil of man is guilt, and who punishes it accordingly (Job 2:10).

The concept of evil has both qualitative and moral categories. Qualitative evil is something bad in nature or a corrupt, displeasing, undesirable, or inadequate condition. It is a misfortune, injuring or threatening to injure or kill people. Sometimes it describes people, their names, temperaments, or reputations. It is also used to refer to deep displeasure in someone else's performance, distress common to humankind, the trouble of the age, speech or intentions, physical harm, situations, land, disease, or animals either useless to the cult or endangering human lives. God can protect those whom God elects from such evils (Ps 23:4; Jer 29:11). It can also refer to natural disasters such as plagues, famines, attacks by foreign enemies, and defeat in battle. And because of this disconnect from the moral overtones, biblical authors could ascribe these evil events to God without impugning God's righteousness—God sends evil spirits to people, brought evil upon a nation (Isa 49:11), and caused the destruction of a city (Jer 21:10). Evil is also used in a moral and spiritual sense, as an attribute of humans, the designation of immorality and unfaithfulness to the covenant. The origin of evil is the human heart (Prov 6:14; 21:10; Eccl 8:11). Evil describes idolatry and apostasy, disobedience to the commandments of God, false prophesy, murder, disobedience to parents, false witness, adultery, fornication, stealing, sin in general, and the inclination of the heart. Evil serves as opposite and contrast to the goodness and righteous (Gen 2:9; 3:5; Prov 11:21; 12:13). Evil is also several times described in the New Testament in terms of the evil one or the devil (John 17:15; Eph 6:16; 1 John 2:13–14; 5:18). The opponent or devil is depicted as the one who wants to lead humankind into evil, although the impression is that he cannot do anything outside the limitations imposed by God (John 12:31; Rev 12:9; 20:1–3).[9] At times it seems as if the New Testament utilizes "the evil one" to refer instead to the evil of the present age as a neuter reference, as in Matthew 6:13. Translating "the evil one"

---

9. That "the evil one" of the New Testament does refer to Satan or the devil is demonstrated by the correspondence between Matt 13:19, Mark 4:15, and Luke 8:12, with their different references to the evil one, Satan, and the devil. The evil one is a title for the devil when it is a substantive formed by the definite article and the masculine nominative of the adjective *ponēros*.

rather than "an evil person" or "evil" in general must be based on both grammar (the form must be masculine substantive) and context. It seems that 1 John 2:13–14; 3:12; 5:18–19's references should be translated as "the evil one," for instance. What is essential is that the New Testament deliberately never attributes evil to God (Jas 1:13), unlike the Old Testament. Evil comes from within a person, not only because of actions but also because of humanity's fallen condition (Matt 15:19; Rom 7:14–25). Paul emphasizes that we must be saved from the evil that characterizes our fallen nature (Rom 1:28–32).

Philosophical Considerations

As little as a century ago, before the twentieth century's titanic world wars, death camps, genocides, and Gulags, and the relentless bombing of civilians, what had previously been called the "problem of evil" had almost disappeared from the philosophical agenda. Some even assumed that evil was the product of human ignorance and superstition that would gradually from its own disappear with the advance of science and education.[10] Hannah Arendt's controversial book with the subtitle, *A Report on the Banality of Evil*, argues that in our time, evil is not merely a question of bad or malevolent people. It has to do with our not being attentive to how our seemingly small roles in complex and intricate societies can result in unspeakable evil.[11] In 1961, Hannah Arendt was asked by the *New Yorker* to cover the trial of Adolf Eichmann, a Nazi SS officer who played a part in the Holocaust. The question she posed for herself was, How could anyone perpetrate evil of such a nature? Wouldn't it need a wicked person, a sociopath, to participate in the *Shoah*? But Arendt was surprised when she interviewed Eichmann; he showed a total lack of imagination. He was a conventional citizen. In the book that she wrote about her impressions of the trial, Eichmann claims that he only did his job as well as he could to ensure that the trains were on time. The fact that those trains were crammed with Jewish children and women, *inter alia*, on their way to Auschwitz did not concern him. Arendt argues that while Eichmann's *actions* were evil, Eichmann himself—the *person*—"was quite ordinary, commonplace, and neither demonic nor monstrous. There was no sign in him of firm ideological convictions." She attributed his immorality—his

---

10. Cox, *How to Read the Bible*, 34.
11. Arendt, *Eichmann in Jerusalem*. See also Arendt, *The Origins of Totalitarianism*.

capacity, even his eagerness, to commit crimes—to his lack to think things through for himself. He did not stop at any stage, deliberate, and think about what was happening in Germany and what role he fulfilled in it. For that reason, Eichmann committed himself to participate in mass murder without realizing or considering the consequences of his deeds. He did not take responsibility for what he did. He argued that he only did his job to the best of his ability, as his employer expected of him. He did not ask the questions that would have allowed him to examine the meaning of things, to distinguish between fact and fiction, truth and falsehood, good and evil.[12]

After two world wars and many other ethnic conflicts with the resultant horrors demonstrated by war, often with unparalleled savagery perpetrated by Christians on both sides,[13] it became necessary to perpetuate the debate about the origins, essence, and appearance of evil.[14] Raised as a problem of logic, philosophers of religion frequently point out the incompatibility of the three propositions that constitute theodicy: God is omnipotent (all-powerful); God is omnibenevolent (all-loving); evil and suffering exists. The affirmation of any two of these negates the other. Theologians who wish to defend the existence and righteousness of God find themselves in the position of proffering a theodicy that justifies

---

12. Sitt, "Before You Can Be with Others, First Learn to be Alone."

13. Merton, *Faith and Violence*, 11.

14. Merton, *Faith and Violence*, 11. Augustine influenced the debate about evil and war, and specifically just war. In his theology, he concentrated on the boundless reality of God and then also considered what he imagined evil to be. Evil exists only as a privation of the good (*privatio boni*), a form of non-being, which is a Neoplatonic commonplace (Augustine, *Concerning the City of God*, 424–26; X:32). A privation of goodness implies in theological language an absence of God. Plotinus was a third-century CE Platonist whose writings revolutionized Augustine's conception of God. Augustine identified evil with matter, while his notion of materiality is one of consummate deprivation, not solid stuff or indeed any kind of subject, but a beckoning, formless nullity, foreign to goodness. Augustine describes the split within the angelic ranks between the angels who fell into themselves and eternally darkened their minds and those who held steady to the deliverances of divine light. He speaks of Satan, the perverted light bearer and father of lies, who shows up in Eden in a serpent's guise and seduces the woman into a fateful transgression, and Adam, her mate, and the model of a human sinner, who sees through the serpent's deception but grievously underestimates the cost to him and his race of his obscurely motivated disobedience. If Augustine's notion of evil were more realistic, his concept of just war would have looked different. Augustine emphasized that human beings are deficient agents. They suffer from total depravity. However, they cannot be moved to will their self-corruption because God makes appropriate and beneficial use of sin.

God in the face of the presence of suffering and evil. The logical problem exacerbated by its existential application in the lives of created human beings is: If God is an omnipotent being, he must be able to destroy all evil. If God is a perfectly good being, God must want to abolish all evil. Yet evil exists. Therefore, God must either not be omnipotent or not be perfectly good. Though it can be argued that human beings have no right to justify God and that sin is in its essence unintelligible, Christianity cannot avoid the question of the existence of evil because it is a genuine logical difficulty.

One philosopher who wrote extensively about evil after his experience of the horrors of the Second World War was Albert Camus. After 1942, he became involved in the French resistance and post-war political left, like his friend Simone Weil, a pacifist,[15] who encouraged him to turn to political philosophy and concentrate on justice questions. Camus wrote a long philosophical essay, *L'Homme Révolté* (1951–52), in which he considers the modern age. Like Hannah Arendt's *The Origins of Totalitarianism* (1951), he wanted to understand how the National Socialist and Stalinist regimes could commit genocide and how twentieth-century enlightened Europe tolerated it. Camus's argument represents a qualified defense of the modern, secularist break with the West's premodern, "Christian" culture. He traces the genealogies of Hitlerite and Stalinist regimes to the current European philosophies of Rousseau, de Sade, Hegel, Marx, and Nietzsche, with their critique of Christian theology, in Camus's words, "the great offensive against a hostile heaven."[16] Modern humanity's dilemma is a confrontation of the human desire for unity and order with "an unjust and incomprehensible condition." The rebel's "blind impulse is to demand order amid chaos," Camus says, "he protests, he demands, he insists that the outrage be brought to an end, and that what has up to now been built on shifting sands henceforth be founded on rock."[17]

Early modern philosophers rebelled against European monarchies' "world of grace" sanctioned by Christian theology. What they argued was that the world should occupy itself again with the problem of evil.[18] It should explain how "natural evils" can exist when Christian theology

---

15. Merton, *Faith and Violence*, 11, 76–84.
16. Camus, *The Rebel*, 26.
17. Camus, *The Rebel*, 10.
18. Sharpe, "Black Side of the Sun," 163.

presupposes an omnipotent, omnibenevolent God. Camus writes that philosophers from Machiavelli to Bayle, Voltaire, and de Sade believed that if an omnipotent God indeed created a world in which natural evils exist, this God must not be omnibenevolent, but "a criminal divinity who oppresses and denies mankind,"[19] given the evident injustices and sufferings of the world. They blasphemed against God, in Camus's evaluation, not at first to supplant God but only to challenge God's works "in the name of a moral value."

Camus thinks the inconsistencies in the Christian responses to the problem of evil justified the rejection of the Augustinian doctrine of a universally inherited original sin as profoundly inadequate, inhumane, and unjust.[20] Harvey Cox's remark is relevant, and this study supports it, that human beings are not cursed by the sin that Adam and Eve did in the garden of Eden or the juice of their fatal apple; we are enmeshed and entangled in the fruits of our own collective narcissism and irresponsibility.[21] Consequently, we are the exiles who now dwell "east of Eden." Today's world is hardly one of "sheer delight" (the probable meaning of the Hebrew word "Eden"). Pentecostal theology concurs with this viewpoint.

A more troubling response in the Latin West was the notion of *nemo bonus* ("no one is good"), resulting in the Catholic Church's longstanding doctrine that unbaptized children are damned to eternal punishment. Camus finds this latter idea morally abhorrent.[22] His book *La Peste* (*The Plague*) is the most precise enunciation of his critique of this doctrine in Christianity. The Jesuit father Paneloux's sermon addressing the challenges of the plague, delivered amidst a storm raging outside the crowded church of Oran, was an extended, pitiless discourse on the "*nemo bonus*." His response to the problem of evil was, "Calamity has come on you, my

---

19. Camus, *The Rebel*, 37.

20. Sharpe, "Black Side of the Sun," 167.

21. Cox, *How to Read the Bible*, 28. See discussion following this subsection on Genesis 3.

22. Camus (*Carnets 1942–1951*, 179) opines, "The only great Christian mind to look at the problem of evil in the face was Saint Augustine. His conclusion was the terrifying 'nemo bonus.' Since then, Christianity has spent its time giving the problem temporary solutions. The result is there for everyone to see. It took time, but men became intoxicated with a poison that dates back two thousand years. They have had enough of evil, or they are resigned to it, which amounts to pretty much the same thing. But at least they can no longer put up with lies on that subject."

brethren, and, my brethren, you have deserved it... too long this world of ours has connived at evil, too long has it counted on the divine mercy."[23]

Camus tells how the secular doctor Rieux and the Jesuit father Paneloux, an expert on Augustine and the early African church, watch the agonized death of a small boy, Jacques Othon.[24] Eventually, the child dies despite the prayers of the priest. Rieux is upset and challenges the father: "Rieux was already going out of the ward, walking so quickly and with such a look on his face that when he overtook Paneloux, the priest held out his arm to restrain him. 'Come now, doctor,' he said. Without stopping as he swept along, Rieux turned around and spat out: 'Ah, now that one, at least, was innocent, and you know it as well as I do!'" He adds, "'I have a different notion of love; and to the day I die I shall refuse to love this creation in which children are tortured.'"[25] The child's death just as profoundly touched the priest as the doctor. The priest acknowledges that he now, for the first time, understands what is meant by talks of grace.

Shortly after these events, the priest preaches again. This time, he distances himself from the initial claims that the plague was punishment for Oran's especial sinfulness, in Augustinian fashion.[26] He admits that there can be no rational divine justification for the plague, in the light of his experience of the child's suffering: "'My brethren,' Father Paneloux said, at last, announcing that he was coming to an end, 'the love of God is a difficult love. It assumes a total abandonment of oneself and contempt for one's person. But it alone can wipe away the suffering and death of children, it alone makes them necessary because it is impossible to understand such things, so we have no alternative except to desire them. This is the hard lesson that I wanted to share with you. This is the faith—cruel in the eyes of man, decisive in the eyes of God—which we must try to recapture. We must try to make ourselves equal to this awful image. On this peak, everything will be confounded and made equal, and the truth will break forth from apparent injustice.'"[27] What is Camus's "solution?" For Camus, in one sense, there is no "solution," because the outrage of the murder of innocent people cannot be justified in any way. Camus suspects that the attempt to rationalize such recalcitrant assaults

---

23. Camus, *The Plague*, 80–81.
24. Camus, *The Plague*, 78.
25. Camus, *The Plague*, 178.
26. Camus, *The Plague*, 182–83.
27. Camus, *The Plague*, 186.

on human order is meaningless. However, he acknowledges that children will still die unjustly, even in the best society. We live amidst natural evil that is no respecter of persons.

Evil cannot be solved in a universal sense. In the struggle with evil and suffering, a specific individual may solve the problem in one way or another, whether by cursing God or trusting God. Still, there is no mandatory answer available, binding on everyone. The crisis of evil is essentially existential; it excludes any impersonal answer binding to everyone.

In thinking about evil, Pentecostal theology utilizes a traditional Christian religious model that views humanity as part of the universe as locked in a titanic struggle between the forces of good and evil, as a reflection of the more profound battle between God and Satan, God's opponent. The battleground is the individual human soul, and the entire meaning of human life revolves around this battle. The question of ultimate significance is whether the individual soul will be won to God or the devil.[28] "Non-cooperation with evil is a sacred duty."[29]

However, this is not the only model available to look at and explain evil, precisely human evil. There are various other models, such as the psychological, biological, psychobiological, sociological, sociobiological, Freudian, rational-emotive, behavioral, and existential models. In speaking about evil, especially in attempting to heal it, combining and synthesizing information and insights from the different models artistically and creatively will be necessary. The fact is that evil has to do with the human soul and its mysteries, which cannot be explained adequately only in one model. And it needs to be admitted that evil in the human soul cannot be confronted and healed without leaving room for a religious model. Human evil is too important and complicated for a one-sided understanding and too large a reality to be explained in terms of a single frame of reference.

In contemporary postmodern theological debates, one finds a negative theology that attempts to describe God by negation, to speak of God only in terms of what may not be said about God in an attempt to gain and express knowledge of God by describing what God is not instead of explaining what God is. This study has affinities with that sentiment; speaking confidentially about God contains the risk that theology says more than what is warranted. Negative theology accepts that it is impossible to describe the essence of God; it is possible only to talk about God's

---

28. Peck, *People of the Lie*, 40–41.
29. Merton, *On Eastern Meditation*, 765.

energies as demonstrated in God's revelation in salvation history. For instance, neither existence nor non-existence applies to God. God does not exist in the usual meaning of the word.

Similarly, God cannot be described in terms of good or evil because our terms limit God to what they mean for us. While God's will cannot be discerned easily, it is difficult to reflect on evil because we do not have access to God's notion of evil. The result is that we may be responsible for evil actions without realizing it because we do not comprehend the ultimate values of evil or good which lie exclusively in God's unknowable judgment. We cannot know what is good and what is evil, nor can we predict the outcome of our actions, whether they are good or evil. With our limited abilities, we know too little.

Seventeenth-century Europe experienced the debacle of the conflict between the church and Galileo that proved hurtful to both science and religion. It led to an unwritten social contract between science and faith, with the world divided into two entities, the natural and the supernatural. Faith and theology agreed that the "natural world" was the sole province of the scientists. In contrast, in its turn, science agreed to stay away from the spiritual and supernatural or anything to do with values. Science declared itself "value-free." For the past three hundred years, there has been a state of profound separation between faith and science, leaving the complex of problems associated with evil in the custody of religious thinkers.

That the breach between science and theology should be restored is a condition for addressing the challenge of evil. To speak about evil, the church should listen to the witness of the Bible but combine it with insights provided by the sciences. The problem of evil involves an immensity of mystery to such an extent that an analytical, reductionist ("left-brain"), as well as an integrative ("right-brain") means of exploration, are needed. In reductionist fashion, the little pieces are examined one at a time in relative isolation. What is required is that one simultaneously employs intuition, feeling, faith, and revelation to approach the mystery of evil in an integrative manner.

One cannot separate the problem of evil from the problem of goodness. If there were no goodness in the world, it would not have been possible to consider the problem of evil. That evil occurs in the world is more understandable than that there is goodness.[30] When people ask why evil exists in the world, they presuppose that the world is inherently

---

30. Peck, *People of the Lie*, 45.

good and that it became contaminated with evil. However, it is easier to explain evil from a scientific point of view. The law of entropy determines that all things decay. That life should evolve into more complex forms is not so understandable, and it is improbable that it would occur. That a child should lie, cheat, or steal is observable and comprehensible from our experience with children (including our own experience as children). That a child grows up and becomes honest and acts with integrity as an adult is not so easily explainable. Laziness is more the rule than diligence, dishonesty more than honesty. Perhaps it is clearer to assume that we live in a naturally evil world that became "contaminated" with goodness than that we live in a good world that became contaminated with evil.

In speaking of good, it is necessary to reckon with God as an element in the sum. However, at the same time, it is impossible to talk theologically about evil without any reference to the devil.[31] Next, the earliest supposed reference to the devil is discussed, placing the difficulty of interpreting the narrative about the first couple's disobedience in Genesis 3 on the table. It is followed by a discussion of evil, its nature and source, Satan, and the implications for theodicy.

Genesis 3's Influence in Theodicean Thinking

The Serpent in the Book of Genesis 2–3 and Satan

Most Pentecostals probably connect the serpent in the garden of Eden with Satan. However, there does not appear to be any evidence in the Hebrew Bible that the snake in the book of Genesis 2–3 was Satan or even a creature under the direction of Satan, except the reference in Revelation

---

31. The existence of the devil as a real figure has been debated by theologians for the past two hundred years. Most Pentecostals believe in the objective existence of the devil, although some are reticent to speak of the devil in personal terms. It is important not to invest the devil with authority that is not rightfully his by focusing too much attention on evil and demonic powers. Some Pentecostals, for instance, share in paranoid worldviews that believe that everyone is demonized in some degree and that all the nations of the world are under the control of unseen princes and powers, such as Jezebel, the prince of Persia, or the Antichrist (partly due to their interpretation of Dan 10:13, illustrating how they employ a text in another context to their own). What must be taken seriously is the fact that Christ is now the head of every ruler and authority and has driven out the prince of this world. The human psyche is neither holy nor demonic in itself; yet when it is orientated towards the devil it becomes a realm of unwholesome demonic activity. One of the most pressing questions we are facing today is: How can we oppose evil without creating new evils and being made evil ourselves?

12:9 that describes Satan or the devil as the "ancient serpent" and the deceiver of the whole world. Wisdom of Solomon (ca. 220 BCE–50 CE) might be the earliest literature to make this connection (2:24). The link between Satan and the serpent is also attested in the book The Life of Adam and Eve (33) and the book of 2 Enoch (31). Both texts state that it was the devil who led Eve astray.[32]

It is submitted that the narrative in Genesis 3 serves to symbolically explain how evil in the world originated and why it persists. It describes the propensity of people to do evil and their God-given capacity to choose for or against God, choosing negatively. It does not accept that the narrative is about two people whose choice determined everyone else's history who lived in their wake. The serpent represents the human inclination to choose evil in selfishness and pride rather than a speaking and walking animal. Sin leads to human beings setting themselves up as rivals of God, as demonstrated by the garden narrative, disqualifying people from realizing the purpose of their creation, as explained in the first two chapters, to stand in a relationship with God.

Reinhold Niebuhr defines "original sin" as the inherent urge of both nations and individuals to identify their own view of what is right or good with what is right and good for everyone. Giving it a more philosophical import, Paul Tillich writes that original sin refers to the sense of "alienation" we experience as finite beings separated from our essential nature. For both, because we are trapped in what sometimes feels like a vast spiderweb, our thrashing around only makes it worse. We need something from the outside to help us, and thus "grace," expressed in diverse ways throughout the Bible, enters the picture as God's benign response to the idea that "original sin" seeks to convey.[33] Based on a literal interpretation of Genesis 2–3, the Christian doctrine of original sin is troubling to many modern believers for several reasons, writes Annette Evans.[34] First, the doctrine views human beings as born sinners without hope of ever conquering their sinful nature. However, it does not fit contemporary society's optimism about the prospects of human beings. Second, believers struggle with the meaning and justice of inherited guilt, as well as its proposed consequences. Third, it is not easy to reconcile concepts of human freedom and responsibility with a doctrine that states that humans

---

32. Seal, "Satan."
33. Cox, *How to Read the Bible*, 29.
34. Evans, "Augustine and Pelagius as a Cameo," 2.

are trapped in sin by their very nature and cannot help themselves. Augustine formulated the doctrine of "original sin" that occurred with the disobedience of Adam and Eve in the garden of Eden, allowing evil and brokenness to enter the world.

In contrast, Jewish rabbi Harold Kushner argued for a God who hurts with hurting people because this God is not actually omnipotent. There are things that God cannot do, such as prevent people from committing evil acts that hurt themselves and those around them.[35] What does the doctrine of original sin consist of, and is it possible to salvage it to make sense to contemporary people?

Augustine's Doctrines of Original Sin and Total Depravity of Humankind

Augustine was born in the fourth and wrote in the fifth century CE. Like Camus, he was born in Africa. The problem of evil preoccupied his mind. He believed in a single creator God who is at the same time the God of salvation. To explain how the world shaped by such a Creator can include so much natural and moral evil became an acute problem. Ultimately, Camus argues, Augustine's theodicean "justification of God" necessitated three kinds of moves.[36] First, Augustine assigned the advent of evil to Adam's sin and so conceived of the evils that humans continued to suffer as so many, and just punishments visited upon subsequent generations because of original Adamic sin. Second, moral evil was slated to human free will. At the same time, in his *querelles* with the Pelagians, Augustine also claimed that Adamic sin meant that humans were unable even and ever to choose the good. Third, Augustine referred to the unplumbable mystery of God's unfathomable will to explain the ongoing evils of the world, developing the doctrine hinted at in Paul of the unfathomable separation of the chosen elect from the rejected.

Although the doctrine of original sin (*peccatum originale* in Latin) emerged in the third century CE, Augustine systematized and developed it formally to explain the origins of humanity's sinful nature by demonstrating that all people are born with an inherited tainted nature and a proclivity to sin through the fact of birth. As a result, they are born with

---

35. Kushner, *When Bad Things Happen to Good People*. The work of Kushner was also referred to in chapter 5 in discussions about God as the omnipotent one.

36. Srigley, "'That Other North African," 53–68.

the built-in urge to do wrong rather than evil things and disobey God. People are born totally and absolutely depraved, without the hope of doing good consistently. Their second nature is to partake in evil. This is an essential doctrine within the Roman Catholic Church. The Council of Trent formalized the concept in the sixteenth century, and it is today still the accepted doctrine in the Roman Catholic tradition. Many believers from the Protestant tradition also subscribe to the doctrine's validity or a part of it, following the lead of Reformers Martin Luther and John Calvin. Luther and Calvin maintained that original sin is to be connected to "concupiscence" (or hurtful, evil desire), implying that all people lost their free will except to sin. While Catholics think that a baby's baptism imparts the life of Christ's grace and erases original sin so that the baby is not doomed when dying at an early age, necessitating the sprinkling of babies, Protestants disagree and argue that nothing can erase original sin except the individual's choice to turn to Christ. The implication is clear: a baby who dies and is not elected by God's grace is lost eternally. Lutherans and Calvinists emphasized that nobody can accept Christ as Savior except those elected by God to do so; in them, the Spirit will commence doing a work of grace, and they will turn to Christ in time before they die. In all cases, the consequences for a sinful nature that is weakened and inclined to evil persist in all believers, and they need to fight against sin in a spiritual battle that only ends at death or with the second coming of Christ.

"Original sin" refers to both the spiritual disease or defect in human nature inherited from the first human couple's disobedience to God and the condemnation and curse that followed on Adam and Eve's sin (Gen 3:14–19).[37] It is used to explain why there is so much wrong in a world created by a perfect God; evil is the result of the first humans' choice to follow the snake's advice. It also explains why all human beings, without exception, continued to do evil and do not stand in the right relationship with God. They need to be saved from the condemnation inherent in their raptured relationship. Significant is that original sin refers to a condition, not something that people do or do not do. Human beings' normal spiritual and psychological state is that they are sinful because they were born as sinners. Original sin does not refer to evil thoughts and actions of human beings. Even newborns are wicked and doomed to hell because they were born that way; they are already damaged by original sin.

37. BBC, "Original Sin."

Original sin resulted from Adam and Eve's disobedience to God in the garden of Eden. The effect was that God judged them guilty and sentenced them to live with guilt outside the garden. The same is true of all people; they are born separated from God, guilty, and therefore liable to be judged at the end of the world. Original sin also explains the genocide, war, cruelty, exploitation, people's almost animalistic and cruel actions, and more; it results from the presence and universality of sin in human history.

R. C. Sproul represents the Reformed position when he states that the doctrine of original sin defines the consequences to humans because of the sin of the first human couple.[38] Adam and Eve's sin resulted in original sin. As a result, the nature of all human beings is under the dominion of the power of evil. He refers to Psalm 51:5: "Indeed, I was born guilty, a sinner when my mother conceived me." David does not assert that he did something evil by being born, but he acknowledges that all human beings have fallen. People are not sinners because they sin; they sin because they are sinners.

Sproul distinguishes between "total" depravity and "utter" depravity. "Utter" depravity implies that human beings are as evil as they could possibly be. "Total" depravity suggests rather that Adam and Eve's fall affects the whole person, captures human nature, affecting even their bodies and leading to illness and death. It affects their thinking, weakening and darkening it. It involves the human will so that people do not exercise their moral power in all cases. The power of sin infects the whole person. Sproul prefers the term "radical corruption" because it concerns the root (Latin term for "root" is *radix*) of being human, penetrating to the core of their being. People are essentially sinful, without exception.

With evil forming the core of human beings, to improve requires more than making some minor adjustments or behavioral modifications. It needs a total, radical renovation from the inside to be regenerated and quickened by the power of the Spirit. What is required is that the Holy Spirit changes the human core, the heart. Being regenerated by the Spirit, however, does not instantly or permanently vanquish sin. Instead, the believer is occupied in a spiritual war against evil until the new world dawns, when evil and sin will be ultimately defeated.

Adherents of the doctrine argue that there is no way that human beings can correct their relationship with God and cure themselves of original sin. Therefore, they need God's grace and the provision of Jesus,

---

38. In Sproul, "TULIP and Reformed Theology: Total Depravity."

who died on the cross, to be saved. What they need to do to be saved is to accept God's offer of salvation by believing that Jesus died on the cross for them and that God forgives those who call on God.

Some contemporary thinkers subscribe to the concept of original sin without accepting that the doctrine is literally true. Instead, they use it to describe the reality of the human condition, that the world is not always an excellent place to live in for all people, and that people do not always act in a good, reasonable, or humane manner. Human beings' behavior is also described in terms of some things outside the individual's control, such as events in the individual's past or family and cultural customs.

Many contemporary Christians find the idea objectionable that babies could share in humanity's total depravity and that they are doomed to eternal hell if they die. How does the curse in Genesis 3:17–19 imply babies? What is critical is to understand that the origins of sinfulness in the garden of Eden do not derive from Augustine's reading of the interpretation of Genesis 3 from Genesis 3 itself; instead, it is based on Paul's epistles. Remarkable is that the Old Testament does not ever refer again to the events in Genesis 3 again. It clearly does not feature in further theological developments of the concepts of sin and grace in the Old Testament. Most contemporary scholars share the consensus opinion that the narrative of Eden, a part of the primeval "history" of Genesis 1–11, is a myth that the author used to emphasize the tendency and inclination of human beings to commit evil instead of good. It was not intended to be a historical record.

This study finds appeal in the Eastern Orthodox tradition's rejection of the Augustine doctrines of original sin, total depravity, and hereditary guilt. It explains that sin originates with the devil, the one who sins from the beginning (1 John 3:8). Original sin is not concerned with transmitted guilt but with transmitted mortality. In Adam's punishment, all humanity shares because of their inclination to sin, but they do not share in his responsibility.

The Eastern Churches follows Johan Cassian (ca. 360–435 CE), who qualified the doctrine of total depravity by teaching that human nature is fallen or depraved, but not totally. All people have moral freedom, implying the option to choose to follow and obey God. Some sparks of goodwill still exist, but all attempts are totally inadequate to impress God, and only direct divine intervention ensures salvation.[39]

---

39. Hassett, "John Cassian."

Eastern Christianity prefers the doctrine of ancestral sin, that original sin is hereditary. Adam and Eve's tendency to sin was passed on to their descendants. Like water flowing from an infected source, from mortal parents infected with sin proceed children infected with sin. Humanity did not inherit guilt from anyone; they inherited their fallen nature. Although they bear the consequences of the first couple's wrong, they do not pay the personal responsibility associated with this sin.

This study accepts that each person is responsible for their own choice to sin, although they share a tendency with all humanity to sin.[40] The origins of evil in human beings cannot be blamed on one couple's foolishness to disobey God. Where the human preference for evil comes from is not explained anywhere in the Bible. That people share the inclination does not imply that they cannot choose to do good instead of evil. Unbelievers are no exception, and it is true that they, in some cases, show more sensitivity and consideration for the needs of other people and the planet than some Christian believers.

Toward a Psychotheology of Evil

In the tradition of Plato, traditional Christian theology stresses that a distinction should be made between moral evil and suffering. Moral evil (*malum culpae*) is inevitably the result of the free will of human and angelic beings. Non-man-made suffering (*malum poenae*) can result from either malevolent spirits permitted by God to punish, correct, or warn human beings or follows as an integral element of the laws of nature, implying that God is not all-powerful.

Evil consists of the desire to control other people in order to further one's own interests. It may foster dependence on someone else, discourage their capacity to think for themselves, diminish their originality to keep them in line and manipulate them to serve their own interest. Erich Fromm writes that the evil person tries to avoid the inconvenience of life by transforming others into obedient automatons, in the process robbing them of their humanity.[41] The good person is characterized by the opposite, as someone who appreciates other people and their contributions and distinct personalities as unique. While goodness promotes life and

---

40. Even (some) mentally challenged people share in the inclination to do evil, even though they cannot be held responsible or accountable for their actions.

41. Fromm, *Heart of Man, Its Genius for Good and Evil*, 124.

liveliness, evil seeks to kill life and liveliness. Both good and evil are a force that resides either inside or outside of human beings.[42]

One of the biggest problems in a scientific discussion of evil is that the existence of a reality outside the natural is to be presupposed, as religion accepts. In terms of a history of religions, it is possible to distinguish between three major theological models of evil. First, Hinduism and Buddhism refer to a nondualism in which evil is envisioned as the other side of goodness. There can be no death without life or decay without growth; in the same way, there cannot be evil without goodness. The distinction between good and evil is, then, an illusion; the one cannot exist without the other, and they are two sides of one coin. A second model depicts evil as distinct from goodness, but both goodness and evil are part of God's creation. Second, the Hebrew Bible represents God in terms that presuppose that God alone creates, decides, and acts, and all other forces are subject to God.

Further, integrated dualism teaches that God creates human beings with the free will to decide for themselves what they choose to do, either good or evil. By creating humanity in God's image, God had to endow them with free will, because free will characterizes God. In this way, God permits human beings the option of choosing evil instead of good. Martin Buber speaks of "yeast" in the "dough," a metaphor also utilized by Jesus (Matt 16:6), referring to the ferment placed in the soul by God and without which the dough could not rise.[43] Thus, evil falls within the range of God's reign and under God's control. The third and final model is diabolic dualism, where evil is regarded as being not of God's creation but a dreadful cancer that God does not and cannot control and falls outside God's reign. Traditional Christianity supports this view, as does the New Testament and the apocalyptic tradition found in a small part of the Hebrew Bible, probably because of Jewish exposure to Persian Zoroastrianism.[44] Traditionally, Pentecostalism shares this apocalyptic worldview.

In discussing human evil, theology's dialogue should partner with psychology and psychiatry, including significant contributions such as Freud's discovery of the unconscious, Jung's concept of the Shadow, and Fromm's analysis of Nazism. After having fled Hitler's Germany with its

42. Peck, *People of the Lie*, 42.
43. Buber, *Good and Evil*, 94.
44. Armstrong, *Fields of Blood*, 18–19; Nel, "View of Time in Ancient Cultures," 207–17; Nel, "Daniel 9 as Part of an Apocalyptic Book?," 1–8; Cox, *How to Read the Bible*, 24.

persecution of, *inter alia*, Jews, Fromm identified an evil personality type as part of his examination of evil people.[45] These evil people were identified by the judgment of history as evil, as in the case of some leaders of the German Third Reich. Fromm, however, never met the subjects of his examination but could only study them through the witness of their writings and other people. Fromm's study might have created the idea that "evil people" are significant political figures contained in history. The man who abuses his wife or the mother disciplining her children in an inhumane way would then not fall within this category.

Fromm was the first scientist to identify an evil personality type clearly and suggest that they be studied separately.[46] The problem, as already stated, is that psychology and psychiatry in acknowledging the existence of evil must at the same time also recognize the presence of the "supernatural," representing a world of powers and forces that cannot be subjected to standard forms of experimentation necessary to qualify for scientific endeavors. However, psychology of evil cannot exist without also being a theology of evil, argues Peck,[47] implying that science needs to incorporate valid insights from different religious traditions.[48] For this reason, the subheading of this section refers to a "psychotheology."

Integrating psychology and theology is needed because Christianity is threatened with its replacement by psychology, which seems to be better adapted to the contemporary climate. Christians must now compete with this secular alternative for the privilege of ordering and providing meaning for human life. Integration, then, is the task of understanding and mediating this competition. And the comprehension of human evil is a central arena in which the struggle is apparent. Hopefully, understanding the nature of this struggle will yield a creative response based on some mutual and necessary understanding of human nature. Integration cannot be accomplished simply by endorsing fabricated constructs,

---

45. Erich Fromm, born as Erich Seligman Fromm to Jewish parents, was one of the world's leading psychoanalysts. He was also honored as a social behaviorist, a philosopher, and a Marxist.

46. Fromm, *Anatomy of Human Destructiveness*, 4.

47. Peck, *People of the Lie*, 50.

48. That psychology and psychiatry at times do not know what to do with evil is demonstrated by the four volumes of *Psychology and the Bible*, edited by Ellens and Rollins, which discusses psychology as an angle to read the Bible. No reference to evil can be found in these volumes.

utilizing "hermeneutic acrobatics," or by accepting quasi-spiritual translations of tradition as valid platforms for compatibility.

Paul Ricoeur is another essential voice that should be listened to when he speaks about the theme of evil, a concern throughout his long career.[49] He designates the phenomenon of evil as a challenge in opposition to the traditional approach, which views evil as a problem of logical coherence between propositions.[50] He argues that this approach does not hold when the concrete experience of evil confronts one. In his phenomenology of evil, evil committed (that is, "sin" in Christian parlance) is at the same time distinct from and entangled with evil suffered (e.g., pain, violation, illness, death, natural disasters, etc.) He then surveys the successive stages of speculation about the origin and *raison d'etre* of evil. The first way is the myth that narrates the origins of evil to account for it. Wisdom is the second way when it asks why. It leads to the following question: Why do I suffer and suffer more (and worse) evil than others? The third way of speculation is in *gnosis*, or the system of knowledge, which proposes an ontological answer to the "all-encompassing problematic."

Augustine responded to Gnosticism by arguing that evil is not a substance but a privation. It consists of human beings choosing to turn away from God. Ricoeur thinks this is significant because it takes the problem of evil away from ontology and relates it to humans' will, action, and morality. However, he rejects Augustine's "false concept" of original sin that combines the heterogeneous notions of biological transmission with individual imputation of guilt that ends in viewing suffering as a consequence of the fall, which "leaves unanswered the protest against unjust suffering . . . by condemning it to silence in the name of a mass accusation of the human race."[51] Ricoeur believes that any theoretical resolution of the enigma of evil leads to aporia. He instead advocates a turn from theory to practice, "a response aimed at making the aporia productive."[52] To turn from theory to practice is not simply turning away from thinking but instead another way of thinking about evil, acknowledging that it is ultimately inscrutable.[53] It requires the realization that it is impossible to make evil comprehensible. The only practical way to

---

49. Ricoeur, *Evil: A Challenge to Philosophy and Theology*.
50. Ricoeur, *Evil: A Challenge to Philosophy and Theology*, 33–34.
51. Ricoeur, *Evil: A Challenge to Philosophy and Theology*, 48–49.
52. Ricoeur, *Evil: A Challenge to Philosophy and Theology*, 65.
53. Ricoeur, *Evil: A Challenge to Philosophy and Theology*, 66.

respond to evil entails acting ethically and politically to decrease the evil that people commit and suffer by diminishing the quantity of violence. He then writes, "All evil committed by one person . . . is evil undergone by another person. To do evil is to make another person suffer. Violence, in this sense, constantly recreates the unity of moral evil and suffering."[54] Action alone is, however, insufficient and requires an emotional response, which lament initiates.[55] One should transform lament into a complaint, enabled by Freud's cathartic process, called the "work of mourning."[56] Lament is "a catharsis of the emotions."[57] The lament needs to integrate ignorance (*docta ignorantia*) because it realizes that it is impossible to discern divine reasons for suffering, especially punishing people. Lament should lead to the complaint and protest against God's involvement, much like the Psalmist's cry, "How long, O Lord?" It implies a complaint against theodicy. But such an accusation also contains (what Ricoeur calls) the "impatience of hope," trusting God to transform reality and engender new possibilities. Lament must also develop to where the suffering person can separate belief in God from the urge to explain evil, believing in God despite evil.[58] The last perspective is the *theologis crucis*, the belief that the Christian somehow participates like God in Christ's suffering, functioning at the apex of renouncing lament.[59]

The cross should be the starting point for a Christian response to sin and suffering. Ricoeur discusses Barth's claim that God confronts *das Nichtige* in Christ and conquers it "by 'annihilating' himself on the cross,"[60] agreeing that evil is a challenge to philosophy and theology.

On the other hand, Jung reproaches and criticizes the Christian church regarding how it thinks about evil. In *The Undiscovered Self*, he describes it as "one of the main prejudices of the Christian tradition, and one that is a great stumbling block."[61] Jung complains that we are told we should eschew evil in the Christian tradition, neither touching nor

---

54. Ricoeur, *Evil: A Challenge to Philosophy and Theology*, 66.

55. Ricoeur, *Evil: A Challenge to Philosophy and Theology*, 645.

56. Quoted in Ricoeur, *Evil: A Challenge to Philosophy and Theology*, 67.

57. Ricoeur, *Evil: A Challenge to Philosophy and Theology*, 646.

58. Ricoeur, *Evil: A Challenge to Philosophy and Theology*, 69–70.

59. See also the discussion in the second chapter about cruciform theology. The practice of lament proposed in a Pentecostal context was described at the end of the previous chapter.

60. Ricoeur, *Evil: A Challenge to Philosophy and Theology*, 60.

61. Jung, *Undiscovered Self*, 109.

mentioning it. This attitude towards evil, he argues, "flatters the primitive tendency in us to shut our eyes to evil and drive it over some frontier or other like the Old Testament scapegoat."[62] If we are to overcome the evil of our day and stop "the monstrous engines of destruction," we must come to terms with that element of the personal unconscious composed of the inferior, weak, primitive, and unreasoned evil that is in and inherent to us. This collectivity is the thing he terms the Shadow. Negligence of this Shadow "is the best means of making [oneself] an instrument of evil. What is even worse, our lack of insight deprives us of the capacity to deal with evil."[63]

Moreover, wholeness and individuation are possible only after one has come to terms with one's Shadow side. By integrating the concepts of awareness of personal evil and acceptance of guilt for one's evil with the notion of growth, Jung does indeed provide a corrective to the tendency to project evil and blame onto others. As he says, this projection stands in the way of self-knowledge. Although this insight or self-knowledge cannot promise the reduction or elimination of evil (because evil is a complex phenomenon), it can contribute to growth. If one can become mindful of one's evil potential as reprehensible, one is forced to see evil's enormity in one's own reflection. Rather than seeing evil as "out there," as something that others do, one is better off if one could see that, as Jung says, "Man has done these things; I am a man, who has his share of human nature; therefore I am guilty with the rest and bear unaltered and indelibly within me the capacity and inclination to do them again any time."[64] Genuine growth would take place. For this reason, the church's emphasis on "sin" and believers' awareness of the need to grow in "holiness" stay important themes.

Buber distinguishes between two types of myths about evil.[65] In the first case, people "slide into evil," while in the second, they have already slid or fallen victim to evil; in some cases, they have been taken over by evil so that they function at its command. The theology of evil allows all people, including believers, to be tempted to do evil, while some have chosen to surrender their lives to evil powers. They have crossed the line and descended into radical evil. They do not only do evil; they have become evil.

---

62. Jung, *Undiscovered Self*, 110.
63. Jung, *Undiscovered Self*, 110.
64. Jung, *Undiscovered Self*, 109.
65. Buber, *Good and Evil*, 139–40.

In this regard, Hebrews 3:7–19 uses the analogy of the people led by Moses from Egypt who angered God with their sins and disobedience; their corpses lay in the wilderness. Because they turned their hearts from God and refused to do what God told them, God took an oath that they would not enter God's place of rest (vv. 10–11). The author allows that believers' hearts can become evil and unbelieving so that they turn away from God (v. 12) and become hardened against God (v. 13). The theme is picked up again in Hebrews 6:4–8 after discussing the rest that awaits those who remain faithful, that some have turned away from God who were once enlightened, had experienced the good things of heaven, shared in the Holy Spirit, tasted the goodness of the word of God, and the power of the age to come. Such people cannot be brought back to repentance; they had surrendered to evil when they kept on rejecting the Son of God (Heb 6:6).

The typical reaction to evil is confusion and disgust, a spontaneous and God-given early-warning radar system, in the words of M. Scott Peck.[66] However, such a countertransference reaction is contraproductive in helping people eliminate and get rid of the destructive evil that is starting to characterize their lives. It is not possible to help an evil person without feeling empathy for their situation. However, it is difficult to empathize with evil people who live to deceive others as they have also successfully deceived themselves. In many instances, they specialize in confusing their audience.

What is needed is that the confusion is penetrated and evil be named for what it is. The requirement for helping an evil person is then that the helper occupies a position of remarkable spiritual and psychological strength, understanding that the evil person is living in fear of self-exposure and the verdict of their own conscience, causing them to be the most frightened of human beings.

In the light of the lack of involvement from most medical specialists in the treatment of evil people, the church needs to take the responsibility upon itself to attempt to rescue evil people from the hell that they have created for themselves and those who share their world, for the sake of society.[67] For the church to get involved, it will need to understand the

---

66. Peck, *People of the Lie*, 73.

67. Saving people from hell is not limited to preaching the good news that Jesus died for the lost but includes taking responsibility to care for the victims of suffering. An example of such caring from the Roman Catholic perspective is the practice of mothering souls through the "church mother," a ministry comparable to that of a

nature of evil to acquire the skill to treat it. Evil should be identified as a specific form of mental illness[68] and treated in terms of what Christians believe about evil, that Jesus has successfully conquered it on the cross. Supposing that illness and disease are defined as any defect in the structure of the human body or personality that prevents a person from fulfilling their potential as a human being, evil qualifies *par excellence* to be called an illness.

In investigating Paul's understanding of the activity of Satan, one finds that Paul had more to say about Satan than one might think. Humans are under his control because "they have participated in the sin of Adam," which R. H. Bell describes by using the concept of "identical repetition."[69] Bell also argues that, for Paul, those "participating in the death and resurrection of Christ" have been "released from Satan's bondage."[70] This is expressed ritually through baptism and the Eucharist, both of which are understood as "speech-event[s]" affecting "existential displacement."[71]

In ending the letter to the Ephesians, Paul states the importance of standing firm in the LORD and God's mighty power. Because their fight is against the devil's strategies, they should put on the whole armor of God. The contest is not against enemies of flesh and blood but evil rulers and authorities of the unseen world, against mighty powers in this dark world, and evil spirits in the heavenly places. Their weapons consist of spiritual instruments such as truth, God's righteousness, peace, faith, salvation, and the Spirit, making them the preferred conquerors who will still stand firm after the battle (Eph 6:11–13).

---

spiritual director. Both the spiritual director and the church mother seek to foster the spiritual growth of others, focussing on how God speaks to a given individual or group (McCray, "Mothering Souls," 290).

68. "Ambulatory schizophrenia" is a term that psychiatrists sometimes use, and its relationship to evil needs to be investigated. It refers to a person who generally functions well in the world and never develops a full-blown schizophrenic illness but who demonstrates a specific disorderliness and disorganisation in their thinking, particularly at times of stress, which resembles that of "classical" schizophrenia. Many who qualify to be called ambulatory schizophrenics are in Peck's (*People of the Lie*, 146) view "evil people." They abrogate responsibility, show consistent destructive and scapegoating behavior and excessive but covert intolerance to criticism, have a pronounced concern with their public image and respectability, and suffer from intellectual deviousness.

69. Bell, *Deliver Us from Evil*, 256.
70. Bell, *Deliver Us from Evil*, 263.
71. Bell, *Deliver Us from Evil*, 279.

In their battle against evil, (some) Christians should fearlessly engage the enemy in order to save its victims, without underestimating its dangerous character. Evil should be named; to name something correctly gives a person a certain amount of power over it. Knowing its name allows one to understand something of the dimensions of its power and force. The evil person must hear that they are possessed to a certain extent by a kind of force destructive to the evil person and the people living along with that person.

Evil people usually are not influenced by gentle words; they only react to sheer power. Gentleness is usually the last thing most of us would associate in any case with the rough-and-tumble world of politics and relationships. Politics, we assume, is about conflict and getting interests satisfied.[72] The many instances of demonized people whom Jesus and his disciples freed underscore this powerful approach to evil people. The episode described in Matthew 8:28–32 may serve as an example. Two demonized men who lived in a cemetery were so violent that people could not go through the area without being endangered by their behavior. When they saw Jesus, they reacted by screaming violently at him. Jesus allowed the demons to leave the men and enter a herd of pigs that plunged down the steep hillside into the lake and drowned in the water. What is important to note is that Jesus commanded them to leave.

Although evil people sin, it is not their sins that define their illness. Instead, their sins' subtlety, consistency, and persistence depict their choice to perpetuate their evil behavior. The reason for their choice has to do with their self-perception; the central defect of the evil is not the sin but their refusal to acknowledge that what they do is evil through and through. As explained, evil is the failure to "meet the Shadow," in the language developed by Jung. Sin is not this or that wrong act, but rather the essential alienation of self from self. Sin is separation. Before sin is done, this state of separation is the very character of human life.[73]

Evil people may be any person living anywhere, rich or poor, young or old, educated or uneducated. They are not necessarily criminals like serial killers or involved in corruption, rape, abortion, sacrifices to the devil, or child trafficking. There is nothing dramatic about them. In many instances, they may be solid citizens, lecturers or teachers, bankers or investors, police officers or soldiers. They cannot be designated as evil

---

72. Hauerwas, "The Politics of Gentleness," 78.
73. Hauerwas, *Unleashing the Scripture*, 74.

people except when they acquire enough political, social, or economic power that their evil deeds affect large groups of people. What characterizes them instead is that they conduct evil subtly and covertly but consistently, without any misgivings. Such people form a separate category, apart from other people who act evilly and sinfully. There is nothing random about these evil people's evil deeds; they are inherently evil and cannot act in any other way. Evil people lie repeatedly and routinely. They have become people of the lie.[74] Their life is a pretense. The lies usually are not gross; they cannot be taken to court for their lies. Yet, the process is pervasive. Evil is characteristically inscrutable. While evil deeds do not make a person evil even though they cause destruction, evil people have evil traits.[75]

All people sin at times. "Sin" is a word defined in the Bible, *inter alia*, in terms of "missing the mark." The result when one misses the mark is that one fails. The difference between a sinner and an evil person is that the evil person consistently does evil while at the same time absolutely refusing to tolerate the sense of their own sinfulness. An analogy of sin is the boomerang that returns when it misses the mark and damages the world of the perpetrator, including the sinner.

Christians commonly believe that their sense and awareness of personal sin, leading to feelings of guilt and remediating action, keeps them from their sin getting out of hand. On the other hand, evil people are never displeasing to themselves; they do not self-recriminate. For that reason, they are uncorrectable, making them arrogant and greedy people who are inherently violent. "A society that lives by organized greed or by systematic terrorism and oppression . . . will always tend to be violent because it is in a state of persistent disorder and moral confusion."[76] All sins destroy, alienate, and isolate, betraying the divine and fellow human beings. And while all sins are reparable, the only sin that cannot be repaired is the belief that one is without sin.

---

74. As described in Peck, *People of the Lie*.

75. Peck, *People of the Lie*, 79.

76. Merton, *On Eastern Meditation*, 638. It is difficult to agree on terrorism as a particular species of violence because "terrorism" as such is difficult to define. The word has so much emotive power and one side always sees "terrorism" as "heroic acts of liberation" while the other side views it as destructive. What all agree on is that terrorism is fundamentally and inherently political even when other motives such as religious, social, or economic motives are involved. It is about power—acquiring it and keeping it (Armstrong, *Fields of Blood*, 312–13.

In their refusal to acknowledge or reproach evil in themselves, evil people lash out at others who try to criticize or accuse them. They are willing to sacrifice other people in their scapegoating to preserve their image of self-perfection. Their scapegoating works through a mechanism called projection. As long as evil people deny that their behavior is bad, they must perceive others as bad, projecting their own evil onto the world around them. As a consequence, they perceive evil in other people. Peck defines evil as the imposition of one's will on others by overt or covert coercion in order to avoid spiritual growth for various reasons.[77] Instead of dealing with their own evil behavior, evil people attack and coerce others because they lack conscience or superego.

While they preserve their own self-image of perfection at all costs, they have to maintain the appearance of moral purity and correctness. They lack any motivation to be good, but they intensely desire to appear good. Their goodness is, however, on a level of pretense, a lie. The lie is designed not in the first place to deceive others but to deceive themselves. They do now allow themselves the luxury of self-reproach because they do not tolerate a sense of sin or imperfection. While the psychopath lacks a sense of morality, evil people deny the evidence of their evil; they are not aware of its existence or effects. The evil they commit is not wicked in itself but rather in the cover-up process. Their evil does not consist of the absence of guilt but in their effort to escape it. This makes it easier to observe the lie rather than the evil that is covered by the lie. The false smile hides the hatred as the velvet glove hides the fist.[78] And since the primary motive of the evil is to disguise, one of the places evil people most effectively hide is within the church. Evil people tend to gravitate toward piety for the disguise and concealment it can offer them.[79]

The fundamental problem of human evil is a particular variety of malignant narcissism or self-absorption characterized by an unsubmitted will. Mentally healthy adults submit themselves to something higher than themselves, be it God, love, or another ideal. They accept what is accurate rather than what they would like to be true. They submit themselves to the demands of their own conscience and react to guilt when they disobey their demands.

---

77. Peck, *People of the Lie*, 25.
78. Peck, *People of the Lie*, 85.
79. Peck, *People of the Lie*, 86.

Evil is the consequence of free will. God created human beings in God's own image, implying that God gave them free will, including choosing the option of evil. While all people have free will, some strong people show a willingness to submit themselves to higher ideals, while others offer a desire to exert their own will over others to control them.

The enigmatic narrative of Cain and Abel demonstrates the difference. It seems that God's acceptance of Abel's sacrifice indicates a rejection of Cain's worth.[80] When Cain refused to acknowledge his imperfection, he became angry and looked dejected (Gen 4:5b). He reacted by taking the law into his own hands and murdering his brother. The narrative and its sequel, referring to the descendants of Cain, illustrate the accumulating disorder within human society. Remarkably enough, the term "sin" is used here for the first time in the Bible. Violence is sketched as the product and manifestation of the power of evil. The fact that the first man on earth, as soon as the human race starts to develop itself outside the garden of Eden, commits a violent crime against the only person available, his brother, is telling.[81] It confirms the parents' choice to disobey God's command in the garden of Eden, continuing the trend they set. Fratricide is the archetype of all violence. Violence against one's brother cannot be disposed of as merely an interpersonal event; it has to do with human beings and their relationship with God, the Creator of life. For that reason, violence can never have the last word; because God is involved in all acts of violence, it makes human beings worthy of punishment, and God

80. The question of why the offering of Cain was not accepted has led to at least three different answers. The first explanation starts with the fact of the absence of an explicit motivation of God's choice itself and one cannot but talk of God's inscrutability and reflecting the experience of sometimes inexplicable blessings or misfortunes, acceptance or rejection. A second explanation seeks to find the motive in the nature of the gifts themselves: a blood sacrifice is more pleasing to God than an offering of grain, or Cain's gift was not accepted because it was taken from the soil while the earth was cursed by God shortly before (in Gen 3:17). A last explanation finds the reason for the rejection of Cain and his sacrifice in the attitude of Cain. Peels ("World's First Murder," 37–38) chooses for this alternative and offers as arguments in favor of the view that there is clearly incongruence in the description of the gifts with a detailed description of Abel's offering and how he brings it while Cain brings only some of the fruits of the soil; that in the context of the pericope the full focus is on the progressive hardening of Cain; that an investigation into the motif of the rejection of sacrifices in both the Hebrew Bible and its *Umwelt* brings to light that the proper attitude and obedience of the person who brings the sacrifice is of crucial importance in deciding whether or not it is accepted; and that a broader reading in the context of Genesis 2–11 also sustains this explanation.

81. Peels, "The World's First Murder," 34.

calls the offender to account for his deed. The biblical account localizes the roots of human violence on the breeding ground of turbid emotions. Violence against one's brother flows from great anger and malice, and this hazardous attitude is described as sin. At the same time, in Genesis 4, a countermovement becomes visible where God stands up in favor of life while man chooses in favor of death. YHWH acts simultaneously as a pastor, *iudex supremus*, and protector.[82]

Evil people are characterized by their willingness to take the law into their own hands and destroy life to defend their narcissistic self-image. Their inability to acknowledge their sinfulness and imperfection leads to haughtiness and arrogance that prompts them to reject any judgment of their inadequacy. They operate with the affirmation of their strengths independent of all findings.[83]

The cause of this overweening pride, excessive and obsessive self-absorption, and arrogant self-image of perfection is unknown. Pathological narcissism may be a defensive phenomenon. Almost all young people demonstrate an array of narcissistic characteristics; psychiatrists assume that they grow out of it in the course of normal development. A stable childhood with loving and caring parents accommodates this development. However, where parents are cruel and unloving, or childhood offers other traumatic experiences, infantile narcissism could be preserved as a kind of psychological fortress to protect the child against the vicissitudes of its intolerable life.[84] Children may become evil to defend themselves against the onslaught of parents and other significant adults who are inherently evil, argues Peck.

It is also possible to think of human evil as a continuum with a small minority who are good and evil, and the vast majority are somewhere between. People can move along the line; the tendency is for good to become better and evil to become eviler, although no rule applies to all people. One's moral choices determine one's situatedness along the line. The more people deliberately make wrong ethical decisions, the more their hearts and consciences harden. The author of Hebrews 10:26 refers to such choices in theological language. Suppose people intentionally and consciously choose to keep on sinning even if they know that what they do is wrong ("after having received the knowledge of the truth"); no

---

82. Peels, "The World's First Murder," 35.
83. Buber, *Good and Evil*, 134.
84. Peck, *People of the Lie*, 90.

sacrifice can atone for their wrongdoing but only the terrible expectation of God's judgment and the punishment for a sinner. The author addresses Christians who know the way but decide deliberately and continuously to do what is wrong.

The opposite is also true. Fromm discusses the phenomenon and concludes that each time a person decides to choose the desirable alternative, self-confidence, integrity, and conviction increase until it becomes more challenging to choose the undesirable than to select the desirable.[85] The other side of the coin is also proper. Each time a person surrenders to the wrong alternative deliberately, the path for more surrender is opened until freedom is eventually lost. If the degree to choose the good is excellent, it needs less effort to choose the good. Most people, Fromm argues, fail in the art of living not because they are inherently wrong, evil, or so without will that they cannot lead a better life. Instead, they fail because they do not wake up and see when they stand at a fork in the road that challenges them to decide. They do not realize that life asks them a question and that they still have alternative answers. And with each step along the wrong road, it becomes increasingly difficult to admit that they are on the wrong road. In any case, they are too lazy to turn back and return to the first wrong turn and acknowledge that they have wasted their lives. In Fromm's view, one is not born or created evil or forced to become evil; one becomes evil slowly over time through a long series of choices. The emphasis is on choice and will.

Nature of Evil

What is the nature of evil in all its seriousness and ugliness? Much of evangelical spirituality and theology, especially in its popular and devotional form, is a "misguided effort in whitewashing the walls of our world with sentimental talk about God's love," opines Veli-Matti Kärkkäinen, because it does not take the radical nature of evil and sin and their effects on human lives seriously.[86] Although evil cannot be equated with sin in private life, it can and should not be downplayed. Martin Luther sees God as the all-determining power in the world who not only allows evil but even causes it to some extent and makes use of it in the divine alien work. Since God takes responsibility for evil, God is not a detached

---

85. Fromm, *The Anatomy of Human Destructiveness*, 173–78.
86. Kärkkäinen, "Toward a Pneumatological Theology of Religions," 232.

observer but a suffering God (dei-passionism). While Luther's theology of the cross takes suffering and death seriously, it is also a theology of hope because it shows how God creates the new out of death, life out of *nihil*. Faith is participation in God (*theosis*); Christ's presence in faith makes Christians "Christs," to serve their neighbors in God's world.[87]

A remark about biblical data needs to be made. Evil in theological terms does not exist independently of God and goodness; evil serves as a perversion of what is good, and sin in theological terms is the greatest of wickedness, the root of all evil. Only God and God's creatures exist. God is good. And because God created everything good, God's creatures are good. It follows then that evil has no independent existence, as Origen and Augustine argued when they viewed evil as an eternal substance, grounded in Scripture. Several Hebrew terms relating to evil connote "nothingness" or "vacuousness," e.g., the four words in Zechariah 10:2 translated as "deceit," "lie," "false," and "vain" (in the New International Version). The first of these, *āwen* (fraud, vanity), was linked to *'ayin* ("there is not, that which is not"), parallel to Isaiah 41:24, 29. The gods of heathenism are *elîlîm*, worthless nothings (Ps 96:5), not *elōhîm* (gods). In Greek, the prefix *a-* is negative (e.g., *adikia*, *anomia*, etc.), as are the common symbols of evil: darkness, disease, and destruction.

If evil is then the absence of good, the implication is not that it is an optical illusion or a mere local imperfection but very real, drawing its reality from created things. It exists as the *perversion* and *corruption* of the good, making it more heinous than if it had an independent existence. "The monstrous and, in a sense, positive fact of a malicious and perverted human will is still not, in itself, a substance. It is the perversion of something inherently and in God's intention good, namely a human being."[88] Biblical evidence supports this theory (by keywords, metaphors, and statements, e.g., in Eccl 7:29; Deut 32:5, "a warped and crooked generation," echoed in Phil 2:15). Evil entered history in the abuse of created freedom (cf. Matt 19:8; Rom 5:12).

The primary evil is sin. Genesis 3 traces life's ills to humankind's disobedience: shame and fear (vv. 7, 10); pain in childbearing; the distortion of male-female relationships (v. 16, see Adam and Eve, man and woman); the painful relationship between humans and the ground; and finally, death (vv. 17–19). Paul agrees that death entered the world through sin

---

87. In Kärkkäinen, "Toward a Pneumatological Theology of Religions," 233.
88. Hebblethwaite, "The Christian-Marxist Dialogue," 85.

(Rom 5:12). Unfortunately, the Bible does not provide any more information about the changes that followed the fall. Only human death is mentioned as a direct consequence. The curse on the ground resulted from human exploitation.

Source of Evil

The mystery of the source of evil has troubled thoughtful human beings from the beginning. At first, it was thrashed out in the language of myth, as in Genesis 1:1–2:4a.[89] P, or the Priest, the assumed writer of the account that appears in Genesis 1, may have wanted to depict a God-shaping-chaos scenario, while the second, J, preferred the creation out of nothing (vv. 2:4b–5). If P is correct, with the God-shaping-chaos description, whence did the chaos come? Did God also create that as well? It becomes a critical question for generations of philosophers because this chaos (not God) is often interpreted as the world's source of evil and disorder. But if the second version (J), the *ex nihilo* account, is correct, then we are left wondering whence this disorder and evil came.[90] What was the "formless void," and who created it? Or was it always there? In terms of newer cosmological models, space and time did not exist before the big bang. Biblical writers advanced their reasoning about violence and disorder, not by turning to history or psychology but using mythic language, which can be a powerful way of speaking about the here and now at the deepest level.[91] The vexing issue of evil, which casts its shadow over the first verses of the Bible, bleeds over from the creation narratives into everything in Genesis that follows. It throbs under the chapters on Adam and Eve, Cain and Abel, Noah, Jacob and Esau, Joseph, and his jealous brothers.

Evil reared its slithery head almost immediately after the creation (Gen 3:1). Adam (meaning "man") and Eve ("life") lived in a paradisical garden; in Hebrew, "Eden" means "delight." They were naked and unashamed, all their wants lavishly provided for, but they soon became impatient with being merely mortal. They longed for complete supremacy. They were not content to be human; they wanted to be "like God" (Gen

---

89. Cox, *How to Read the Bible*, 24.
90. Cox, *How to Read the Bible*, 24.
91. Cox, *How to Read the Bible*, 27.

3:5). Ironically, they craved to possess precisely the kind of total control God had just been relinquishing.[92]

A later tradition in the Hebrew Bible, continued in the New Testament, allows for an evil force that opposes the Creator, a personified power of evil to whose aggressive deception human beings are exposed both internally and externally.[93] This power manifests itself as the adversary of God and human beings, like Satan or the devil, who is like "a roaring lion" and who "prowls around, looking for someone to devour" (1 Pet 5:8). Some Christian believers used texts that do not specifically refer to Lucifer or Satan (Ezek; Job) to depict this figure's genesis when he served as God's second-in-command and chief among the angels who organized a heavenly rebellion against God. Initially, God used him to test and tempt God's children (like "the satan" in Job 1:6–12 and its repetition). After his revolution and being expelled from the presence of God, he carried on his intention of undermining God's good creation. Hence, Protestant diabology is drawn almost entirely from traditional rather than scriptural sources. This does not suggest that Protestant diabology is untrue, merely that the claim to follow the Scripture is a complicated matter in a world constructed of tradition and authority.[94]

Some theologians view Satan as a myth whose shelf-life has expired as materialism gains an insolent and mindless triumph in the Western intellect; that is until the tragedy of a severely beaten and abused child, a mass murderer's coy smile, the mass horrors of the socialist Gulag, or the national socialist death camps confront them. Theologians have responded to the problem of evil in at least four general ways. First, they offer a theodicy that attempts to provide God's (actual or possible) reasons for permitting evil. Second, some theists seek to show that arguments purporting to demonstrate a problem of evil for theism are flawed and that such arguments may involve a questionable inference from "As far as we know, there is no reason that would justify God in permitting horrors" to "There is no such reason," a response that can be called "skeptical theism." Third, some theologians admit that the problem of evil is a special difficulty for theism; nevertheless, natural theology and/or religious experience provide adequate reasons or warrant for theism. Fourth, some

---

92. Cox, *How to Read the Bible*, 28.
93. Bell, *Deliver Us from Evil*.
94. Some modern authors like Georges Bernanos, Thomas Mann, and Flannery O'Connor seem to have faced evil clearly enough to see a grace beyond human understanding.

theologians argue that, although theism does not explain the presence of all evils well, it gives an explanation that is as good as (or better than) the answer provided by some (or all) of the metaphysical rivals.

Pentecostals' reading of the Bible allows for the existence of Satan. Especially in the Third World context, believers experience the interference of Satan and his evil powers continuously and in continuation with their existence within, e.g., the African world of ancestor honoring and witchcraft. Satan's rebellion and fall with his angels created a counterweight to God's Spirit pleading in human beings' hearts to faithfully serve and honor God.

Pentecostal services that typically emphasize healing sometimes find it necessary to minister deliverance when evil spirits manifest. This practice is especially the case among Africans, where superstition and *sangomas* are inherent in their culture. When the "spirit" is interrogated at its manifestation during deliverance, it typically identifies itself as an agent of the devil or Satan, displaying the evil intention of the evil powers for human beings.

A central problem in the theodicy is: Why did God allow evil to exist? If God created Satan and the powers united behind him when he rebelled (if such rebellion took place at all), why did God not destroy these powers at the moment of their uprising? The question should be answered in conjunction with the question concerning evil among human beings. Why does God allow evil to exist among people? Why did God not eradicate it when it first manifested?

The standard theological argument is that God created human beings with free will and, in that sense, limited his own power to interfere in human affairs to a certain extent. The same argument can be applied to the existence of evil forces and their evil intentions with God's creation. Perhaps the Creator gave Satan and the powers free will as well. And the Creator does not destroy, not even evil, but only creates.

A Theology of Evil

In reflecting on God's goodness, love, and power in terms of suffering, evil is the other element that needs to be defined carefully. In philosophical terms, evil is classically defined as the "absence of the good" (*privatio boni*). It denotes the "depravation, corruption, and perversion of the good of creation," as darkness consists of the absence of light and silence of the lack of sound.[95] The Westminster Confession (6.6) provides a theological definition that sin is "a transgression of the righteous law of God."[96] Few Christians would disagree with this definition.

Nevertheless, the Confession's definition of sin is not complete enough because while it expresses a truth about sin, it says too little to discriminate sin from evil. Sin certainly involves the transgression of divine law, but so does any evil, and not every evil counts as sin. Natural evils, for instance, such as the damage and destruction that earthquakes and hurricanes can do, are not sinful. Therefore, the Confession falls short in that it underspecifies the kind of evil that sin is. A distinction between natural and human evil seems to be necessary. Human evil consists of humans' participation in acts like murder, corruption, or other crimes, while natural evil consists of destruction due to fire, earthquake, floods, etc.

The concept of human evil has been central to religious thought for as long as humans have penned their thoughts. During the last few decades, however, such discussions have become conspicuously absent in the part of the church that caters to postmodern human beings, such as third-wave Neo-Pentecostals.

Suffering and death bring us to the problem of evil. "Evil" is what ought not to be. Mordecai M. Kaplan is rightly acclaimed as one of the greatest Jewish thinkers to have emerged from the American Jewish context. Writing shortly after the Holocaust in his *The Future of the American Jew*, he insists that "'[evil] seems to be a necessary condition of life which we accept as part of existence. 'Good' is no less part of that mystery [of existence].'"[97] Traditionally evil has been divided into the three categories of "natural" (suffering arising from natural causes: floods, earthquakes, etc.), "moral" (suffering arising from human causes, from minor mistreatment to murder), and "metaphysical" (suffering arising from basic facts about the human situation, such as the inevitability of death). However, other discussions limit their understanding of the concept of moral evil, which is the most troubling from a theological perspective (e.g., why did God not allow human beings to suffer but gave them the capacity to make others suffer as well?)

---

95. Scott, *Pathways in Theodicy*, 13.
96. Westminster Divines, "The Westminster Confession of Faith."
97. Kaplan, *Future of the American Jew*, 181.

The three basic responses to the primary problem of evil are the religious response that life can be affirmed because evil is in some way justified or redeemed;[98] the ethical response that life can be affirmed in the struggle to eliminate evil; and the Sisyphean response that life can be affirmed despite evil, which cannot and should not be either justified or eliminated.

The religious response is, however, not unanimous. Kaplan, for instance, writing from the perspective of Judaism, states that all of religion calls upon human beings to believe that the element of helpfulness, kindness, and fair play is not limited to humans alone but is diffused throughout the natural order.[99] It asks them to obey the moral law so that they may call to their aid those forces in the world that operate towards human life and its enhancement. They cannot claim to comprehend why evil should be necessary, but in affirming the existence of God, they deny to evil the nature of absoluteness and finality.

It is possible to distinguish between physical/metaphysical evil (misfortune, woe) and moral evil (offense, wrong). The Bible recognizes both kinds. The Hebrew word for "evil," *ra'*, occurs about 640 times, and 40 percent of these cases refer to some calamity. There are other words for mishaps (e.g., *šō'â*, trouble, storm) and moral fault or sin. In New Testament Greek, the word *kakos* has a wide application: it is used to denote Lazarus's poverty and sores (Luke 16:25), the harm caused by a venomous snakebite (Acts 28:5), and the moral evil of which Jesus and Paul are innocent (Mark 15:14; Acts 23:9) and which issues from the human heart (Mark 7:21). The word and its cognates occur 121 times. The other common terms used in the New Testament for evil are *ponēros* and *ponēria* (derived from *ponos*, toil or pain, Col 4:13; Rev 16:10–11). It occurs eighty-five times and refers to physical evil, the bad condition of the eye (Matt 6:23), and pain resulting from the plague (Rev 16:2), but more often to that which is wicked and worthless, the store from which men and women, being evil, draw the evil things they do and say (e.g., Matt 12:35 uses *ponēros* three times). In classical Greek, *ponēros* may have been the more substantial term, suggesting hardened malignity. Still, while it is used more frequently than *kakos* to refer to moral evil in the New Testament, the latter is an equally strong word (cf. Mark 7:21; Matt 15:19).

---

98. This statement complicates the issue of how one convicted of murder is to be punished. The Hebrew Bible is clear; Gen 9:6 states that whoever sheds the blood of a human, by a human shall that person's blood be shed (Knight, "Can a Christian Go to War?," 495).

99. Kaplan, *Future of the American Jew*, 75–76.

Evil and Suffering Attributable to Spiritual, Human, and Natural Causes vs. Spiritual Causes

When God created human beings with the capacity to choose between good and evil, as a part of their being created in God's likeness, did God create an imperfect world? Should God not take responsibility for at least a part of the results of the human choosing for evil? Does it not demonstrate that God's creation of human beings was a flaw?

The question is related to another, which asks to what extent God is involved in creation daily. Does God cause everything that happens? If the answer is positive, then one can reason that everything that happens does happen because it is related to God's choice that it happens. Then a natural disaster may indicate that God is punishing some people and an illness that the sick person has sinned against God. God did this because of what an individual or a group of people did. However, to use such determinism to "speak for God" or justify God cannot be supported by biblical evidence, philosophical consistency, or daily experience. Such determinism, deism, and dualism are not acceptable ways to account for the brokenness that characterizes all creation, such as the universe's state of entropy and the existence of diseases among all living beings, the occurrence of hatred and strife, conflict and war, etc.

What is true is that God, as primordial reality, is the primary cause of everything that happens, including evil, because God brought everything into existence and is responsible for its existence. But the kind of universe and the way human beings were created show that they are moral agents with the capacity to determine their own lives to a certain extent. For example, driving a vehicle at high speed while being in a drunken stupor and causing an accident that claims the lives of other people is clearly a personal choice. The same is true of people who abuse their bodies by overindulging in food and drink, smoking or using drugs, and then experience health problems. People are born with talents and capacities that are in some cases genetically determined; how they apply their talents and utilize their capabilities is their own choice.

God is indeed responsible for the secondary causality of everything globally, but the primary responsibility for a world war or genocide lies with people, politicians, and military leaders. The same is true of floods and droughts caused by global warming as a verifiable result of human abuse of resources. What exists is called to flourish by participating in

God and God's purposes with creation; when these purposes are ignored, it is done at risk to human survival.

Suppose God would have forced human beings to serve God and do good, even if only by denying them the ability to choose between good and evil. It would have deprived them of the fulfillment of the ability to negotiate and grow in a relationship with God. Instead, God's love created freedom for humans to exist as they do, as self-determining beings. Love that is not free to reject the object of love cannot be real love determined by loyalty.

Christians view the source of goodness as God, who is good. In contrast, moral evil did not exist in God, nor was it created. Evil is instead the faulty exercise of good-created things, such as free will, freedom to choose, and self-determination. It is the abuse of choices and actions that turn them into evil. Evil is the result of the abuse of God-given freedom; human beings act in evil ways when they choose what is anti-good and anti-God. In the Pentecostal tradition that blames Satan and his demonic forces for all kinds of evil manifestations, it is imperative to see human culpability in evil acts for what it is: wrongly exercised human choices. And when people continue with such evil deeds, they might eventually become evil people.[100]

What about natural disasters, sometimes referred to as natural evil?[101] Stanley Hauerwas emphasizes the importance of building what he calls a "community of character" capable of facing tragedy without resorting to self-deceiving explanations.[102] Natural disasters are "tragedies" because they create great suffering for humans and animals, and they are caused by powers that no human being can control. Whether or not a particular explanation is "self-deceiving" may depend more on the question to which the explanation responds and its purpose rather than on the content of the explanation itself. Many Christians refer to Paul's remarks in Romans 8:22–23 and reason that such disasters are examples of creation groaning in labor pains. Daniel Castelo refers to

---

100. See, e.g., the significant work of the psychiatrist Peck, *People of the Lie*, referred to earlier in this chapter.

101. For instance, a tsunami in the Indian Ocean on December 26, 2004, killed more than 150,000 people in a dozen countries. In 2010 an earthquake in Haiti left 230,000 people dead and in 2011 an earthquake in Japan killed 29,000 people. In 2019, 7.1 million people were suffering from starvation as a result of famine in southern Sudan and since 2016 more than 85,000 children have died in Yemen alone from starvation (Orr-Ewing, *Where Is God in All the Suffering?*, 87).

102. Hauerwas, *A Community of Character*.

Terence Fretheim, who distinguishes between a "good creation" and a "perfect creation," explaining that natural disasters represent a part of God's creational purposes.[103] What is called "evil" is actually, in many cases, the result of geological and atmospheric patterns that characterize the earth's development and shaping. Creation was not a finished product when God created it, but it evolved with all biological life forms. When such evolution results in the loss of human lives and property, human beings call it evil, leading to the quest to find out why such things happen. This question is anthropocentric because it views natural catastrophes as not scientific explanations but human perceptions. Thus, to call such disasters "natural evil" is a misnomer.[104]

The relation between the theological category of "sin" and "evil" is in the faulty exercise of human self-determination, resulting from the freedom humans received in creation. Sin can be defined as human arrogance and the decision to deliberately choose for the non-realization of the purpose for which humans were created, in contrast to God's goodness to create human beings. They miss the mark the Creator set.

The tragedy is that sin can become a collective endeavor due to cultural and religious baggage, as in the case of racism, sexism, and genderism. Collective behavior becomes evil when people are stereotyped as "the other" and rejected in generalized terms. For example, a political ideology in Germany after the First World War turned Jews into subhuman beings that needed to be weeded out. Later, communists grouped all non-communists together, calling them "capitalists" and declaring them the state's enemies. The same happened in many Western countries during the Cold War, stereotyping all people striving for socialist ideals as "communists." In conservative religious circles, the same phenomenon still occurs in terms of people of other sexual orientations. They are grouped together as "sinners" and rejected out of hand, without distinguishing between the widely diverse groups of lesbians/gays, bisexual, transgender, intersexual, and queer people. The result is structural or systemic sin built on prejudice. The sinning person or community misses the mark by using a boomerang that proverbially returns and injures the person using it as a weapon. Sin always destroys, and the victims regularly include the innocent, because sin is by nature anti-God, anti-creation, and therefore

---

103. Fretheim, *Creation Untamed*. See also Carlson, "Open God of the Sodom and Gomorrah Cycle."

104. Castelo, *Theological Theodicy*, 51.

anti-human.[105] Humans who sin are behaving in a substandard way to what the Creator intended for them. In discussing theodicy, it is crucial to remember that much of the evil that human beings suffer is related to the choices to act contrary to the purpose human beings were intended to realize.

Satan and Theodicy

As far as Satan is concerned, blamed by many Christians for the woes in the world, it needs to be stated that Christian belief about the devil is in many cases not related to the viewpoints and different perspectives found in the Bible. "Satan" is a Hebrew word that translates as "the one who opposes, obstructs, or accuses." The Greek term literally means "adversary." Sometimes the New Testament uses the term as a title or a name: (the) Satan. David Seal, in *The Lexham Bible Dictionary*, writes that the Old Testament uses "satan" as a noun to refer to a human opponent, and it is usually translated as "adversary" or "enemy."[106] For instance, when he built the temple, King Solomon stated that it was a good time to do so because he did not have any "satan" or "adversary" that might want to hinder him from this endeavor (1 Kgs 5:4). David refers to Abishai in the same terms as an opponent or adversary (2 Sam 19:22). At times, the word "satan" is also used to refer to a supernatural figure, as in Numbers, where an angel of the Lord is called a "satan" because he obstructs Balaam and his donkey's way (Num 22:22). That does not imply that the angel is a "satan," only that he is opposing Balaam in his purpose to thwart God's will. The book of Job also refers to a supernatural "satan" figure. This entity functions in God's court, reports to God, and can only act in conjunction with God's wishes when he tests Job's faithfulness (Job 1:6). The term is used with a definite article, suggesting that the term does not refer to a specific person but rather to a title or an office. The entity functions on the same level as an angel ("messenger"). As a participant in the divine council along with the sons of God, it seems that his task is concerned with the observation of human beings on earth. "The satan" functions as an accuser, not as a rebellious being undermining God's good purposes. One finds something similar in the book of Zechariah, where the term "satan"

---

105. N. T. Wright (*Evil and the Justice of God*, 19) remarks that Satan is not only opposed to Israel, Jesus, and the church but also to creation itself.

106. Seal, "Satan."

is applied within the context of a trial (Zech 3:1). The high priest Joshua stands before the Angel of the LORD, and he is being accused by "the satan." "The accuser" is not acting maliciously; he serves as a prosecuting attorney, seemingly questioning whether Joshua is fit for the priesthood. In 1 Chronicles, "satan" is also connected to some type of supernatural being (1 Chron 21:1; cf. 2 Sam 24:1). The impression is that the LORD incites David by using a "satan." Clearly, "the satan" does not refer to the devil that Christians refer to, portrayed in later literature as God's chief rival, but to an office or function that falls under God's direct control. In the entire Old Testament, nowhere does one find a presentation of the "satan" as the personification of evil.

There might be two passages (Isa 14:12–15; Ezek 28:11–19) that seem to describe Satan's rebellion, as such interpreted by the Life of Adam and Eve, originally from the first century BCE or CE. The text analyzes the fall of the Day-Star (*Lucifer*) as the fall of Satan and his angels (Life 12–15; see 2 Enoch 29:4–5). Several passages also refer to angels as stars (Jud 5:20; Job 38:7; 1 Enoch 104:1; Testament of Moses 10:9). Satan is a part of those creatures God cast out of heaven because of their rebellion in this tradition.

One finds in Second Temple literature (second and first centuries BCE) the first references to "satan" as a proper name (The Assumption of Moses 10:1; Jubilees 2:23–29). This figure is the archenemy of God and humanity, linked in the Wisdom of Solomon with the phenomena of death (Wis 2:24). His aim is death; for that reason, Satan had to bring human beings to sin, to separate them from the source of their life, God.[107] Satan is also called Belial, Mastema, and Satanail (Testament of Gad 4:7; Testament of Benjamin 7:1; Testament of Reuben 4:7; Testament of Simeon 5:3; Testament of Asher 3:2; Jubilees 11:5; 2 Enoch 31:6). Now believers verbalize the hope for Satan's speedy destruction as the author of evil and sin (Testament of Levi 18:12; Testament of Judah 25:3).[108]

The New Testament connects to the figure that developed in the intertestamental period; Satan is viewed as the primary enemy of God and believers. Satan is directly opposing Jesus from the start. Before beginning with his ministry of proclaiming the coming of the kingdom of God, Jesus is tested in the wilderness by Satan, a place of desertion and death connected to Satan. By winning over Satan by relying on what the

---

107. Wright, *Evil and the Justice of God*, 19.

108. The snake as a possible "satan" in Genesis 3 was discussed earlier in the chapter.

Bible teaches (Matt 3:17; 4:1–11), Jesus obeys God's will, in a symbolic way undoing Eve's and Israel's disobedience.

The New Testament describes some individuals as afflicted with demons. Luke 13:11, 16 connects an ill woman with "a spirit that had disabled her" with the words, "whom Satan bound for eighteen long years." Whether "Satan" in 13:16 and "spirit" in 13:11 refer to the same entity is unclear. John relates Judas's betrayal of Jesus to "Satan" who entered him (John 13:27). Does this refer to possession by Satan or oppression? The text does not make it clear. According to Jesus, the devil is a busy enemy, trying to undermine the arrival of the kingdom of God. He is the evil one that snatches away the seed that falls along the path (Matt 13:19; Mark 4:15), causing people to neglect the message of the kingdom of God, and wicked people are referred to as followers or children of the devil (John 8:44; Acts 13:10; Rev 2:9; 3:9; 1 John 3:8).

Satan is also viewed as a defeated enemy (Matt 13:36–43; Rom 16:20; Heb 2:14–15; 1 John 3:8; Rev 20:2); the enemy is already conquered (Rev 12:7–10). However, that does not deny that Satan is aggressively attacking people, and several texts encourage believers to be on guard against his attacks (2 Thess 3:3; Jas 4:7; Rev 2:24).

Satan is called a dragon (Rev 20:2), a serpent (Rev 12:9), the evil one (John 17:15; Eph 6:16), and a tempter (Matt 4:3; 1 Thess 3:5) that prowls like a lion (1 Peter 5:8), characterizing him as the enemy of God. He is a ruler of the kingdom of the air and leader of the demonic realm (Eph 2:2). The belief aligns with and accommodates the first century CE's cultural beliefs, which accept that spirits exist somewhere between heaven and earth. Satan is also referred to as "Beelzebul" (e.g., Matt 12:27; Luke 11:18), "lord of the house," or "lord of the heights." Perhaps it implies that Beelzebul or Satan is in charge of the demons.

Whence does Satan come? According to Revelations 12:7, Satan lost a war in heaven at the genesis of the world, and Michael and his angels cast out the devil and his angels from heaven (Rev 12:7). First John describes the devil as one who "has been sinning from the beginning" (1 John 3:8). The phrase "from the beginning" might refer to the Genesis account, linking the devil with the serpent, although it is improbable and implausible. The New Testament suggests that the "great dragon," or "ancient serpent," who is called "the Devil and Satan, the deceiver of the whole world," was cast from heaven, that is, God's presence, down to the earth along with his followers, who were also angels. His fall was due to pride (1 Tim 3:6); he is a "murderer from the beginning," devoid of any truth (John 8:44).[109]

There are two dangers in terms of the devil's existence. The first is to assert that such an entity does not exist except in the imagination and mythology of ancient people. The result is that evil is seen as a problem that requires a rational explanation and solution. The other is taking the devil too seriously, making him an easy scapegoat for people who are unwilling to take responsibility for their behavior, as argued above.[110] Especially among Pentecostals, it seems that the last danger occurs. The concept of warfare led many Pentecostals to become engaged in actively pursuing tactics that they assume assist the case of God. In the process, many of their efforts serve the unintended purpose of overemphasizing Satan's powers. What should not be forgotten is that the war was already won on the hill of Golgotha, and believers are part of a cleanup process.

It cannot be denied that the New Testament argues in terms of a provisional cosmic dualism that consists of good and evil powers and that threaten God's purposes with creation. Christians recognize it and experience the tension of being involved in a battle between the forces of light and darkness, with their own choices, decisions, and behavior contributing to the good of tolerance and recognizing the dignity of all people or the evil of decay and chaos.

---

109. Seal, "Satan."
110. Castelo, *Theological Theodicy*, 54.

7

Conclusion

THE DISCUSSION CONCLUDES THAT Christians are not able to justify what God does because God *per se*, as well as God's ways, are a mystery to them. The puzzle of theodicy remains unsolved until the missing variables are inserted. That will only happen with the consummation of the present world and the establishment of the new earth and heaven.[1] The most Christians can do in speaking about God is to adore and worship the great God who created everything and revealed the divine self to human beings. Christians are not called to compile information about God but to encounter God through the divine Spirit and worship God as the Master of the universe. The role of Christians is not to answer the challenges that theodicy poses to human logic but to busy themselves with their calling, to serve the *missio Dei* to reach the lost world with God's love. The primary Christian response to evil, suffering, and human sin is, in Daniel Castelo's words, not to explain and try to justify God's ways in allowing people and the rest of creation to suffer but to move to action, to realize the kingdom of God in the world through their acts of compassion to the needy and helpless.[2] Instead of theorizing about evil, Christians can spend their time judiciously by combating the roots of evil, as far as it is in their capacity to do so effectively.

This study argues, like open theism, for non-exhaustive divine foreknowledge in the face of theodicy's challenges, because God is finite and

---

1. Scott, *Pathways in Theodicy*, 207.
2. Castelo, *Theological Theodicy*, 69.

dependent on the world.³ At the same time, unlike process theology, it affirms that God is infinite, necessary, ontologically independent of the world, transcendent, and omnipresent, all orthodox teachings of Christianity. To be valid, theology should be dialectical when speaking about God. Furthermore, it argues that God is open to new experiences and flexible in how God works in the world. Because God has not predetermined the future, it can hold surprises, even for God. The problem this study has with open theism is that its statements about God are propositional and dogmatic. It is made with the assurance that it is possible to describe God's essence with confidence. Pentecostal hermeneutics affirms that knowledge of God's essence can be encountered in charismatic experiences with the Spirit, but it is impossible to develop it into theological propositions or dogmatic statements. God as the one who falls outside the human frame of reference can be experienced but not described. It is possible to understand God's heart and follow suit, in one's own life, without limiting God with words to refer to the divine that is necessarily and essentially anthropomorphic.

Jürgen Moltmann refers in this regard to the provisionality of theodicy, a perspective that this study supports.⁴ He argues that there are no definitive, final answers to the attempt to vindicate divine justice and explain suffering. Such answers are not a condition for understanding suffering; instead, what is needed are the resources to engage the problem of suffering by addressing its diverse roots. Moltmann emphasizes that no one in the world can answer the theodicy question; suffering remains the "open wound of life" in our world. To live with the open question of theodicy is to be willing to suspend final judgments until the arrival of the eschatological future while keeping one busy with the realization of that new kingdom in the present reality. Christians pray for the coming of God's kingdom while at the same time they spend their energies to realize it in their personal world.

Bernard Adeney-Risakotta argues that human tragedies do not have a single, fixed ontological meaning.⁵ The meaning of suffering is not fixed for all time; each human being creates a specific meaning or concludes that it is meaningless. However, the meaning they verbalize is not merely subjective or arbitrary; they are not free to create any meaning.

---

3. Zeeb, "Open Theism and the Problem of Theodicy," 301.
4. Moltmann, *Trinity and the Kingdom*, 49.
5. Adeney-Risakotta, "Is There a Meaning in Natural Disasters?," 229.

Instead, the meaning is substantively objective and developed in terms of the social surroundings and personal perceptions. The meaning may also be evolving. In the case of natural tragedies, Adeney-Risakotta argues that all the affected people create collective meaning in relation to each other. At first, such meaning may be superficial and wrong, but in time, meaning may be established that the majority of the affected community accepts. Such meaning then has the potential to change the meaning of the remembered event and the future of the community shaped by the memory.

Adeney-Risakotta refers to Nietzsche, who wrote, "One must still have chaos in oneself to be able to give birth to a dancing star."[6] Natural disasters are concerned with the facts of suffering, the chaos in us; human beings must find meaning in it for themselves. They use different sources, sometimes in combination, including folk wisdom, religious language, and scientific discourse. In each case, meaning represents symbolic moral systems based on assumptions that cannot be proven. No one system of discourse is more important or valid than the others. People need such symbolic and extended vocabularies to find and describe meaning in suffering because such events can easily confound their conventional understanding.

In surveying evidence of such discussions about meaning in suffering in the Old and New Testament, one finds several such discourses, relating suffering to, *inter alia*, the retribution for sin, human freedom to decide about individual participation in good or evil actions, or as disciplining, testing, conditional to the development of character, participation in the suffering of Christ, etc. The fact that several discourses exist implies that believers in earlier times also utilized different discourse systems based on their own perceptions and probably shifting perspectives. Thus, it permits and requires contemporary believers to find meaning for themselves in their own suffering, developing a discourse that reflects their experience.[7]

To contribute to the redemption and healing of the world requires Christians to look for the underlying cause of the evil that oppresses human beings and concerns themselves in addressing and solving it as far as it is in their power. In South Africa, which condemns millions of

---

6. Adeney-Risakotta, "Is there a Meaning in Natural Disasters?," 242.

7. As an example I refer to two friends, both believers and ministers of the gospel, who have daughters of nearly the same age (in their mid-twenties) and suffering from the same physical and mental challenges. They (and their wives) interpret their situation differently, assigning different meanings to their experiences with such a child.

its inhabitants through structural inequality to a life of poverty, believers only need to look past the privileged neighborhoods to the squatter camps and shantytowns that litter the outskirts of South African cities and towns.[8] While attending to the most pressing needs of the needy, they also need to address the historical, political, and economic causes of such inequality. The calling of Christians includes that they carry evangelical standards into politics, economy, health care, and education. They should follow the early Christians, who opted to avoid explanation for the sake of living communally to support and care for the poor and hungry. As Stanley Hauerwas explains, the suffering around us is not a metaphysical problem that requires philosophical debates to find a solution but a practical and existential challenge that urgently requires a response, because people are dying.[9]

One's response to suffering forms a crucial part of realizing the significance and meaning of one's life. The way one responds to one's own suffering, and those of others, show how one responds to being a human and mortal. Faith offers the structure to address these challenges, not by presenting answers to our "why" questions but by participating in the *missio Dei*.

In this regard, the most crucial element is probably cultivating the potential to feel empathetically with another who suffers, a feeling that requires genuine engagement. Christian compassion is not only a feeling for the victims of suffering but requires that one's hands get dirty in taking care of those in need.

What is advocated, in conclusion, is not a philosophical theodicy but a pastoral one, where the priesthood and prophethood of every believer imply the empathic involvement of believers in the lives and suffering of other people constructively and lovingly. They care for and bear the burdens of fellow believers in the first place but then selflessly reach out to others who cross their roads, living sacrificially to change their world for the better. What they need is the courage and boldness to live ex-centrically, finding their center outside themselves in shared commitments

---

8. South Africa suffers from one of the highest levels of inequality when measured by the commonly used GINI index. For instance, the top 20 percent of the population holds over 68 percent of income, compared to a median of 47 percent for similar emerging markets while the bottom 40 percent holds 7 percent of income, compared to 16 percent for other emerging markets and countries (IMF, "Six Charts Explain South Africa's Inequality.").

9. Hauerwas, *God, Medicine, and Suffering*, 51.

to the coming kingdom of God, among the poor, the suffering, and those who need the message of God's grace and power.[10] Their attention is especially directed to the marginalized in society; like early Pentecostals, they look with Christ's eyes at alcoholics who are abusing their families, uprooted migrants who are not welcomed in the host society, those who are rejected due to their alternative sexual orientations, the unemployed and unemployable, etc. They contribute to shifting the faith community into a caring community and into its surrounding world, by resisting the temptation to speak for others and explain away the agony of those who struggle with loss, avoiding easy solutions and answers like, "God is in control, and it will work out," or "I know what you are experiencing." They take care not to dehumanize the needy and suffering by being present and listening patiently to them while at the same time addressing the preventable causes of suffering due to human cruelty or callousness.[11] At times they find themselves in awkward and difficult situations, but as representatives of the one who died on the cross, they wait hopefully for the final restoration of creation.

---

10. Kritzinger, "Ministerial Formation," 44.
11. Schmidt, *When Suffering Persists*, 111–21.

Bibliography

Adams, Marilyn M. "Horrendous Evils and the Goodness of God." In *The Problem of Evil*, edited by Marilyn M. Adams and Robert M. Adams, 297–323. New York: Oxford University Press, 1990.

———. *Horrendous Evils and the Goodness of God*. Ithaca, NY: Cornell University Press, 1999.

———. "Redemptive Suffering: A Christian Solution to the Problem of Evil." In *The Problem of Evil: Selected Readings*, edited by Michael L. Peterson, 169–87. Notre Dame, IN: University of Notre Dame Press, 1992.

Adeney-Risakotta, Bernard. "Is There a Meaning in Natural Disasters? Constructions of Culture, Religion and Science." *Exchange* 38 (2009) 226–43.

Albertz, Rainer. *Israel in Exile: The History and Literature of the Sixth Century BCE*. Translated by David Green. Leiden: Brill, 2004.

Albrecht, D. E. *Rites in the Spirit: A Ritual Approach to Pentecostal/Charismatic Spirituality*. JPTS 17. Sheffield, UK: Sheffield Academic, 1999.

Allan, Deborah Joy. "Sertraline, Suffering, and the Spirit: How do Pentecostal/Charismatic Christians Respond Faithfully to Depression?" DPhil diss., University of Aberdeen, 2018.

Allan, Richard. "Contemporary Pentecostal Hermeneutics: Toward a Critical Realist Epistemology." MPhil diss., University of Birmingham, 2008.

Anderson, Alan. *To the Ends of the Earth: Pentecostalism and the Transformation of World Christianity*. New York: Oxford University Press, 2012.

Apostolic Faith Mission of South Africa. "History of the AFM." https://afm-ags.org/about-us/history-of-the-afm/.

Archer, Kenneth J., and Andrew S. Hamilton. "Anabaptism-Pietism and Pentecostalism: Scandalous Partners in Protest." *Scottish Journal of Theology* 63.2 (2010) 185–202.

Archer, Kenneth J. *The Gospel Revisited: Towards a Pentecostal Theology of Worship*. Eugene, OR: Pickwick, 2011.

———. "Pentecostal Hermeneutics: Retrospect and Prospect." In *Pentecostal Hermeneutics: A Reader*, edited by Lee Roy Martin, 131–48. Leiden: Brill, 2013.

Arendt, Hannah. *Eichmann in Jerusalem: A Report on the Banality of Evil*. New York: Viking, 1963.

———. *The Origins of Totalitarianism*. 2nd enlarged ed. Cleveland: Meridian, 1951.

Armstrong, Karin. *Fields of Blood: Religion and the History of Violence*. London: The Bodley Head, 2014.

Arrington, F. L. "The Use of the Bible by Pentecostals." *Pneuma* 16.10 (1994) 101–07.

Asamoah-Gyadu, J. Kwabena. "'From Every Nation under Heaven': Africa in World Pentecostalism." In *Global Renewal Christianity: Spirit-Empowered Movements Past, Present, and Future: Vol. 3: Africa*, edited by Vinson Synan, Amos Yong, and J. Kwabena Asamoah-Gyadu, xxvii–liv. Lake Mary, FL: Charisma House, 2016.

Audi, Robert M. "Theodicy." In *The Cambridge Dictionary of Philosophy*, edited by Robert Audi, 910–11. 2nd ed. Cambridge, UK: Cambridge University Press, 1999.

Augustine of Hippo. *The Confessions of Saint Augustine*. Translated by E. B. Pusey. https://www.gutenberg.org/ebooks/3296.

———. *The City of God*. Translated by Marcus Dods. Peabody, MA: Hendrickson, 2009.

———. *Concerning the City of God against the Pagans*. Translated by H. Bettenson, edited by D. Knowles. Middlesex, UK: Penguin, 1972.

———. "De Trinitate." In *Nicene and Post-Nicene Fathers, First Series, Vol. 3*, translated by Arthur W. Haddan. Buffalo, NY: Christian Literature, 1887. http://www.newadvent.org/fathers/130115.htm.

———. "Enchiridion." In *Nicene and Post-Nicene Fathers, First Series, Vol. 3*, translated by J. F. Shaw. Buffalo, NY: Christian Literature, 1887. https://www.newadvent.org/fathers/1302.htm.

Barth, Karl. *Church Dogmatics I.2: The Doctrine of the Word of God*. Translated by T. H. L. Parker. London: T. & T. Clark, 1957.

———. *Church Dogmatics II.1: The Doctrine of God*. Translated by T. H. L. Parker. London: T. & T. Clark, 2010.

———. *Church Dogmatics III.1: The Doctrine of Creation*. Translated by T. H. L. Parker. London: T. & T. Clark, 2010.

Bartleman, Frank. "Frank Bartleman and Azusa Street." In *Azusa Street: The Roots of Modern-Day Pentecost*, edited by Vinson Synan, i–xxvi. 1925. Plainfield, NJ: Logos, 1980.

———. "How Pentecost Came to Azusa Street." In *Witness of Pentecost: The Life of Frank Bartleman*, edited by Donald Dayton, 39–53. New York: Garland, 1985.

Barton, John, and John Muddiman. *The Oxford Bible Commentary*. Oxford: Oxford University Press, 2001.

BBC. "Original Sin." https://www.bbc.co.uk/religion/religions/christianity/beliefs/originalsin_1.shtml.

Bell, R. H. *Deliver Us from Evil: Interpreting the Redemption from the Power of Satan in New Testament Theology*. WUNT 216. Tübingen: Mohr Siebeck, 2007.

Berkhof, Louis. *Systematic Theology*. Grand Rapids, MI: Eerdmans, 1938.

Bierma, Lyle. "The Heidelberg Catechism." *Ligonier*, April 1, 2008. https://www.ligonier.org/learn/articles/heidelberg-catechism.

Boer, Harry R. *An Ember Still Glowing: Humankind in the Image of God*. Grand Rapids, MI: Eerdmans, 1990.

Bonhoeffer, Dietrich. *Letters and Papers from Prison*. Edited by Eberhard Bethge et al. Dietrich Bonhoeffer Works 8. Minneapolis: Fortress, 2010.

Borrowed, "Gebruik die Middel (Use the Means)." *Comforter and Messenger of Hope* 1.1 (May 15, 1932) 3–4.

Bosman, J. E. "Teorieë vir 'n Genesingsbediening in die Apostoliese Geloof Sending van Suid-Afrika (Theories for a Ministry of Healing in the Apostolic Faith Mission of South Africa)." MTh diss., University of South Africa, 1988.

Boyd, Gregory A. *God at War*. Downers Grove, IL: InterVarsity, 1997.

Brown, C. Gunther. "Introduction: Pentecostalism and the Globalisation of Illness and Healing." In *Global Pentecostal and Charismatic Healing*, edited by C. Gunther Brown, 523. Oxford: Oxford University Press, 2011.

Brueggemann, Walter. *Isaiah 40–66*. Louisville: Westminster John Knox, 1998.

———. *The Message of the Psalms: A Theological Commentary*. Minneapolis: Augsburg, 1984.

Bryant, Antony, and Kathy Charmaz. "Grounded Theory Research: Methods and Practices." In *The SAGE Handbook of Grounded Theory*, edited by Antony Bryant and Kathy Charmaz, 1–28. London: SAGE, 2007.

Bryant, Barry E. "John Wesley: On the Origin of Evil." *Wesley Fellowship Occasional Paper* 7 (1992) 111–26.

Buber, Martin. *Good and Evil*. New York: Charles Scribner's Sons, 1953.

Bultmann, R. "The Problem of Hermeneutics." In *New Testament Mythology and Other Basic Writings*, 69–93. Philadelphia: Fortress, 1984.

Burger, Isak. *Die Geskiedenis van die Apostoliese Geloof Sending van Suid-Afrika (1908–1958)*. Braamfontein, South Africa: Gospel, 1987.

Burger, Isak, and Marius Nel. *The Fire Falls in Africa*. Vereeniging, South Africa: Christian Art, 2008.

Burrell, David B. *Deconstructing Theodicy: Why Job Has Nothing to Say to the Puzzle of Suffering*. Grand Rapids, MI: Brazos, 2008.

Cairns, Alan. *Dictionary of Theological Terms*. Belfast, UK: Ambassador Emerald International, 2002.

Calvin, John. *Institutes of the Christian Religion*. Translated by Henry Beveridge. 1536. Peabody, MA: Hendrickson, 2012.

———. *Opera Quae Supersunt Omnia, Vol. XIII*. Brunsvigae, Germany: C. A. Schwetzke Et Filium, 1875.

———. "Sermon on Job 1:6–8." In *Calvin's Doctrine of the Word and Sacrament*, edited by R. S. Wallace, 3–43. Edinburgh: Oliver and Boyd, 1953.

Campbell, Courtney S. "What More in the Name of God? Theologies and Theodicies of Faith Healing." *Kennedy Institute of Ethics Journal* 20.1 (2020) 1–25.

Camus, Albert. *Carnets 1942–1951*. Translated by P. Thody. London: Hamish Hamilton, 1966.

———. *The Plague (La Peste)*. Translated by Stuart Gilbert. New York: Vintage, 1947.

———. *The Rebel (L'Homme Révolté)*. Translated by Richard Clouet. London: Penguin, 1951–52.

Carlson, Reed. "The Open God of the Sodom and Gomorrah Cycle." *Journal of Pentecostal Theology* 21 (2012) 185–200.

Carny, Pin'has. "Theodicy in the Book of Qohelet." In *Justice and Righteousness: Biblical Themes and their Influence*, edited by Henning G. Reventlow and Yair Hoffman, 71–81. JSOT Suppl 137. Sheffield, UK: JSOT Press, 1992.

Carson, D. A. *How Long, O Lord? Reflections on Suffering and Evil*. Grand Rapids, MI: BakerAcademic, 1990.

Carter, Jason A. "The Book of Job Through Central African Eyes: Theodicy, Suffering and Hope Amongst Fang Protestant Christians in Equatorial Guinea." DPhil diss., University of Edinburgh, 2014.

Cartledge, Mark. *Testimony in the Spirit: Rescripting Ordinary Pentecostal Theology*. Explorations in Practical, Pastoral, and Empirical Theology. Farnham, UK: Ashgate, 2010.

Castelo, Daniel. *Theological Theodicy.* Eugene, OR: Cascade, 2012.

———. "What If Miracles Don't Happen? Empowerment for Longsuffering." *Journal of Pentecostal Theology* 23 (2014) 236–45.

Chan, Simon. *Pentecostal Theology and the Christian Spiritual Tradition.* Eugene, OR: Wipf and Stock, 2000.

Charnock, Stephen. *Discourses upon the Existence and Attributes of God, Vol. 1.* Grand Rapids, MI: Baker, 1979.

Childs, Brevard S. *Isaiah.* Louisville: Westminster John Knox, 2001.

Clifton, Shane. "The Dark Side of Prayer for Healing: Toward a Theology of Well-Being." *Pneuma* 36 (2014) 204–25.

———. "Theodicy, Disability, and Fragility: An Attempt to Find Meaning in the Aftermath of Quadriplegia." *Theological Studies* 76.4 (2015) 765–84.

Cobb, John B., Jr., and David Ray Griffin. *Process Theology: An Introductory Exposition.* Philadelphia: Westminster, 1976.

Copeland, Kenneth. *Our Covenant with God.* Fort Worth, TX: Kenneth Copeland Ministries, 1980.

———. *You Are Healed.* Fort Worth, TX: Kenneth Copeland Ministries, 1979.

Cox, Harvey. *How to Read the Bible.* New York: HarperCollins, 2015.

Crane, R. A. "Why Believers Experience Sickness." *Comforter and Messenger of Hope* 3.8 (August 1934) 9–10.

Crenshaw, James L. *Defending God: Biblical Responses to the Problem of Evil.* Oxford: Oxford University Press, 2005.

———. "Shift from Theodicy to Anthropodicy." In *Theodicy in the Old Testament,* edited by James Crenshaw, 1–16. Philadelphia: Fortress, 1983.

———. "Theodicy and Prophetic Literature." In *Theodicy in the World of the Bible,* edited by Antti Laato and Johannes C. de Moor, 238–55. Leiden: Brill, 2003.

Cross, F. L., and Elizabeth A. Livingston, eds. "Hell." In *The Oxford Dictionary of the Christian Church,* edited by F. L. Cross and Elizabeth A. Livingston, 753. Oxford: Oxford University Press, 2005.

Dankbaar, W. F. *Kerkgeschiedenis.* Groningen, Netherlands: Walters-Noordhoff, 1974.

Davies, E. W. *The Immoral Bible.* London: T. & T. Clark, 2010.

De Chardin, Pierre T. *The Future of Man.* Translated by Norman Denny. New York: Harper and Row, 1969.

Dell, Katharine. *"Get Wisdom, Get Insight": An Introduction to Israel's Wisdom Literature.* London: Darton, Longman and Todd, 2000.

Dostoevsky, Fyodor. *The Brothers Karamazov.* Translated by Constanze Garnett. New York: Modern, 1996.

Duff, Nancy J. "Recovering Lamentation as a Practice of the Church." In *Lament,* edited by Sally A. Brown and Patrick D. Miller, 3–14. Louisville: Westminster John Knox, 2005.

Editor. "Healing Helps." *Comforter and Messenger of Hope* 10.11 (November/December 1918) 15.

eHymnbook.org. "Though Shadows Deepen and My Heart." http://ehymnbook.org/CMMS/hymnSong.php?id=pd16252.

Ellens, J. Harold, and Wayne G. Rollins, eds. *Psychology and the Bible: A New Way to Read the Scriptures.* 4 Vols. Westport, CT: Praeger, 2004.

Elliger, Karl. *Deuterojesaja in Seinem Verhältnis zu Tritojesaja.* Stuttgart: Kohlhammer, 1933.

Ellington, S. A. "Pentecostals and the Authority of Scriptures." *Journal of Pentecostal Theology* 4.9 (1996) 16–38.
Engelbert, Pamela F. *Who Is Present in Absence? A Pentecostal Theological Praxis of Suffering and Healing.* Eugene, OR: Pickwick, 2019.
Evans, Annette H. M. "Augustine and Pelagius as a Cameo of the Dilemma Between Original Sin and Free Will." *Scriptura* 120.1 (2021) 1–12.
Evans, G. R. *Augustine on Evil.* Cambridge, UK: Cambridge University Press, 1982.
Evans, Rachel H. "The Problem of Biblicism." January 16, 2012. https://rachelheldevans.com/blog/biblicism-christian-smith-bible-impossible.
Executive Council of the AFM of SA. "Minutes." Meeting of General Conference. January 22, 1909. Johannesburg: Auckland Park Theological Seminary Library.
———. "Minutes." Meeting of General Conference. April 2, 1918. Johannesburg: Auckland Park Theological Seminary Library.
———. "Minutes." Meeting of General Conference. July 16, 1918. Johannesburg: Auckland Park Theological Seminary Library.
———. "Minutes." Meeting of General Conference. October 18, 1919. Johannesburg: Auckland Park Theological Seminary Library.
———. "Minutes." Meeting of General Conference. December 11, 1919. Johannesburg: Auckland Park Theological Seminary Library.
———. "Minutes." Meeting of General Conference. April 11, 1920. Johannesburg: Auckland Park Theological Seminary Library.
———. "Minutes." Meeting of General Conference. April 1, 1931. Johannesburg: Auckland Park Theological Seminary Library.
———. "Minutes." Meeting of Workers' Conference. April 2, 1931. Johannesburg: Auckland Park Theological Seminary Library.
Fee, Gordon D. *Gospel and Spirit: Issues in New Testament Hermeneutics.* Grand Rapids, MI: BakerAcademic, 1991.
Fettke, Steven M. "The Spirit of God Hovered Over the Waters: Creation, the Local Church, and the Mentally and Physically Challenged: A Call to Spirit-led Ministry." *Journal of Pentecostal Theology* 17 (2008) 170–82.
Fettke, Steven M., and Michael L. Dusing. "A Practical Pentecostal Theodicy? A Proposal." *Pneuma* 38 (2016) 160–79.
Fretheim, Terence E. *Creation Untamed.* Grand Rapids, MI: Baker Academic, 2010.
———. *The Suffering of God.* Philadelphia: Fortress, 1984.
Fromm, Erich. *The Anatomy of Human Destructiveness.* New York: Holt, Rinehart and Winston, 1973.
———. *The Heart of Man, Its Genius for Good and Evil.* New York: Harper and Row, 1964.
Frost, Stanley B. "The Death of Josiah: A Conspiracy of Silence." *Journal of Biblical Literature* 87 (1968) 369–82.
Geivett, R. Douglas. "Augustine and the Problem of Evil." In *God and Evil: The Case for God in a World Filled with Pain*, edited by Chad Meister and James K. Dew Jr., 65–79. Downers Grove, IL: InterVarsity, 2013.
Gericke, Jacobus G. "A Comprehensive Typology of Philosophical Perspectives on Qohelet." *Verbum Ecclesia* 36.1 (2015) 1–7.
Godet. "Is the Bible Verbally Inspired?" *Comforter and Messenger of Hope* 5.9 (September 1936) 25.
Goldingay, John. *Isaiah for Everyone.* Louisville: Westminster John Knox, 2015.

Goldingay, John, and David Payne. *Isaiah 40–55, Vol 2*. London: T. & T. Clark, 2006.
Gordis, Robert. *The Book of God and Man: A Study of the Book of Job*. Chicago: University of Chicago Press, 1965.
Green, Chris E. "Crucified God and the Groaning Spirit: Toward a Pentecostal *Theologia Crucis* in Conversation with Jürgen Moltmann." *Journal of Pentecostal Theology* 19 (2010) 127–42.
Green, Ronald M. "Theodicy." In *The Encyclopedia of Religion, Vol. 14*, edited by Mircea Eliade, 430–41. New York: Macmillan, 1987.
Grey, Jacqueline. *Three's a Crowd: Pentecostalism, Hermeneutics, and the Old Testament*. Eugene, OR: Pickwick, 2011.
Griffin, David Ray. *Evil Revisited: Responses and Reconsiderations*. Albany, NY: State University of New York Press, 1991.
———. *God, Power, and Evil: A Process Theodicy*. 1976. Philadelphia: Westminster, 2004.
Gutiérrez, Gustavo. *On Evil: God-Talk and the Suffering of the Innocent*. Translated by Matthew J. O'Connell. Maryknoll, NY: Orbis, 1987.
Hagin, Kenneth, Jr. *Executing the Basics of Healing*. Tulsa, OK: Faith Library, 2006.
Hagin, Kenneth E., Sr. *Exceedingly Growing Faith*. Tulsa, OK: Kenneth Hagin Ministries, 1973.
———. *I Believe in Visions*. Tulsa, OK: Faith Library, 2003.
Hanekom, A. R. "Wonder of Vergissing? 'n Teologies-Kritiese Evaluering van Moderne Genesingswonders (Wonder or Mistake? A Theological-critical Evaluation of Modern Miracles of Healing)." MTh diss., University of Stellenbosch, 1985.
Hanson, Paul D. *Isaiah 40–66*. Interpretation: A Bible Commentary for Teaching and Preaching. Louisville: Westminster John Knox, 1995.
Harris, W. Hall, et al., eds. *The Lexham English Bible*. Bellingham, WA: Lexham, 2012.
Hart, L. D. "A Critique of American Pentecostal Theology." PhD diss., Southern Baptist Theological Seminary, 1978.
Hassett, Maurice. "John Cassian." *The Catholic Encyclopedia*. http://www.newadvent.org/cathen/03404a.htm.
Hauerwas, Stanley. *A Community of Character*. Notre Dame, IN: University of Notre Dame, 1991.
———. *God, Medicine, and Suffering*. Grand Rapids, MI: Eerdmans, 1990.
———. "The Politics of Gentleness." In *Living Gently in a Violent World: The Prophetic Witness of Weakness*, edited by Stanley Hauerwas and Jean Vanier, 77–99. Downers Grove, IL: IVP, 2008.
———. "Timeful Friends: Living with the Handicapped." *Journal of Religion, Disability and Health* 8.3 (2004) 11–25.
———. *Unleashing the Scripture: Freeing the Bible from Captivity to America*. Nashville: Abingdon, 1993.
Hauerwas, Stanley, and Richard Bondi. "Memory, Community and the Reasons for Living: Theological and Ethical Reflections on Suicide and Euthanasia." *Journal of the American Academy of Religion* 44.3 (September 1976) 439–52.
Hebblethwaite, Peter. "The Christian-Marxist Dialogue: Beginnings, Present Status, and Beyond." *Sociology of Religion* 39.1 (Spring 1978) 84–89.
Henning, Johannes G. "Vragen en Antwoorden (Questions and Answers)." *Comforter and Messenger of Hope* 3.5 (August/September 1923) 7.
Heraclitus. *Readings in Ancient Greek Philosophy: From Thales to Aristotle*. Edited by S. Marc Cohen, Patricia Curd, and C. D. C. Reeve. Indianapolis: Hackett, 1995.

Hick, John. *Evil and the God of Love*. London: Fontana, 1968.
Hollinger, Dennis. "Enjoying God Forever: A Historical/Sociological Profile of the Health and Wealth Gospel." In *The Gospel and Contemporary Perspectives: Viewpoints from Trinity Journal*, edited by Douglas Moo, 13–26. Grand Rapids, MI: Kregel, 1997.
Holm, Randall. "Healing in Search of Atonement: With a Little Help from James K. A. Smith." *Journal of Pentecostal Theology* 23 (2014) 50–67.
Holmén, Tom. "Theodicean Motifs in the New Testament: Response to the Death of Jesus." In *Theodicy in the World of the Bible*, edited by Antti Laato and Johannes C. de Moor, 605–51. Leiden: Brill, 2003.
Hoover, J. N. "Divine Healing." *Comforter and Messenger of Faith* 17.196 (March 1948) 9.
Houtman, Cornelis. *Exodus, Vol. 1*. Historical Commentary of the Old Testament. Kampen, Netherlands: Peeters, 1993.
———. "Theodicy in the Pentateuch." In *Theodicy in the World of the Bible*, edited by Antti Laato and Johannes C. de Moor, 151–82. Leiden: Brill, 2003.
Hume, David. *Dialog Concerning Natural Religion*. New York: Penguin, 1990.
Hymnary.org. "Every Promise in the Book Is Mine." https://hymnary.org/hymn/YL1982/63.
———. "Standing on the Promises." https://hymnary.org/text/standing_on_the_promises_of_christ_my_ki.
IMF. "Six Charts Explain South Africa's Inequality." *International Monetary Fund*, January 30, 2020. https://www.imf.org/en/News/Articles/2020/01/29/na01282osix-charts-on-south-africas-persistent-and-multi-faceted-inequality.
Jackson, Christopher D. "Luther's Theologian of the Cross and Theologian of Glory Distinction Reconsidered." *Pro Ecclesia* 43.4 (2020) 352–65.
Jacobsen, D. *Thinking in the Spirit: Theologies of the Early Pentecostal Movement*. Bloomington, IN: Indiana University Press, 2003.
Jamieson, J. A. "Divine Healing." *Comforter and Messenger of Hope* 2.1 (January 1933) 23–24.
Japhet, Sara. "Theodicy in Ezra-Nehemiah and Chronicles." In *Theodicy in the World of the Bible*, edited by Antti Laato and Johannes C. de Moor, 429–69. Leiden: Brill, 2003.
Jones, C. B., and J. J. Jones. "Yielding to the Spirit: A Pentecostal Approach to Group Bible Study." *Journal of Pentecostal Theology* 1 (1992) 109–34.
Jones, L. "Is Divine Healing for Everybody?" *Comforter and Messenger of Hope* 4.10 (October 1935) 7–8.
Jung, Sigmund. *The Undiscovered Self: Answers to Questions Raised by the Present World Crisis*. Oxford: Routledge, 1958.
Kaplan, Mordecai M. *The Future of the American Jew*. New York: MacMillan, 1948.
Kärkkäinen, Veli-Matti. "Toward a Pneumatological Theology of Religions: A Pentecostal-Charismatic Inquiry." *International Review of Mission* 91.361 (2002) 178–98.
Käsemann, Ernst. *Exegetische Versuche und Besinnungen 2*. Göttingen: Vandenhoeck and Ruprecht, 1970.
Keener, C. S. *Spirit Hermeneutics: Reading Scripture in Light of Pentecost*. Grand Rapids, MI: Eerdmans, 2016.
Keller, James A. "Process Theism and Theodicies for the Problems of Evil." In *The Blackwell Companion to the Problem of Evil*, edited by Justin P. McBrayer and Daniel Howard-Snyder, 321–62. Malden, MA: John Wiley, 2013.

Kgatle, Mookgo Solomon. "Triumphalist Theology in the Context of Prophetic Pentecostalism in South Africa." *Journal of the European Pentecostal Theological Association* 41.2 (2021) 141–52.

Klein, William. *The New Chosen People: A Corporate View of Election*. Grand Rapids, MI: Zondervan, 1990.

Knight, G. W. "Can a Christian Go to War?" In *Readings in Christian Ethics, Vol. 2: Issues and Application*, edited by D. K. Clarke and R. V. Rakestraw, 495–500. Grand Rapids, MI: BakerAcademic, 1996.

König, Adrio. *Here Am I! A Believer's Reflection on God*. Grand Rapids, MI: Eerdmans, 1982.

Kritzinger, K. "Ministerial Formation in the Uniting Reformed Church in South Africa: In Search of Inclusion and Authenticity." In *Between the Real and the Ideal: Ministerial Formation in South African Churches*, edited by M. Naidoo, 33–47. Pretoria: Unisa, 2012.

Kuenen, A. *Historisch-kritische Einleitung in die Bücher des Alten Testaments*. Leipzig: Otto Schulze, 1887.

Kushner, Harold S. *When Bad Things Happen to Good People*. New York: Avon, 1993.

Laato, Antti. *The Servant of YHWH and Cyrus: A Reinterpretation of the Exilic Messianic Programme in Isaiah 40–55*. Stockholm: Almqvist and Wiksell, 1992.

———. "Theodicy in the Deuteronomic History." In *Theodicy in the World of the Bible*, edited by Antti Laato and Johannes C. de Moor, 183–235. Leiden: Brill, 2003.

Lake, John G. "Die Genade van Goddelike Genesing. (The Grace of Divine Healing): Speech at a Convention at Chicago, July 16, 1920." *Comforter* 12.8 (1954) 15–16.

———. "Does God Ever Heal?" In *Jesus: God's Way of Healing and Power to Promote Health*, edited by W. H. Reidt, 10–31. Tulsa, OK: Harrison House, 1981.

———. *John G. Lake's Life and Diary*. Edited by Talbert Morgan. Bloomington, IN: AuthorHouse, 2006.

———. *The John G. Lake Reader*. Wayne, NJ: Low Tide, 2017.

———. *The New John G. Lake Sermons*. Edited by Gordon Lindsay. Dallas, TX: Christ for the Nations, 1971.

———. *The John G. Lake Sermons on Dominion over Demons, Disease, and Death*. Edited by Gordon Lindsay. Dallas, TX: Christ for the Nations, 1979.

———. *Tune in for Adventures in Religion: Radio Sermons*. Edited by Wayne C. Anderson. Morgantown, WV: Stand Sure, 1991.

———. "Vrae Met Betrekking tot Genesing (Questions About Healing)." *Comforter* 30.8 (August 1960) 25–27.

Lake, John G., and Kenneth Copeland. *John G. Lake: His Life His Sermons His Boldness of Faith*. Fort Worth, TX: Kenneth Copeland Ministries, 1994.

Lambert, W. G., ed. "The Babylonian Theodicy." In *Babylonian Wisdom Literature*, edited by W. G. Lambert, 63–91. Oxford: Clarendon, 1960.

Land, Steven J. *Pentecostal Spirituality: A Passion for the Kingdom*. Cleveland, OH: CPT, 1993.

Leibniz, Gottfried W. *Theodicy*. Chicago: Open Court, 1990.

Le Roux, P. L. "The Pentecostal Signs." *Comforter and Messenger of Hope* 15.175 (June 1946) 3, 19.

Lewis, B. Scott. "Evil, Problem of." In *Dictionary of Pentecostal and Charismatic Movements*, edited by S. M. Burgess and G. B. McGee, 186–89. Grand Rapids, MI: Zondervan, 1988.

Lewis, C. S. *The Problem of Pain*. 1940. New York: HarperOne, 2001.
Lewis, P. W. "Towards a Pentecostal Epistemology: The Role of Experience in Pentecostal Hermeneutics." *The Spirit and Church* 2.1 (2000) 95–125.
Liardon, Roberts. *The Azusa Street Revival: When the Fire Fell*. Shippensburg, PA: Destiny Image, 2006.
Lindström, Fredrik. "Theodicy in the Psalms." In *Theodicy in the World of the Bible*, edited by Antti Laato and Johannes C. de Moor, 256–303. Leiden: Brill, 2003.
MacArthur, John. *The Power of Suffering: Strengthening Your Faith in the Refiner's Fire*. Colorado Springs, CO: David C. Cook, 1995.
MacIntyre, Alasdair C., and Paul Ricoeur. *Religious Significance of Atheism*. New York: Columbia University Press, 1969.
Mangum, Douglas. "Idolatry." In *Lexham Theological Wordbook*, edited by Douglas Mangum et al. Lexham Bible Reference Series. Bellingham, WA: Lexham, 2014.
Mbugua, Michael O. "Misunderstanding the Bible." In *Prosperity? Seeking the True Gospel*, edited by Michael O. Mbugua et al., 15–32. Nairobi: Africa Christian Textbooks Registered Trustees, 2015.
McCray, Donyelle C. "Mothering Souls: A Vocation of Intercession." *Anglican Theological Review: Women and Prayer* 98.2 (Spring 2016) 285–301.
McDowell, John C. "Karl Barth Having No-Thing to Hope For." *Journal for Christian Theological Research* 11.2 (2006) 1–49.
McGee, G. B. "Brought into the Sphere of the Supernatural: How Speaking in Tongues Empowered Early Pentecostals." *Encounter* 4.1 (2007) 1–16.
McGuire-Moushon, J. A., and Rachel Klippenstein. "Eternity." In *Lexham Theological Wordbook*, edited by Douglas Mangum et al. Lexham Bible Reference Series. Bellingham, WA: Lexham, 2014.
McKinley, J. E. "What Do I Do with Contexts? A Brief Reflection on Reading Biblical Texts with Israel and Aotearoa New Zealand in Mind." *Pacifica* 14 (2001) 159–71.
McLean, Mark D. "A Pentecostal Perspective on Theodicy." Paper presented at the Twenty-Seventh Annual Meeting of the Society for Pentecostal Studies, Cleveland, OH, 1998.
———. "Pentecostal Responses to the Problem of Evil: Walking the Razor's Edge between Deism and Calvinism." Paper presented at the Thirtieth Annual Meeting of the Society for Pentecostal Studies, Tulsa, OK, 2001.
Meeks, Charles. "Trinity." In *Lexham Bible Dictionary*, edited by John D. Barry et al. Bellingham, WA: Lexham, 2016.
Merton, Thomas. *Faith and Violence: Christian Teaching and Christian Practice*. Notre Dame, IN: University of Notre Dame Press, 1968.
———. *On Eastern Meditation*. New York: New Directions, 2012.
Michel, D. "Ein Skeptischer Philosoph: Prediger Salomo (*Qohelet*)." *Universität im Rathaus* 7 (1987) 1–31.
Miller, J. Maxwell, and John H. Hayes. *A History of Ancient Israel and Judaism*. London: SCM, 1986.
Moltmann, Jürgen. *The Crucified God: The Cross of Christ as the Foundation and Criticism of Christian Theology*. Translated by R. A. Wilson and John Bowden. Minneapolis: Fortress 1993.
———. *The Trinity and the Kingdom: The Doctrine of God*. Translated by Margaret Kohl. Minneapolis: Fortress, 1993.
Morgan, G. D. "Goddelike Genesing (Divine Healing)." *Comforter and Messenger of Hope* 2.6 (June 1933) 17.

Murray, John C. *The Problem of God Yesterday and Today*. New Haven, CT: Yale University Press, 1964.

Murray, Michael J. "Theodicy." In *The Oxford Handbook of Philosophical Theology*, edited by Thomas P. Flint and Michael C. Rea, 360–62. New York: Oxford University Press, 2009.

Nel, Marius. *African Pentecostalism and Eschatological Expectations: He Is Coming Back Again*. Newcastle upon Tyne, UK: Cambridge Scholars, 2019.

———. "Bible-Reading Practices in the AFM." https://issuu.com/afm_ags/docs/bible_reading.

———. "Daniel 9 as Part of an Apocalyptic Book?" *Verbum et Ecclesia* 34.1 (2013) 1–8.

———. "Die Leerstelling van Goddelike Genesing Soos dit in die Apostoliese Geloof Sending van Suid-Afrika Ontwikkel het: 'n Kerkhistoriese Perspektief (The Doctrine of Divine Healing as it Developed in the Apostolic Faith Mission of South Africa: A Church-Historical Perspective)." DDiv diss., University of Pretoria, 1992.

———. "Isaiah 53 and Its Use in the New Testament and Classical Pentecostal Churches in Southern Africa." *Australasian Pentecostal Studies* 21.1 (2020) 70–90.

———. "Moedertaal in die Kerk: Die Apostoliese Geloof Sending van Suid-Afrika (AGS van SA) en Afrikaans as 'n Illustrasie van die Rol wat Moedertaal in die Kerk Speel (Mother Language in the Church: The Apostolic Faith Mission of South Africa [AFM of SA] and Afrikaans as an Illustration of the Influence of Mother Language in the Church)." *Tydskrif vir Geesteswetenskappe (Journal of Humanities)* 59.2 (2019) 177–91.

———. "'n Aktualisering van die Apokaliptiese Openbarings in die Daniëlboek (Actualisation of the Apocalyptic Revelations in the Book of Daniel)." MDiv diss., University of Pretoria, 1997.

———. "'n Teologies-Hermeneutiese Ondersoek na Daniël 1 en 2. (A Theological and Hermeneutical Investigation into Daniel 1 and 2)." PhD diss., University of Pretoria, 2001.

———. "The Pentecostal Movement's View of the Continuity of Tongues in Acts and 1 Corinthians." *In Luce Verbi* 51.1 (2017) a2198.

———. "Pentecostal Spirituality in Dialogue with Early Fathers of the Eastern Orthodox Tradition: A Question of Continuity." *Journal of Early Christian History* 8.2 (2018) 1–26.

———. "Pentecostal Talk about God: Attempting to Speak from Experience." *HTS Teologiese Studies/Theological Studies* 73.3 (2017) 1–8.

———. "Pentecostalism and the Early Church: On Living Distinctively from the World." *Journal of Theology for Southern Africa* 153 (2016) 141–59.

———. *The Prosperity Gospel in Africa: An African Pentecostal Hermeneutical Consideration*. Eugene, OR: Wipf and Stock, 2020.

———. "Rethinking Hell from a Classical Pentecostal Perspective: Some Ethical Considerations." *Stellenbosch Theological Journal* 7.1 (2021) 1–24.

———. "View of Time in Ancient Cultures, and the Origin of Apocalypticism in Jewish Thought in the Centuries Before Christ." In *Stimulation from Leiden: Collected Communications to the XVIIIth Congress of the International Organization for the Study of the Old Testament, Leiden, 2004*, edited by H. M. Niemann and M. Augustin, 207–17. Frankfurt: Peter Lang, 2006.

Nelson, P. C. "Instruction to Those Seeking Healing." *Comforter and Messenger of Hope* 5.1. (November 1936) 23.

Ngong, David T. "Protesting the Cross: African Pentecostal Soteriology and Pastoral Care." *Journal of Theology for Southern Africa* 150 (November 2014) 5–19.

Noth, Martin. *Überlieferungsgeschichtlichen Studien: Die Sammelnden und Bearbeitenden Geschichtswerke im Alten Testament*. Tübingen: M. Niemeyer, 1957.

Nsiku, Edouard K. "Isaiah." In *Africa Bible Commentary: A One-Volume Commentary Written by 70 African Scholars*, edited by Tokunboh Adeyemo, 809–52. Nairobi: WordAlive, 2006.

O'Connor, Kathleen M. "Lamenting Back to Life." *Interpretation* 62 (2008) 34–47.

Onyinah, Opoku. "God's Grace, Healing and Suffering." *International Review of Mission* 95.376/77 (January/April 2006) 117–27.

Orr-Ewing, Amy. *Where Is God in All the Suffering?* Epsom, UK: Good Book, 2020.

Ortlund, Ray. "The Book of Job." *Gospel Coalition*. https://www.thegospelcoalition.org/blogs/ray-ortlund/book-of-job/.

Osterhus, C. S. "Have They Real Faith?" *Comforter and Messenger of Hope* 1.5 (September 1932) 4.

Pannenberg, Wolfhart. *Systematic Theology, Vol. 1*. Translated by Geoffrey W. Bromiley. Grand Rapids, MI: Eerdmans, 1991.

Parker, P. G. "Die Sewevoudige Evangelie (The Sevenfold Gospel)." *Comforter and Messenger of Hope* 4.7 (July 1935) 3–5.

Peck, M. Scott. *People of the Lie: The Hope for Healing Human Evil*. New York: Touchstone, 1983.

Peels, Eric. "The World's First Murder: Violence and Justice in Genesis 4:1–16." In *Animosity, the Bible, and Us*, edited by J. T. Fitzgerald, Fika J. van Rensburg, and Harry van Rooy, 19–39. SBL Global Perspectives on Biblical Scholarship 12. Atlanta, GA: SBL, 2009.

Pelikan, Jaroslav. *The Christian Tradition: A History of the Development of Doctrine, Vol. 2*. Chicago: University of Chicago Press, 1971.

Perkins, Anna K. "Just Desert or Just Deserts? God and Suffering in These Perilous Days." *Black Theology* 14.3 (November 2016) 179–92.

Perriman, Andrew. *Faith, Health and Prosperity*. Carlisle, UK: Paternoster, 2003.

Pfeiffer, R. H. "The Peculiar Scepticism of Ecclesiastes." *Journal of Biblical Literature* 53 (1934) 100–109.

Phillips, D. Z. "Theism without Theodicy." In *Encountering Evil: Live Options in Theodicy*, edited by Stephen T. Davis, 145–80. Louisville: Westminster John Knox, 2001.

Pinnock, Clark H. "From Augustine to Arminius: A Pilgrimage in Theology." In *In the Grace of God and the Will of Man: A Case for Arminianism*, edited by Clark H. Pinnock, 15–30. Grand Rapids, MI: Zondervan, 1989.

———. *Most Moved Mover: A Theology of God's Openness*. Carlisle, UK: Paternoster, 2001.

———. "Systematic Theology." In *The Openness of God: A Biblical Challenge to the Traditional Understanding of God*, edited by Clark H. Pinnock et al., 91–115. Downers Grove, IL: InterVarsity, 1994.

———. "The Work of the Holy Spirit in Hermeneutics." *Journal of Pentecostal Theology* 1.2 (1993) 3–23.

Pinnock, Sarah K. *Beyond Theodicy: Jewish and Christian Continental Thinkers Respond to the Holocaust*. Albany, NY: State University of New York Press, 2002.

Potgieter, Raymond. "Divine Exultation and Agony in the Face of Evil, a Creation Theodicy of Divine Restraint." *Acta Theologica* 33.1 (2013) 196–213.

———. "Etty Hillesum: *Esse Quam Videri*—Reformed Christian Perspectives on a Spiritual Journey." *In Luce Verbi* 54.1 (2020) 1–11.

Price, C. S. "Healed by the Lamb." *Comforter and Messenger of Faith* 12.143 (April 1943) 2.

Quayesi-Amakye, Joseph. "Coping with Evil in Ghanaian Pentecostalism." *Exchange* 43 (2014) 254–72.

Reidt, W. H., ed. *Jesus: God's Way of Healing and Power to Promote Health. Featuring the Miracle Ministry of Dr. John G. Lake*. Tulsa, OK: Harrison House, 1981.

———. *John G. Lake: A Man without Compromise*. Tulsa, OK: Harrison House, 1989.

Renkema, Johan. "Theodicy in Lamentations?" In *Theodicy in the World of the Bible*, edited by Antti Laato and Johannes C. de Moor, 410–28. Leiden: Brill, 2003.

Rice, Richard. "Biblical Support for a New Perspective." In *The Openness of God: A Biblical Challenge to the Traditional Understanding of God*, edited by Clark H. Pinnock et al., 1–48. Downers Grove, IL: InterVarsity, 1994.

Ricoeur, Paul. *Evil: A Challenge to Philosophy and Theology*. London: Bloomsbury Academic, 2007.

Ridderbos, Herman. *Heilsgeschiedenis en Heilige Schrift*. Kampen, Netherlands: J. H. Kok, 1955.

Robinson, C. R. "Keeping Healing." *Comforter and Messenger of Hope* 4.2 (February 1935) 3–4.

Rowley, Harold H. "Book of Job and Its Meaning." In *From Moses to Qumran: Studies in the Old Testament*, edited by Harold H. Rowley, 141–83. London: Butterworth, 1963.

Runia, Klaas. *Karl Barth's Doctrine of Holy Scripture*. Eugene, OR: Wipf and Stock, 1962.

Sanchez, Jonathan. "John Wesley on the Etiology of Evil: A Pastoral Reconstruction of Wesley's Theodicy Based on Genesis 1:31." *Apuntes: Theological Reflections from a Hispanic-Latino Context* 34.4 (2014) 137–49.

Sanders, John. "Historical Considerations." In *The Openness of God: A Biblical Challenge to the Traditional Understanding of God*, edited by Clark H. Pinnock et al., 49–90. Downers Grove, IL: InterVarsity, 1994.

Santrac, Aleksandar S. *An Evaluation of Alvin Plantinga's Free Will Defence: Whether Our Power to Do Bad Is Something Good*. New York: Edwin Mellen, 2018.

Schmidt, Frederick W. *When Suffering Persists: A Theology of Candor*. Harrisburg, PA: Morehouse, 2001.

Schoors, Antoon. "Theodicy in Qohelet." In *Theodicy in the World of the Bible*, edited by Antti Laato and Johannes C. de Moor, 375–409. Leiden: Brill, 2003.

Scott, Mark S. *Pathways in Theodicy: An Introduction to the Problem of Evil*. Philadelphia: Fortress, 2015.

Seal, David. "Satan." In *The Lexham Bible Dictionary*, edited by John D. Barry et al. Bellingham, WA: Lexham, 2016.

Sharp, Shane. "Monotheistic Theodicy as Imaginary Face-Work." *Sociological Forum* 29.4 (December 2014) 873–92.

Sharpe, Matthew. "The Black Side of the Sun: Camus, Theology, and the Problem of Evil." *Political Theology* 15.2 (March 2014) 151–74.

Simojoki, Anssi. *Apocalypse Interpreted: The Types of Interpretation of the Book of Revelation in Finland 1944–1995 from the Second World War to the Post-Cold War World*. Turku, Finland: Abo Akademi University Press, 1997.

———. "The Book of Revelation." In *Theodicy in the World of the Bible*, edited by Antti Laato and Johannes C. de Moor, 652–84. Leiden: Brill, 2003.

Sitt, Jennifer. "Before You Can Be with Others, First Learn to be Alone." *Aeon*. https://aeon.co/ideas/before-you-can-be-with-others-first-learn-to-be-alone.

Smith, Jan. "Wonderbare Genesings (Wonderful Healings)." *Comforter* 3.8 (1982) 158–59.

Smith, Kevin G. "Spiritual Warfare in African Pentecostalism in the Light of Ephesians." *Conspectus* Special Edition (December 2018) 70–80.

Snyman, Gerrie. *Om die Bybel Anders te Lees: 'n Etiek van Bybellees*. Pretoria: Griffel, 2007.

Spong, John Shelby. *Rescuing the Bible from Fundamentalism*. New York: HarperOne, 1992.

Sproul, R. C. "TULIP and Reformed Theology: Total Depravity." *Ligonier*, May 25, 2017. https://www.ligonier.org/learn/articles/tulip-and-reformed-theology-total-depravity.

Srigley, Ronald. "'That Other North African': Camus on Augustine and His Legacy." In *Brill's Companion to Camus: Camus Among the Philosophers*, edited by Matthew Sharpe, Maciej Kałuża, and Peter Francev, 53–68. Brill's Companion to Philosophy 5. Leiden: Brill, 2019.

Stewart, Robert. "N. T. Wright's Hermeneutic: An Exploration." *Churchman* 117.2 (2003) 153–75.

Stuart, Eva. D. "Goddelike Genesing vir die Gemeente (Divine Healing for the Congregation)." *Comforter and Messenger of Hope* 2.2 (February 1933) 4.

———. "Gods Wil in Genezing (God's Will in Healing)." *Comforter and Messenger of Hope* 1.12 (February 1922) 6.

Sundkler, Bengt G. M. *Zulu Zion and Some Swazi Zionists*. London: Oxford University Press, 1976.

Surin, Kenneth. *Theology and the Problem of Evil*. New York: Blackwell, 1986.

Swinton, John. *Raging with Compassion: Pastoral Responses to the Problem of Evil*. Grand Rapids, MI: Eerdmans, 2007.

Tada, Joni E. *A Place of Healing: Wrestling with the Mysteries of Suffering, Pain, and God's Sovereignty*. Colorado Springs, CO: David Cook, 2010.

Tchividjian, Tullian. *Glorious Ruin: How Suffering Sets You Free*. Colorado Springs, CO: David Cook, 2012.

Thompson, Michael E. W. *"Where Is the God of Justice?" The Old Testament and Suffering*. Eugene, OR: Pickwick, 2011.

Torr, Stephen C. *A Dramatic Pentecostal/Charismatic Anti-Theodicy: Improvising on a Divine Performance of Lament*. Eugene, OR: Pickwick, 2013.

———. "Lamenting in Tongues: Glossolalia as a Pneumatic Aid to Lament." *Journal of Pentecostal Theology* 26 (2017) 30–47.

Trible, Phyllis. *Texts of Terror: Literary-Feminist Readings of Biblical Narratives*. Philadelphia: Fortress, 1984.

Uffenheimer, Benjamin. "Theodicy and Ethics in the Prophecy of Ezekiel." In *Justice and Righteousness: Biblical Themes and Their Influence*, edited by Henning G. Reventlow and Yair Hoffman, 200–227. JSOT Suppl 137. Sheffield, UK: JSOT, 1992.

Van de Beek, A. *Why? On Suffering, Guilt, and God*. Translated by John Vriend. Grand Rapids, MI: Eerdmans, 1990.

Van Woudenberg, René. "A Brief History of Theodicy." In *The Blackwell Companion to the Problem of Evil*, edited by Justin P. McBrayer and Daniel Howard-Snyder, 177–79. Malden, MA: Wiley Blackwell, 2013.

Verweij, André C. *Positioning Jesus' Suffering: A Grounded Theory of Lenten Preaching in Local Parishes.* Delft: Eburon, 2014.

Vicchio, Stephan J. *The Book of Job: A History of Interpretation and a Commentary.* Translated by John Vriend. Eugene, OR: Wipf and Stock, 2020.

Volf, Miroslav. "Theology for a Way of Life." In *Practicing Theology: Beliefs and Practices in Christian Life,* edited by Miroslav Volf and Dorothy C. Bass, 245–63. Cambridge, MA: Eerdmans, 2002.

Voltaire. "Author's Preface to the Lisbon Earthquake." In *The Works of Voltaire, Vol. X: The Dramatic Works: Part 1.* New York: E. R. DuMont, 1901.

Vondey, Wolfgang. *Pentecostalism: A Guide for the Perplexed.* London: Bloomsbury, 2013.

Von Rad, Gerhard. *Old Testament Theology, Vol I.* 1975. London: SCM, 1996.

Vroegop, Mark. *Dark Clouds, Deep Mercy: Discovering the Grace of Lament.* Wheaton, IL: Crossway, 2019.

Warrington, Keith. *Pentecostal Theology: A Theology of Encounter.* London: T. & T. Clark, 2008.

Webster, J. *Holy Scripture: A Dogmatic Sketch.* Cambridge, UK: Cambridge University Press, 2003.

Weinandy, Thomas G. *Does God Suffer?* Notre Dame, IN: University of Notre Dame Press, 2000.

Welker, Michael. "Theodicy, Creation, and Suffering: Drawing on God's Spirit and Love." In *The Spirit is Moving: New Pathways in Pneumatology,* edited by Gijsbert van den Brink, Eveline van Staalduine-Sulman, and Maarten Wisse, 280–92. Studies in Reformed Theology 38. Leiden: Brill, 2019.

Wesley, John. "A Letter to His Father." In *The Works of the Rev. John Wesley: in Ten Volumes,* edited by John Wesley and Joseph Benson, 108. New York: J. & J. Harper, 1827.

———. "Sermon 56: God's Approbation of His Works." In *The Sermons of John Wesley,* edited by Thomas Jackson. http://wesley.nnu.edu/john-wesley/the-sermons-of-john-wesley-1872-edition/sermon-56-gods-approbation-of-his-works/.

West, Gerald. *The Stolen Bible: From Tool of Imperialism to African Icon.* Pietermaritzburg, South Africa: Cluster, 2016.

Westminster Divines. "The Westminster Confession of Faith." *Ligonier.* https://www.ligonier.org/learn/articles/westminster-confession-faith.

Willis, W. Waite. *Theism, Atheism, and the Doctrine of the Trinity: The Trinitarianism of Karl Barth and Jürgen Moltmann in Response to Protest Atheism.* Atlanta, GA: Scholars, 1987.

Wikipedia. "Apostolic Faith Mission of South Africa." https://en.wikipedia.org/wiki/Apostolic_Faith_Mission_of_South_Africa.

World Bank. "Disability Inclusion." https://www.worldbank.org/en/topic/disability#1.

World Health Organization. "World Health Report: Mental Disorders Affect One in Four People." https://www.who.int/news/item/28-09-2001-the-world-health-report-2001-mental-disorders-affect-one-in-four-people.

Wright, N. T. *Evil and the Justice of God.* Downers Grove, IL: InterVarsity, 2006.

Yong, Amos. *The Bible, Disability, and the Church: A New Vision of the People of God.* Grand Rapids, MI: Eerdmans, 2011.

———. "Disability and the Love of Wisdom: De-forming, Re-forming, and Per-forming Philosophy of Religion." *Evangelical Review of Theology* 35.2 (2011) 160–76.

———. "Many Tongues, Many Senses: Pentecost, the Body Politic, and the Redemption of Dis/Ability." *Pneuma* 31.2 (January 2009) 167–88.

Yrigoyen, Charles. *John Wesley: Holiness of Heart and Life*. Nashville: Abingdon, 1996.
Zeeb, Janelle. "Open Theism and the Problem of Theodicy." *Churchman* 130.4 (Winter 2016) 299–317.
Zheng, Honge, Wei Wang, and Libin Wang. "Rural Christians' View of Sickness Treatment Behavior: A Case Study from a Shandong Village, China." *Anthropology and Medicine* 22.2 (2015) 114–26.

www.ingramcontent.com/pod-product-compliance
Lightning Source LLC
Chambersburg PA
CBHW050343230426
43663CB00010B/1967